JOURNEY OF THE WILD GEESE

To Amy + Harold

Edwin Stephenson

JOURNEY OF THE WILD GEESE

A Quaker Romance In War-Torn Europe

BY MADELEINE YAUDE STEPHENSON
and
EDWIN "RED" STEPHENSON

Intentional Productions

Published by Intentional Productions; PO Box 94814; Pasadena, CA 91109

Cover, map and book design by Gabriel Graubner, The Electronic Monastery 7899 St. Helena Road; Santa Rosa, CA 95404

Typography: Adobe Garamond, Optima and Isadora
Cover stock: 10pt Carolina; text paper: 55lb Glatselter Antique-White

Printed by Gilliland Printing; Arkansas City, KS 67005

Cover Painting of Monan's Rill scene by Caroline Neel Yaude, 1975

Library of Congress card number 98-074015

ISBN 0-9648042-3-9

First printing 1999 in the United States of America

Second printing 1999 in the United States of America

ACKNOWLEDGEMENTS

When Madeleine knew that she was dying, she began to look for someone who could edit and finish her book. She met and interviewed Carol Caldwell-Ewart, with whom she signed a contract. Madeleine left over 400 single-spaced typewritten pages. For more than four years, Carol has worked to make these pages into a readable book, while maintaining the integrity of Madeleine's purpose.

For these four years, I had the joy of working with Carol and supporting her efforts by being sure that people are correctly identified, names are correctly spelled, and supplemental data has been available.

My thanks to Susan Forrest and Jeanne Lohman who read the manuscript during its formative stages and were most helpful in their comments and support.

My thanks to Roger Moss who read the manuscript and helped guide me in my search for potential publishers.

Claire Gorfinkel, who had published a book on her own, offered to publish this book for me and guide me in obtaining information necessary for the copyright page. In addition, her suggestions were invaluable in making the book readable and presentable.

To have the book designer as a neighbor so that I could follow his efforts on a daily basis was a thrill. Gabriel Graubner spent many days and nights using his artistic talents in making this a beautiful book. To him I am grateful.

Of course, the book and the adventures leading to it would not have happened had it not been for American Friends Service Committee and Friends Service Council. Their willingness to sponsor young idealists who wanted so much to help repair a war torn world made all of this possible. In recognition of their Humanitarian Services in Europe and elsewhere, these two agencies received the Nobel Peace Prize in 1947.

In preparing this book, we have chosen to retain the language and tone of the letters for the sake of authenticity.

This book is dedicated to our grandchildren
Erika, Elijah, Gabriel, and Isaiah

WILD GEESE

Wavering lines, unerringly directed,
High cries that call to us on Earth—
We, too, must take our journey through the void
To land—we know not where.

Your journey seems the easier,
Guided by patterns, mem'ries in your cells,
Finding land-falls that you have never seen,
But known to generations of your kind.

But of you too obedience is required,
To leave familiar pasturage and wood,
To venture forth, commit yourselves to air,
To trust in that which never can be known

Until the moment of arrival.

—Madeleine Stephenson

EUROPE 1946-1947

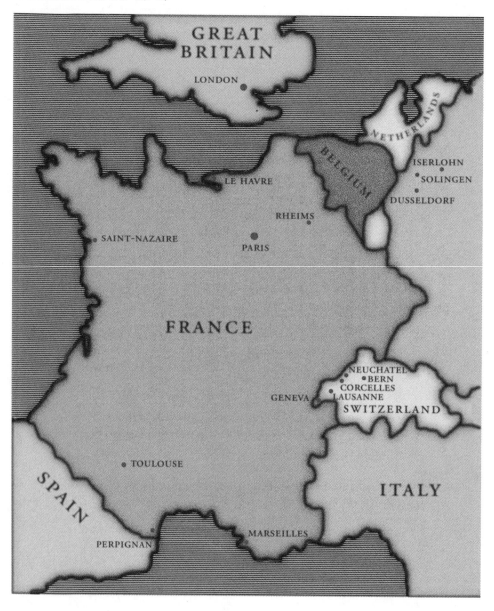

ACRONYMS

AFSC	American Friends Service Committee
APO	Army Post Office—U.S. Army
CPS	Civilian Public Service—Camps for conscientious objectors during WW II
ETU	European Transport Unit—an AFSC entity
FRS	Friends Relief Service—British Quakers
GMC	General Motors Company trucks
IGC	Intergovernmental Committee on Refugees—French
MP	Military Police—U.S. military
NAAFI	Navy, Army, and Air Force Institute—organized canteens and provided other welfare services for British armed and civil defense forces
POW	Prisoners of war
PX	Purchasers' exchange—U.S. military
RAF	Royal Air Force—British
UNO	United Nations Organization
UNRRA	United Nations Relief and Rehabilitation AGENCY

INTRODUCTION

In the 1930's, an anti-war movement surfaced on college campuses throughout the United States. These were not "America Firsters," but people with a revulsion against the destruction and terrible loss of young life in World War I and against the armaments profiteers. They were convinced that there had to be a better way of resolving international conflicts than by killing millions of people. At the University of Rochester (1936-40), I was one of many students caught up in this passionate conviction. Then came Pearl Harbor. The United States entered the war, and overnight, attitudes changed. But some of us did not change. I didn't change. Edwin "Red" Stephenson, who became my husband, didn't change.

Men who opposed war went into Civilian Public Service (CPS) camps or to prison because they wouldn't register for the draft or cooperate with military service. Women of pacifist conviction faced the dilemma of finding meaningful work that did not contribute to the war effort.

As my French was fairly fluent, I offered my services to the American Friends Service Committee (AFSC) as a relief worker in France. No civilians, however, could leave the country during the war. For about three years, until the war was over and relief workers could be sent abroad, I worked in the central Philadelphia office of AFSC.

OUR GROUP OF SIX QUAKER RELIEF WORKERS PHOTOGRAPHED BEFORE BOARDING THE SS BRAZIL. FROM LEFT TO RIGHT, THEY ARE MARLIS GILDERMEISTER, MADELEINE YAUDE, EDWIN "RED" STEPHENSON, VAN CLEVE GEIGER, REED SMITH, AND JOHN ROBBINS.   -PHOTOGRAPHER UNKNOWN

During the war, Red spent more than four years working in CPS camps. He and other men who believed that fighting was wrong worked with no pay under government direction. He expected to do work of national importance, and some of the work *was* important: fighting forest fires, reforestation, medical research on the effect of starvation and jaundice. But much of it—weeding little trees in the snow, digging trenches, building public parks—seemed unimportant when one thought of the hundreds of thousands of soldiers fighting and dying in Europe and the Pacific.

Finally, in 1945, first in Europe and then in the Pacific, the war was over. Troops began coming home. Now the men from CPS and women like me who had been waiting for the opportunity to help were free to volunteer for relief and reconstruction work: feeding the starving and helping to rebuild the devastated cities in Europe.

Six of us, bound to do relief work for AFSC, gathered on a New York dock March 14, 1946. Waiting to board the SS Brazil were: John Robbins, Reed Smith, Van Cleve Geiger, and Red (all of whom had worked in CPS) and two women, Marlis Gildermeister, and me. I was twenty-seven years old, and Red turned twenty-eight soon after we arrived in Europe. The men were part of the European Transport Unit (ETU), a group of truck driver/mechanics who would be hauling building materials to bombed out areas where sometimes not one stone was left standing on another. The women's roles were not as clearly defined; we would be working with refugees in feeding programs and medical case work.

Formerly a banana boat, the SS Brazil had been converted to a troop ship to take soldiers to Europe and was now bringing them home. Going to Europe, the Brazil carried hundreds of young people working for the State and War Departments and the United Nations Relief and Rehabilitation Association (UNRRA), as well as AFSC.

On the boat, we met a woman from Geneva who told us of the "wide human radius" of Quaker Centers in Europe during the war. "So many people were helped just by knowing you were there," she said. "I am so very glad that Americans like you are going now to live among the French people. Europe's experience of Americans needs to be completed; Europeans know the tourists and the enterprising businessmen and the GIs, but they also need to know young people with concerns like yours."

I'd never been on shipboard before, and I frequently walked the rolling deck in the cold mist, stepping over ropes, greeting the sailors and my fellow passengers, and enjoying the damp wind in my face.

On the second day at sea, Red —a tall, lanky, red-headed southerner—stepped forward to help me over the coils of rope and afterward slowed his pace to mine. For the rest of the trip, we spent most of our time together, often just strolling along the deck. We weren't thinking of romance then. I was still in love with Philadelphian Herb Hauck, and he and I were trying to come to some understanding about what our relationship would be. Red always said he couldn't imagine romancing a girl five-foot-two when he was six-foot-four. But we began a friendship that was important to both of us.

The *Brazil* landed in Le Havre after nightfall; even through the darkness we could see the docks in ruins. The harbor had been one of the most beautiful in the world before the Allied bombing. We saw building after building with walls missing and no chance of ever being useful again. It was our first exposure to the ravages of war.

The Le Havre delegation of AFSC met us and shepherded us through the red tape of customs. We had a simple supper with them and then boarded the night train for Paris. The six of us fit neatly into one compartment, feet resting on the opposite seat and gray uniform greatcoats covering one another. As we traveled east, the sky cleared, the moon rose, and our first view of the French countryside was touched with magic: ancient stone houses, quiet fields, the Seine. This was also our first view of a war-ravaged countryside with bombed villages, ruined homes, blown bridges. One small blue bulb lit our compartment; most of the group went to sleep despite a blaring radio and loud celebration that went on most of the night in the adjoining compartment. Red and I were too fascinated by the passing scene—and if truth be known, by each other—to sleep much.

MADELEINE WALKING THE DECKS OF THE S S BRAZIL EN ROUTE TO LE HARVE
-PHOTOGRAPH BY AN ETU MEMBER

The next morning, we rolled into Paris under cold gray skies to begin our work. This book is a collection of the letters, reports, and journal entries we wrote over the next 17 months.

Madeleine Yaude Stephenson
Monan's Rill
Santa Rosa, California

To venture forth, commit yourself to air,
To trust in that which never can be known
Until the moment of arrival

                                    -Madeleine

To Venture Forth

can walk on the grass! The
floor is surrounded by tiny
tables and chairs, like a
café; there are palms and
chestnut trees, lit by Hollywood-like indirect lighting.
It's a beautiful night
again — full moon, luminous
sky, warm and fresh. The
music was soft; we
laughed a great deal and
danced with each other. I
got on well with Charles
Thurn, who's over 6', so I
figure I should do the
same with you. I did so
wish you there! It was
one of the rare times when

April 1946 ~ Report from Madeleine to AFSC in Philadelphia

(Madeleine's assignment was to report on conditions in France, and Quaker Service efforts there, as part of The American Friends Service Committee's public education, outreach and fundraising efforts.)

To you who have seen Paris in what a colleague calls the grumpy months, our enthusiasm must seem extravagant, but it is spring. We saw the countryside first by moonlight and then by dawn on the train from Le Havre, and Paris grows lovelier every day! We've seen Notre Dame through a haze of green buds, the sun on the Seine, and the countryside bedecked with pink and white fruit blossoms. The shabbiness is still here, of course: the clop of wooden-soled shoes on the streets, the endless queues for food, the pathetic little shops, the patient, tired people who still manage to be gay.

Our first day here, Marlis Gildermeister and I were riding the Metro beside a red-cheeked French woman. She eyed our insignia for a time and then gathered up courage to speak to us. For four years she had been a political prisoner, and only the Quakers had been able to bring any help to her and people like her. She felt she owed her life to Friends, and since she had never been able to thank any of those who had helped her, she wanted to express her gratitude to us.

I haven't definitely been assigned a job as yet, so I divide my time between the vestiaire (clothing room), visiting for Assistance Sociale, and making the European Transport Unit's (ETU) quarters more habitable.

ETU seems to be the most alive and growing part of the program in Paris right now. In spite of the fact that the place is furnished only with army cots and a board table, the garage has become a social center. When the men aren't off with the trucks or working under jeeps, they're scrubbing the floors (for a week now, a wheelbarrow has been making regular trips through the bedroom) or whipping up an American dessert. Hester, Lois, Marlis, and I are supposed to provide the feminine touch, which up to now consists of eight pairs of hastily sewn curtains and a bunch of ivy in a jam jar.

The courtyard of the ETU garage shows the contrast that one sees all over Paris between the new hopefulness of spring and the ruin of the war. Beside the little plot that the concierge gardens determinedly is a great heap of rubble. The trucks are parked beside the red and black striped former German sentry box. The new life in trees and flowers has brought new life to the people. Team members say the change in them in just the past two or three weeks is amazing: more smiles, more energy, a little more hope.

· From Rheims, where they go to pick up trucks, the ETU boys brought back these stories:

German prisoners of war (POWs) are assigned to help ETU drivers scrounge for spare parts in the army dumps to repair the U.S. Army trucks that AFSC has bought for the transport unit. One of the ETU drivers, pointing to the red and black star, asked a prisoner if he had ever heard of the American Friends Service Committee. No, he hadn't. Well, had he ever heard of the Quakers? The man's face brightened. Of course, they were the people who fed children after World War I. He had been in school then and could still remember just how much soup they were served and what kind of bread went with it!

The POWs are entirely cut off from contact with their homes and families and are terribly anxious to talk. Those who say they were anti-Nazi feel keenly the current lack of distinction between Nazi and German. They seem to look on the United States as a deliverer, but the fact that we haven't delivered very well doesn't excite their animosity. They still look to us for whatever hope there is in the postwar world. One of them asked an ETU driver, "Say, this Truman is a pretty good President, isn't he?" Said the cautious Quaker, "Well, I haven't made up my mind yet. Guess we'll have to wait a little longer and see."

"I think he's a good man," persisted the POW; "after all, he's a Quaker too, isn't he?"

I don't feel that I've done much relief work yet, but I'm having time to settle into the life here, and I think I can see the big push ahead. I'm very happy and am having a better time than one should, perhaps, in a job like this. Even running around Paris looking for living quarters is interesting. It's good to feel all of you in Philadelphia backing us up. One has very clearly the feeling of being an instrument for the concerns of people many miles away; that makes for humility and responsibility and also for the strength of shared ideas. Thanks for all you've done in getting us here. I hope we do you proud.

April 1946 ~ Red in Paris to friends at home

One of the men due to go to Poland with the ETU cannot go because of serious illness in his family. I'm to go in his place. So I shall stay in Paris for a while and await orders from Poland.

This means that I shall not be going with the fellows to Saint-Nazaire on the ETU's first project. As soon as we can get the trucks serviced, six to eight men will leave for Saint-Nazaire to help move people back into the town. It was almost completely destroyed, and the people were evacuated to nearby towns. Now temporary structures are being built, but the people have no other means of moving their bits of furniture back.

There is plenty of other work that our team can do if we have the time and manpower, plus trucks. Someone has suggested a milk supply route, since there is milk nearby, but transportation is so inadequate that few people benefit from it.

At last we have all the trucks we expect to get for some time, having obtained all the fifteen trucks we bought from the army. All of them are used, and some went through the African campaign, so they are in pretty poor shape, but we hope to put them on the road without major overhauls.

The building which garages the trucks also houses our office and living quarters. They are like barracks—all the beds are in two rooms. We each have a canvas cot with a sleeping bag. The kitchen is in an adjoining room which has the only tap with safe drinking water. Somehow we were able to buy an electric stove, so we live in luxury! Our latrine is next door, where the U.S. Army has a garage. We have no shower or bath facilities, but we have made arrangements to take showers and go swimming at the municipal pool for twenty francs plus tip.

Food is very good, since there is a commissary in Paris for U.S. citizens residing here. The rations are provided by the army, but each month there is a rumor that the commissary will close soon. This month they are cutting rations in order to have enough to go around. We get fresh meat once a week and some fresh fruit, which I had not expected to see again for many months.

Yesterday morning I saw an elderly woman searching through the garbage cans along the street, collecting morsels of food that had been thrown out. Then I saw another old woman ride by on a bicycle, slowing down at each garbage can and peering into it with anxious eyes. It really hurt to think that I had just feasted on half a grapefruit, hot cereal, and an egg. For the French, breakfast still consists of ersatz coffee and rationed bread.

Americans who stay at the big hotels eat very well, but most of the food is bought on the black market. Because the French still suffer from lack of food, they resent the luxurious way Americans here are living. Many old people sell their ration points in order to have enough money for bread. There won't be enough bread until the next wheat crop is harvested.

Russia is sending wheat to France, and you can imagine the favorable response that receives here. I remember the days when American housewives complained about standing in line to get fresh meat. Here I have seen lines where people wait to get their ration of bread. I have seen children who were as happy to get a dry piece of bread as you are to get a piece of good candy. And yet they say that France is in excellent shape considering conditions in central and eastern Europe.

April 3, 1946 ~ Madeleine in Paris to Herb Hauck

How I'm beginning to admire and covet strength! Only the strong can be gentle; only the strong can compromise; only the strong can buck convention and stupidity and inertness. The dangers of power and strength (I'm not sure how far they are equivalent and coexistent) are appalling, but they are a necessary risk. You can no more beg off from them than you can beg off the dangers of high-voltage electricity.

Oh Herb, I wish I were a genius! All around I see a desperate need for syntheses of all kinds: of means with use; of political aims with human understanding; of wisdom and courage; of devotion and savoir-faire. Parties and politicians and just plain ordinary people are making such a hell of a mess of things, trying to work out problems on the impossible basis of every person or nation for itself. And the people who have a different basis, such as the people I'm working with, are mostly so damned impotent. Having got hold of a piece of a splendid idea, they can't seem to do anything with it except to keep hanging on, which is, obviously, something in a time like this.

I spent a week with the ETU at Saint-Nazaire. As great a bunch of guys as God ever made. But some of them think we shouldn't eat so much; some of them won't drink; some of them won't smoke; some of them won't drink coffee because they're afraid they'll get to be "dependent" on it. Some of them react as a Republican does to "red" if you say the word "army." Lord, the world's falling apart, and they sit there and piddle over what they call pacifism!

I try to startle the ETU men with the necessity and basis of compromise for action, and they wander round the issue somehow and come up with one of the old hackneyed phrases. The times I wished for your incisive comments to clear the brush and expose the fundamental problem. I keep on liking these men; maybe the careful way they load up the few sticks of furniture and junk that the bombed-out people of Saint-Nazaire have saved expresses more to the French than advanced philosophical inquiry could.

RELIEF SCENE NEAR SAINT-NAZAIRE. 1946
-PHOTOGRAPH COURTESY OF AFSC ARCHIVES

Trouble is, it's philosophical inquiry, or the lack of it, that lay behind those bombings. And if I had a mind like a tent, I'd try to include all these conflicting factors and make something of them. Try to put together the opposites that don't fit in any system yet, and see if they wouldn't work. Feeling isn't enough; it's essential, but it isn't all. And Herb, though I know there's no need to say this, let me say it anyhow, just for my own satisfaction: whatever else you may or may not do, keep on trying to figure things out! If we fill every Liberty Ship full of food and coal and don't bring hope and ideas, Europe is sunk.

France is hungry and cold partly because she has an incredible bureaucracy; she has a black market because she's selfish; she has homeless people because she doesn't know how to cooperate. That isn't all. Everything is aggravated by the war and the occupation, but I've never before been so acutely aware that the spirit giveth life, and in most of Europe, the spirit seems lacking. I don't see the whole picture, of course; I hope the spirit is there despite my blindness.

April 12, 1946 ~ Madeleine in Paris to family and friends at home

It's a warm Saturday afternoon; "spring is busting out all over." The trees below my windows are in full leaf, and horse-chestnut blossoms are just beginning to show white. I've moved since coming to Paris; this is the rue de Varenne apartment, the home of a wealthy French woman who has given us the use of the fourth floor of her lovely house rent free. The rooms are large and bright. I'm writing in front of a deep French window that looks out over the garden of the Rodin Museum; to the right is the black and gold dome of Les Invalides and farther off the tracery of the Eiffel Tower.

MADELEINE AT THE EIFFEL TOWER. 1946
-PHOTOGRAPHER UNKNOWN

We're about twenty minutes' walk from the office in rue Notre Dame des Champs and fifteen from the Place de la Concorde. You can imagine how beautiful it is now, that great open space with the white marble statues, new green all around the embassies, and flower vendors at every corner. Daffodils are ten francs a tight bunch; vendors have violets, lilacs, tulips, and daisies spread out on little stalls covered with evergreen boughs. Apartments and offices have flowers all the time, and even the poorest people, going out to buy their 300 grams of bread, stick a bunch of flowers in their string bag along with the watercress.

There's so much to tell you that I feel as if I would explode! I want you to know about everything: the wooden-soled shoes (there is no leather); how polite people are in the Metro; how crazy the traffic is; how beautiful the boulevards; how clean the city (every morning the hydrants flow for several hours, and men with twig brooms sweep down the gutters); how people carry their sticks of bread with them everywhere; how pretty the children are; how shabbily people are dressed.

Thursday night, half a dozen of us walked down the river to the Ile de la Cité (the oldest part of Paris, the island in the Seine where the city began) to see Notre Dame in the moonlight. I hadn't been greatly impressed with the cathedral the first time I saw it as it seemed dingy and crumbling and cold. When I saw the fabulous jewels of the Treasure of Notre Dame, all I could think of was how useless a lot of gems and tons of gold and silver are when France is almost starving. But at night it was magic: the square towers rising beside the black river, the slender spire at the crossing, the flying buttresses with the deep blue night sky between them. The moonlight and shadows brought out the massiveness and delicacy of the stone work, and it was awesome to remember how long that great building, raised on an island to the honor of Our Lady, has stood there. While we leaned against the stone railing by the river, the clock in the tower boomed out eleven, and by the time it finished, clocks all over the city were answering it.

The public gardens, full of sun and color, are for the daytime. Tulips have just been set out in the Tuileries, and on Sunday there were thousands of people there, strolling under the trees, playing with their children, sailing bright toy sailboats across the fountains. Near our office are the Luxembourg Gardens where students from the Sorbonne come at noon to eat their lunches and study in the sunshine. There's a marionette show under the trees, statues of all the queens of France in

PALAIS DE CHAILLOT FROM THE EIFFEL TOWER. 1946
-PHOTOGRAPH BY MADELEINE

a great circle around a pool, and formal gardens just being planted.

Children are everywhere, lots of them, mostly toddlers. Since the end of the war and the return of soldiers and deportees, the birth rate has shot up. France takes good care of her children, as far as I can see, both government and parents. They get special rations, of course; whatever milk and chocolate and butter there is, goes to them. French parents seem very affectionate and solicitous. Too much so, some young Frenchmen think. Family ties are very strong, and sometimes children remain spoiled and dependent all their lives. I've seen men in their forties or fifties excuse themselves during discussions of business to go and ask maman what she thinks best.

The war has hurt France very deeply, more than one sees at first glance. There aren't starving people on the streets, but the average Frenchman is suffering from hidden starvation. For five years they've been on insufficient rations, and now a big proportion of the population is pretubercular. They have no resistance, they work slowly. Until this year's harvest is in, they're never more than a month's bread supply from acute hunger. They stand in line every day for everything, and they have severe inflation. A franc is worth less than a cent, which makes the exchange easy to figure out but is very hard on the average workingman's income. The only cheap things in Paris are bread and the Metro. A day's bread ration (300 grams) costs about five cents; you can ride anywhere in the city for two cents. Shoes are 1,500 francs, a cotton blouse 3,000 francs, and one must have ration stamps to buy everything from clothing to dishes.

Around Paris there was not very much destruction, but cities like Le Havre lost a third to a half of their houses and public buildings. The damage is being repaired very slowly; materials are scarce, and people are just too tired to be energetic about rebuilding. The gaiety of the French—showing again now that it's spring and they're getting warm and a little hopeful—is a kind of courage, really. They have had to build and rebuild so many times; it's wonderful that they ever laugh at all.

The tradition and the reminders of war are always present: still a lot of soldiers; many women in deep mourning; plaques all over the city, each commemorating a Parisian who died—always gloriously or heroically—on August 25 for the liberation of the city. Sometimes we Americans are irked by so many plaques, but I guess we can't understand what an occupation means. That August 25 was like the Day of Judgment for the French. You never talk to a Frenchman that he doesn't tell you what happened to him that day. Hatred of the Germans is deep and very bitter. Beside the plaques of 1945 are others from the war of 1870; you wonder if it will just go on and on.

So, although it's spring and Paris and moonlight and flowers, there's an undercurrent of sadness and questioning.

The problems of the world seem very much more complex and difficult here. Tangled strands reach back into the past; nothing is simple and direct. Sometimes I wonder if we're watching the death of a civilization: an old country, thinking more on its past than on its future; thinking in terms of the glory of empire and power when the day for that is long gone by; looking chiefly for security; bound by an incredible bureaucracy (the ETU men had to go to eight offices and ministries to get licenses to drive trucks!); its people being drained of vitality and hope. It's easy to see why the eyes of Europeans turn toward America as toward a Promised Land. To have to tell them that even America isn't all that is dreamed of is shaming and heartbreaking.

Our setup for living and working is great. I often feel guilty for being so very comfortable and happy, but there's no point in not enjoying what is here now. There will be times coming when the going will be tough. Here at the Varenne apartment, we have an excellent French cook and housekeeper who even does our laundry on the side. We take turns getting breakfast, which is porridge, tea (half of us are English), French bread, marmalade, and fruit once or twice a week. Dinners are wonderful: meat (American commissary rations) or chicken, potatoes (which are a luxury in France now), a vegetable or salad, French bread, and a pudding or fruit and cheese for dessert.

At noon, all Quaker workers eat together on French rations, which gives us an idea of what French food is like now: pottage (usually a gooey soup thickened with barley or rice); macaroni and potatoes, cooked together, sometimes with a dab of meat; French bread (everyone brings his own); water to drink; and for dessert, rice pudding. As one American said: "The thing that's wrong with the meal is—no starch!"

For the French, it's a good meal; at least it fills them up. We think it's so bad that we either eat somewhere else at noon or contribute rations so there can be some cheese, chocolate pudding, and coffee. Now that green vegetables are available, the meals are improving.

Way down on the list is my job! I did come here to work, but so far I've mostly enjoyed myself. The French program is in the process of closing down. There is still great need here, but it's eclipsed by that of other countries in Europe. The ETU has gone off to Marseille, Saint-Nazaire, and Rheims to help move supplies—food, building materials, furniture—to isolated villages and cities. One little town in the south where they are working is going hungry though there is food within a ten-mile radius. There simply is no transportation. Even here in Paris, much of the trucking is done in handcarts.

My first job was to look for a hotel where all the English and Americans—about fifteen of us—could stay until the work here closes down in June. That was a lark. I just poked all over Paris for a week, talking to people, seeing quaint streets and grand boulevards, and viewing dozens and dozens of red plush rooms. I finally found a place, which is an achievement in a city overflowing with American, British, and French army personnel and getting ready for the Peace Conference in May. I really gave my French a workout! I think now I could go anywhere and ask for anything.

I've done some visiting for the Refugee Committee, looking for people who lived here before the war and whose relatives are now looking for them. Interesting, but sometimes terribly pathetic.

I have a refugee case of my own, the sixteen-year-old Austrian nephew of my German teacher in Philadelphia. The boy's mother died in a concentration camp, but he and his sister escaped to France. They are now in an American-supported orphans' home, and their uncle wants them to come to America. The boy came to the office yesterday to see me and brought a comrade, a blond, bright Polish boy who has no relatives left. There are thousands like these two, unwanted, too old for their years, looking for a country that will give them a home and a future. Their adventures make our lives seem tame. They were interned, escaped, were sought by the SS, hidden by friendly French, worked for the Maquis (the French Resistance), all while they were still children. The boys asked me to come to the school and meet the director. In the midst of very grown-up talk, they said we could go boating on the river, and their eyes shone, and they were like any American kids free on Easter holidays. Somehow, that was heartbreaking.

Today, April 12, the first anniversary of Roosevelt's death, is commemorated all over France, in the schools and newspapers. Yesterday was the first anniversary of the liberation of Buchenwald, celebrated here by three masses. My two young visitors, the Pole and the Austrian, went to one; they were told that perhaps Roosevelt died when he did so that he would not have to know of the horrors of Buchenwald. The boys seemed to find this very fitting.

1993 ~ Madeleine from Monan's Rill

In the Quaker Service safe in Paris were jewels, rings, watches, and money given to Quaker workers during the war as they walked through the trains carrying deportees to the east for forced labor, often for death.

When the trains halted in Toulouse, for example, where the railway station was just across the street from the Quaker office, the staff would have prepared huge kettles of soup or hot cocoa, which the Germans allowed to be distributed to the deportees. During the distribution, people hastily wrapped valuables in bits of paper, with the addresses of family or friends to whom they wished them to go, and these were surreptitiously put into the pockets of the workers.

With these bits of paper, I poked around the streets of Paris looking for lost relatives, getting into quarters that I probably would never have otherwise seen. Some were like little villages, neighborhoods unto themselves, where people lived their lives without venturing into parts of the city that are world famous, to say nothing of having seen other provinces of France.

LOIS PLUMB AND WINSLOW AMES, AN AFSC COMMISSIONER OF EUROPE IN PARIS. 1946
-PHOTOGRAPHER UNKNOWN

Finding streets was not easy; during the Occupation, street names had sometimes been changed to confuse the Germans; after liberation, streets were re-named to honor heroes of the Resistance. Naturally, none of these changes appeared on the maps we had! It was seldom that I found the people to whom the sad treasures had been confided; most often they had moved or died or disappeared.

And then at last, a REAL job, in which both Red and I were involved! There were serious food shortages all over France, but along the Mediterranean coast, conditions were severe. There was a scarcity of local produce and existing food stocks had been diverted to the black market. While northern France was occupied, many children were sent south to large homes for safety. Sanatoria were established there because of the fine climate. At this time, all these institutions were unable to provide even minimum rations for their patients. Small, isolated communities were also suffering because of lack of transport. Secours Quaker had undertaken an emergency food distribution of seven tons of supplies over a six-week period, April 15 to May 31, 1946, under the direction of the Marseille delegation. The food was to be sent from Paris by truck. Red was one of the drivers, along with John Jones, an eighteen-year-old Quaker and conscientious objector, who had just been assigned to the ETU. I went along to write publicity in the hope that it would help raise additional funds in the U.S. for the relief effort.

April 1946 ~ Madeleine in Paris to friends and family in New York

John, Red, and I left Paris for Marseille on Good Friday, April 19, in two General Motors trucks (GMCs), six-by-sixes, loaded with about six tons of powdered milk, cocoa, sardines, and sugar—all foods more precious than money in Europe these days.

About 9:15 a.m., we rolled out of the garage. It was beautiful weather, cool and bright, the countryside just washed by a rain. Inside of an hour, we had two flats, the first of a score or more. The bombed roads are full of holes and shrapnel still lies about; the tire repair kit was as much a necessity as petrol.

The countryside here looks so French. It surprises us that fields and trees can look so different in another country. Plots of ground are small and perfectly tended. Everything is in miniature: little orchards with neat rows of lettuce planted between the flowering trees and small stone buildings, roofed with red tile, that look as if they had grown from the soil, along with the stone walls and trees.

Villages are close-set, always crowned with a church tower. Sometimes little streams run through, and buildings coming down to the water's edge are reflected there as in a green mirror. Lilacs were blooming everywhere, and wisteria dripped over courtyards and fences.

Going through these quiet, almost medieval villages in huge trucks makes us feel out of place. They seem to fill the streets from wall to wall, and we tower above everyone else. The roar of the motor brings heads popping out of every window and shop door, scattering the pedestrians like a flurry of chickens. Little kids wave to us, especially on the slow uphill grades where they can get a good look at us, and lots of them, even toddlers, still give the V-sign.

When we really got rolling, we didn't want to stop, not even to eat. It's a good feeling, seeing the speedometer eat up the miles, following the truck ahead of you through the winding streets of the town and watching the boxes marked with the Service Committee star disappear over a hill and come into sight again. You look at a road differently when you're in a truck. A downgrade is where you try to get up enough speed to go up the next hill without shifting; on the long slow pulls, you have time to see every flower and blade of grass along the roadside. I came to appreciate machinery, even if not to understand it.

Life here is terribly hard because people haven't learned how to use machines, and also because there aren't the machines to use. You see more ox-carts—two-wheeled, high, and unsteady-looking—than cars; you see men and women laboring under enormous burdens. Everything is slow and deliberate. Life is quiet and more whole, but that isn't enough. People starve for lack of trucks like ours. It seems necessary to learn to use machinery in a more fitting way than we have in America, perhaps, but not to give up using it. Over here, people do live more graciously—and less conveniently. But when the lack of convenience involves medieval sewage systems and dirty, vile, and polluted water, you begin to appreciate the mechanics of living.

Early in the afternoon, having used both spares in the first fifty miles, we stopped at a garage. I was delegated to do the talking— try asking for a hot patch in French! We got one, finally, and some lunch, too. In a little place, one can always get eggs (the omelets are so light they float), and bread and vin ordinaire, which taste wonderful after a few hours in an open cab with the wind whipping through and the sun on your face.

About five o'clock we wound our way through a tiny village, and that's a road test for the best drivers. The eight-foot-wide streets are filled with pedestrians, all more interested in their conversations than in getting out of the way. We encountered handcarts, bicycles, cows being driven home, sharp turns, no signs, and to cap it all, a troop of Girl Scouts marching down the street, making straight for us!

Once out into the open countryside, we made time until about nine o'clock, when we started to look for a place to spend the night. French villages really shut up shop. All the windows are shuttered tight. There are no street lights, and going through a village after dark, you'd think it was deserted.

In Digoin we finally called a halt. There was no garage for trucks, so the fellows drove them into the courtyard of the biggest hotel (not so very big), and Red slept with the trucks. John and I (John because he was the youngest and me because I was the girl) wallowed in the luxury of beds and hot water.

French beds are made for short people, but they're very wide, almost square. They have square puffs, filled with feathers, and bolster pillows. This hotel had French provincial furniture and was beautifully clean. My window gave on the main street of the town, and when I looked out, mine was the only open window for blocks! There were stars and in my room a handful of lilies of the valley that the concierge had given to me, and it was heaven to sleep.

Before we slept, we ate: more eggs, soup, sole, and ersatz coffee in the hotel dining room. Good Friday seems to be a family holiday here; there were several parties in the dining room. Two of the older women wore fine, full black dresses and exquisite lace head dresses, starched until they looked like wings. We were a dusty, greasy lot to be sitting down with them, but we were so tired we didn't care. I have found something curious: When you're tired, your tongue just doesn't cope with a foreign language. After a long day, it's all I can do to say the simplest thing in French, though the rest of the time, French is so natural that we fall into it even when talking with Americans and British.

Saturday was beautiful. The country began to look poorer and wilder as we got further south. We began to see the reason for the food crisis in the Midi.

It is the most peaceful of countrysides, broken here and there, incongruously, by ruins: farmhouses riddled by shelling, sections of stone villages smashed flat, and always, always, the blown bridges. After a while you learn to look for the differences in color and building material that mark the line between the old foundations and new temporary bridges. Many of them have not been replaced. The cleanness with which they are sliced off at the abutment always surprises me. Such neat destruction.

At one point, we rode for miles between rusty, burned-out trucks, jeeps, and antitank guns piled up man-high along the road. It was a grim path. And at Toulouse, they told us of riding for miles between boxes of unexploded shells and machine gun bullets! There just isn't any place to get rid of the ammunition, so it's piled up along the road and left.

At noon we stopped in a field and sprawled in the sun for an hour. Relief workers' lunch: canned butter, fresh bread, canned cheese, peanut butter, marmalade, and water still cool in a canteen brought from Paris. A little boy came sidling up to us when we'd almost finished. He wouldn't say much, but he probably knew that around an army truck there would be something to eat, and he looked as if he could use it. Skinny—as most French children are—bare legs stuck in shorts made of khaki canvas so stiff they would have stood without him, and heavy, clumsy shoes broken through at the toes. His daddy had gone to war and hadn't come back, he said. That was all we could get out of him, but he devoured every scrap left from lunch. We filled his pockets before we sent him home.

Late in the afternoon, one of the motors began missing, but we decided to try to make Avignon anyway, since the chances of finding a truck garage there were better than in a small town. We kept on rolling, and about ten o'clock we hit Avignon. Here we were "deceived," as the French say. People didn't seem to know the streets of their own city; for an hour we were chasing in and out of the gates of the old wall—which weren't built with trucks in mind.

Finally we gave up, drove out of the city, parked beside a field, unrolled our sleeping bags and called it a day. There was a new moon in the sky, adding a special tenderness to the moment.

Easter morning! Church bells from the ancient city of the Popes woke me, or maybe it was the birds. In the dark, we had picked a good place, a meadow full of yellow daisies and pink clover and buttercups. It was a warm, sparkling day, perfect for an Easter parade. What a contrast with last year when frilled and veiled and flowered I set off for Washington Cathedral. This year I sported slacks in which I had slept; my face was streaked with dirt (no water to wash in); my hands were raw from having washed them in gasoline; and my corsage was of field flowers. Still, a beautiful Easter!

While the fellows tinkered with the truck, I went cross-lots to the nearest farmhouse for water and breakfast. The people were kindly and didn't seem half as surprised to see an American girl at their door as I was to be there. John cooked a K-ration breakfast, very good and very filling. I can see how, after the thirtieth time, you could get tired of it, but this was satisfying.

Before we'd finished breakfast, three men from the farmhouse came over. One of them jumped up on a fender of the truck, stuck his head inside the motor, and started taking it apart. Somewhat startled, we asked him what he was doing; he said it was okay, he was an airplane mechanic with the French army, home on leave. In half an hour he had the motor purring. We passed around K-ration cigarettes and candy and started off again.

As one goes south, the land gets drier and poorer. Rows of dark, pointed cypress cut across the landscape. They were planted for windbreaks against the Mistral, the cold, bitter wind that sweeps down from the mountains. There were a few vineyards, some scraggly olive trees, and fields of bright red poppies, just like those that veterans sell on the streets at home on Armistice Day, November 11. Early in the afternoon, we bumped into Marseille over roads full of shell holes.

Still grimy and hot, with greasy clothes and dust-filled eyes, we were escorted into the swankest hotel in Marseille, the Grand Hôtel de Noailles. Requisitioned by the American army for billets, it has beautiful high-ceilinged rooms with private baths and a paneled dining room with white linen tablecloths, red roses on each table, and a string orchestra! The contrast floored us. It took a day until we felt comfortable among all the army brass in the mess, but the ways of luxury are easy to learn, and pretty soon we were going to army movies and eating PX (Purchasers' Exchange U.S.Army) ice cream as if we'd never been relief workers on the road.

1993 ~ Madeleine from Monan's Rill

I spent several days in Marseille and then went on to Toulouse to report on conditions there. Red worked for several weeks with the Marseille delegation before returning to Paris briefly and then leaving for Poland.

The Quaker delegation in Marseille distributed food to groups of children and young people medically ascertained to be of greatest risk from malnutrition. This was done through goûters (that untranslatable cross between a tea and a snack) and a package service. Six days a week, children were given a hot milk drink containing chocolate and malt and either cheese, sardines, or chocolate to be eaten with bread.

The seven tons of food, along with the two trucks and two drivers that we had brought, meant that the relief program in Marseille could be extended to orphanages, old people's homes, and isolated villages along the Côte d'Azur. For John, Red, and me, being part of this effort was a heady experience. Our delivery routes took us along the magnificent Grande Corniche, where red rock cliffs plunge into the intensely blue Mediterranean waters for which the Azure Coast is named. The beauty and the poverty of the region, the walled medieval towns set on almost inaccessible heights, and the history going back to Greeks and Romans dazzled our naive American eyes.

Touched by the romance of the Midi, our truck trips were high adventure. We were finally doing a tangible relief job in an ancient land of surpassing beauty, and Red and I were becoming more and more aware of the exciting attraction between us. "But at our backs we always hear Time's winged chariot hurrying near." We were together for only a few days. Eventually Red would be sent to Poland, and we could not know what our shared fate might be.

April 1946 ~ Madeleine in Marseille to AFSC in Philadelphia

The younger children tear in after school carrying their bowls in bright cloth bags or wrapped in layers of newspaper. They're bright-eyed and noisy as children ought to be, in spite of their pipe-stem arms, the sores on their legs that betoken vitamin deficiency, and their much-patched clothing.

A few, smaller and thinner than the rest (and all of them look undersized by several years), come in slowly dragging a twisted leg or stumbling along in misshapen shoes and lean wearily against a wall while their more energetic comrades whoop it up. The hot drink disappears in one long gulp. Then the boys rush out into the courtyard, munching chunks of bread and the cheese or chocolate or fish that is provided that day. For many, it is their supper. They have to be carefully watched to see that the precious food isn't taken home to a small brother or sister. One must be sternly selfish; food goes to those who most need it and can best use it.

TWO CHILDREN FROM THE SPANISH REFUGEE FEEDING PROGRAM
-PHOTOGRAPHER UNKNOWN

This feeding, which to an American seems little more than the snack the average youngster gets on coming home from school, produces amazing results. As a rule, the children gain weight at once, sometimes as much as two kilos (about four-and-a-half pounds) the first month. They grow, too. Dispositions change. Many a problem child has become friendly and cooperative after a month or two of goûter. They study better. They regain their appetites. Many pretubercular children lose the taste for the poor French rations, but after supplementary feeding, they are able to relish and assimilate the coarse food they ordinarily get.

Doctors say that two or three months of goûter saves many children from tuberculosis. Those who have gained weight continue to do so after the goûter has been stopped. Of forty-seven children who were entered in a goûter program, forty-three showed gains in weight at the end of one month ranging up to five-and-one-quarter pounds.

CHILD FEEDING PROGRAM AT TOULOUSE, FRANCE FOR SPANISH REFUGEES. 1946
-PHOTOGRAPH BY DICKIE AND TONY CHAPELLE

For the children who need additional feeding, there is a package service. Once a week they file into the office, a ragged shopping bag clutched in one hand. Inside are empty dried milk cans and a bottle for the week's ration of oil. The very little ones rush in and throw their arms around Madame in a burst of affection and gratitude. Then they slip off their sandals or their clumsy shoes (very few have socks or stockings) and solemnly climb on the scales. Most of them gain at a satisfying rate; those who do not are investigated to see whether they are really getting all of the extra food at home or whether they are too ill to benefit from our feeding and need medical care. We fill the bag with precious things: oatmeal, dried milk, rice, sugar, oil, a malt preparation, fruit paste, cheese, margarine—all foods high in calories and rich in the proteins so badly lacking in the French diet.

In Nice, we visited an orphanage that one entered by a dank, shadowy alley and then climbed hundreds of stone steps to come out at last into a courtyard on top of a hill. (No question of getting a truck up there; boxes had to be carried up those steps.) Here were sunshine, grass, and trees. Sober little girls—all dressed in black, their thin bare legs stuck into great clumsy shoes—were working at jobs that we in America would think too dull and difficult for young hands: cleaning, sewing, washing in great stone tubs. They looked as if they could very well do with supplementary feeding.

Another, more cheerful home was a day nursery for little tots. The sweet-faced Red Cross worker told the children that we were Americans come to bring them good things to eat and that they should say thank you. Embarrassing moment for both the children and us! Finally one adorable little boy in a pink checked apron lisped, "Merci pour le chewing gum!" Months ago some Americans had given the children gum, and the association stuck fast.

I had a concern to do something
constructive where there had been war,
and the rest followed naturally
                                    -Red

Yes, Paris Is For Lovers

August 23

Dear my Red,

I've found a quiet place at las—
I'm in a convent! No, I haven
taken the veil — a heck of a nun
I'd make! But it seems quite
the thing hereabouts to retire for
a week-end or even a vacation.
Some convents take in people a
pensionaires — like a hotel, almo
others take in people for sweet
charity.

I went to mass at 6:30 this
morning — not so much from
piety as because the bell
clanged right outside my
window. A sweet-faced
soeur just came in to ask m
why I hadn't eaten break
fast. It seems the mother

April 29, 1946 ~ Red in Marseille to Madeleine in Toulouse

Nine o'clock last night has been uppermost in my mind since you left; it was as if part of me left on that train with you. I walked out beside the station where the lights of the lower section of Marseille could be seen. The night and the lights brought back Le Havre, and from there I relived many of the moments we have had together since then. It was like a lifetime wrapped up in a few short weeks.

Coming down the long stairs, I nearly ran. I wanted to sing and shout and cry all at the same time. It was very tempting to walk down to the Old Port, but I knew I needed some rest. Today I looked at the stairs where we walked together and felt great tenderness for them, tenderness that I never thought I could feel for something as cold and hard as stone steps. They seemed to symbolize that we had taken a few steps together until we were up where we had the whole world before us.

The expected has happened: Martha, John Munsey, and I have received notices to vacate the hotel. We plan to look for an apartment where we can live and eat together. We don't even know whether we can get commissary privileges here. If not, we may fare pretty common for awhile. Maybe we can get a better feel of what it is like to live like the French. Certainly we have lived in a world of our own since arriving here. Darling, already I am looking forward to the first letter from you.

April 29, 1946 ~ Madeleine in Toulouse to Red in Marseille

I blessed you and the army this morning, the army for having dreamed up K-rations and you for having made me bring some with me. Here at Toulouse one gets off the train and enters a restaurant that serves coffee in bowls but nothing else. Everybody pulled out hunks of bread and cheese, and I pulled out my K-rations and shared them with an uncommunicative French woman sitting beside me who didn't seem to have anything. They tasted good, but I like them better out in a field on an Easter morning.

Tonight, I'm in a hotel room that's a Sears & Roebuck nightmare: red and pink wallpaper and a brilliant blue satin comforter! Toulouse is fun, a lively delegation and a beautiful view of the Pyrenees, like a luminous cloud below the clouds. The city seems small after Marseille, quaint and quiet. Toulouse is nice. I like it.

May 1946 ~ Report from Roger Craven to AFSC in Philadelphia

(Roger Craven was one of the early members of the ETU.)

Some of us had a most gratifying experience last week. I happened to be in Toulouse, where I had taken a load of clothing, and Friday afternoon I went along on one of the regular visits to the POW camp at Mauzac. We took some food and medical supplies and walked around the camp visiting the prisoners.

Conditions were terrible. There were almost no beds, and the men slept crowded together on straw mats on the floor. I tasted some of the stuff that had been given them for a meal: soy bean flour with all the oil removed. After eating a spoonful of it, one could well understand why forty of the prisoners had vomited it up after trying to make a meal of it. Each day for lunch they are given that stuff, and if they do not eat it, they get nothing. We talked with the men about their families and their experiences. Certainly gloom hung over them as they faced the prospect of eventually returning to a Germany where, as they say, "Alles ist kaputt."

We learned that on the following morning, 150 of these men were to be transferred on foot to another camp, twenty-four kilometers away. Each man would have to carry all of his belongings.

When we got back to Toulouse, we busied ourselves with plans. Madeleine Chevalier, Andy Maisano, and I were chosen to try to be of some help in the situation. Next morning early, the three of us set out with a truck, a jeep and trailer, and supplies for making many gallons of hot chocolate. We met the troop on the road about half an hour after they had started. They had covered about two kilometers, carrying on their shoulders all manner of packs, boxes, and sacks with all their worldly possessions therein. Each man was carrying around fifty or sixty pounds. A few words of negotiation (Madeleine was our go-between) and soon the men were lined up behind the truck while two of them climbed inside to pack the baggage. We weren't sure at first whether there would be room for everything, so only the heaviest bags were accepted. But the prisoners who were doing the packing fully realized their responsibility, and as the very last corner of space was taken, the last pack was placed aboard. What a relief! The men set out again on their march, this time with a little sprightliness in their step. I inquired as they filed past, "Geht's besser?" "Ja, danke!" came the resounding reply.

Madeleine and Andy went with the jeep back to Mauzac, and with the cheerful cooperation of the prisoner kitchen crew, prepared two huge kettles of hot chocolate. Back down the road they went, Andy driving the jeep and Madeleine riding behind in the trailer, holding the lids on the kettles. They overtook the prisoners at just about mid-distance; a halt was called and serving of chocolate began. Everybody was in on the refreshments, including the French soldiers in charge and the Senegalese guards, some of whom wore evidence of their African tribal customs in the form of scars, cut in elaborate patterns, on their faces. Every man had two cups of hot chocolate and one or two sweet biscuits. Hot chocolate! They had not tasted any for such a long time. Expressions of gratitude were simple but heartfelt.

I drove ahead with the truck full of luggage, carrying a prisoner with an injured foot and a Senegalese guard who directed me in French. The prisoner and I chatted in German and became quite good friends. His name was Herbert. He came from Leipzig, had been captured in Africa, and had been in the USA as a prisoner. He told me, "My comrades are so happy that you came." Later on, as the miles rolled by, he remarked that the men simply could not have made the journey without our help.

We finally arrived at the new camp, and many hands were there, ready to unload the truck. I noticed one of the prisoners scooping up a few handfuls of dirty rice and macaroni that lay strewn on the floor of the truck, where they had fallen when some paper bags broke on an earlier trip. So I scraped up all the grains I could, put them into a bag, and gave it to him. That, he said, would give him the best meal he had had for a long time, once he washed the dirt off.

Just before I drove off, I jumped down from the truck, reached through the still-open gate of the barbed wire fence and shook hands with Herbert. His smile was something to remember.

May 1, 1946 ~ Madeleine in Toulouse to Red in Marseille

Happy Premier Mai! Are you wearing lilies of the valley, like everybody else this morning? This is a holiday! Our concierge says, "This is the day of the workers, which means that nobody works!" Not even the trams run. You walk.

This afternoon I'm going to the POW camp at Mauzac, and tonight—I wish you were here—there's a dance in honor of two delegates who are leaving. All the staff and personnel—cooks, drivers, students, everybody—are invited. It should be a fun time! Do come and visit this delegation if you have a chance, Red. It's a lively group but not a very democratic one, which you wouldn't like.

Toulouse is picturesque, but it smells to high heaven. In addition to all the usual problems of France, it has the Spaniards, an eloquent, impassioned, miserable lot of people. Coming into the waiting room of the center here is like walking into a Hemingway novel.

Tomorrow I go back to Paris. Have you been to Nice yet? Throw a kiss to the Mediterranean for me. I miss you.

May 1946 ~ Madeleine in Toulouse to AFSC in Philadelphia

Quaker workers from Montauban, driving through the Département of the Dordogne early in 1945, first noticed the prison camp at Mauzac because of the pitiable condition of the men behind the rusty barbed wire. Mauzac is a camp for political prisoners, one of the many in France crowded with men condemned, justly or unjustly, as collaborationists. (German POWs are also held here.) The Quakers asked to go into the camp to leave supplies for the infirmary. They were refused. For six months they tried. Finally in August of 1945, they were allowed to leave supplies but not to visit. At that time, no other agency could get into the camp; not even pastors were permitted to see the prisoners.

In February 1946, after much negotiation, a parcel service was started. Given the camp rations, extra food was absolutely necessary. Of the 1,300 prisoners, those who received nothing from their families or who were especially in need of supplementary food were selected by the prisoners themselves to receive the Quaker parcels.

The situation was a difficult one to work in. Guards inside the camp and French outside were quick to resent undue concern for those whom they considered traitors. There is much bitterness still, but from the months when Quaker workers were not allowed inside the barbed-wire gate, relationships with the camp officials have progressed to the point where now a truck painted with the red and black star can drive unquestioned into the camp with whatever personnel are necessary to distribute the parcels.

On their July trip to the camp, the Quakers were accompanied by a French Red Cross worker and a social service worker from

Entr'Aide Française. The parcels were made up from Entr'Aide and Quaker stocks, and the distribution was made jointly. From here on, the French agencies are taking over responsibility for the parcel service, for medical supplies to the infirmary, and for social service work in the camp. This is in line with the general policy of Quaker Service to encourage local agencies to take over work started by the Quakers, so it will become part of a permanent, indigenous program. In the case of the political prison camps, this relationship is especially significant, for it marks the beginning of a concern by the French for a group of people who represent a grave problem in national unity and understanding.

May 3, 1946 ~ Madeleine in Paris to Red in Marseille

I just came back from Notre Dame des Champs and found a fistful of mail, your letter among it, for which I was terribly glad. It was a beautiful train ride from Toulouse yesterday. Coming north it was spring again, in a rolling, peaceful countryside. The hills were crowned with châteaux, stone houses seeming to grow from the friendly soil. The train's big corridor windows were open, and one could stand there

SECOURS QUAKER (FRENCH) TRUCK AND WORKER
-PHOTOGRAPH COURTESY OF AFSC ARCHIVES

in the sun, watching the landscape flash by. In the evening a thin red moon hung in the west with a single star blazing over it, and I wished you there.

I must work. I'm dead tired in a comfortable way, but I must do that report. I feel a hurting humility; I wish somehow I could be an instrument to make people at home see the need and move them to be compassionate and wise and understanding. Not only for the food, but for the whole tremendous need of the world for brotherhood and honesty and vision. I'm not the one who can do it, but I have to try.

May 5, 1946 ~ Madeleine in Paris to Red in Marseille

A week ago, we visited Château d'If and Notre Dame de la Garde, and walked the steps to the station. Yesterday and today, I've been making up for those leisurely days in the south, by working hard on reports. I'm not half done. I came back from Toulouse just bursting with impressions and ideas, and in a few days, I think, I'm slated to go to Saint-Nazaire.

Yesterday the ETU gave a tea—very pleasant, very successful, except for two distinct lacks: no cookies and no Red. I picked up on my back transport gossip: ten men are going to Poland the first of June, you among them, of course, and maybe John Jones.

Winslow Ames is back; he's going soon to Austria to investigate transport needs there. Three fellows on their way to Italy were passing through, and we have more to come from Pendle Hill. How the world doth move! Joe Howell is up in Norway or Denmark getting barracks to take back to Le Chambon. Howard Wriggins and Steve Cary are going to the Côte d'Azur to see about an extended feeding program there, which makes me happy. (Minor note: I sure would like to know what's going to happen to me.)

One of the things that's been burning inside me ever since Toulouse and my first visit to a POW camp is the great need for literature in German for those men. They sit there, trying to sort things out, with nothing to do or else doing dangerous and unrewarding work, such as de-mining fields. There I am, in the middle of about 100 Germans, and they ask me, "Why do the Quakers want to go into Germany?" And in my halting German, I try to tell them, sounding like a five-year-old.

They want literature about Quakerism, and I thought they might like to chew on some material about co-ops. They're going back into a hell of a difficult society, and somebody ought to be giving them something new to think about, new patterns to work with, the best that we know from experience. It seems such a distinctively Quaker job, and so far we haven't touched it. I got a few Quaker pamphlets and a little co-op literature from Del Eberhardt, and I'm going to try to translate and mimeograph it for a start.

Can't you see what might happen if Friends and the co-op movement really got into this? It's political dynamite for sure for men who are going back into the Russian zone, for example, but everybody else can go around setting off capitalistic and reactionary and nationalistic dynamite; why can't we set off a little of our own brand?

Damn! I wish I knew more! I wish I were five people! I wish I didn't get tired. I wish I could see you, right now, walking in the door.

May 7, 1946 ~ Red in Marseille to Madeleine in Paris

Tuesday morning I was enjoying a leisurely breakfast, knowing I did not have to rush, thinking I might even take time off to write some letters, when John Munsey, head of mission, rushed in. "Where is John? Get him quick! Two trucks have been stolen!" This seemed so unreal that, if not for how very upset he was, I would not have believed him.

The two of us hurried to the warehouse while he told me what he knew. The two men who guard the warehouse are Spanish refugees, a man and his son who have been with Secours Quaker for nearly six years. Felix, the father, also works in the warehouse, and the son works as a mechanic in the garage. When we arrived, Felix broke out crying like a baby; I have seldom seen a man as upset and broken as he was.

Armed, masked robbers had tied their feet together and their hands behind their backs, blindfolded and gagged them, then roped them to their beds. This was at 2 a.m. With the watchmen safely tied, the robbers took four hours to load the best foods: all the chocolate (worth at least one million francs on the black market), all the sugar, all the sardines, and all the rice—which hasn't been seen in France for over five years. They had taken time to open various cases that were not clearly marked, and food and clothing were scattered about. Our usual time for leaving is early morning, so the robbers left at the same time, which facilitated their passing through a guarded gate. My truck had been full of gas and was standing waiting. It was as though half my life was gone when I looked at the empty space that the evening before had held my truck!

After the robbers were gone, Felix's son was able to ease from under the ropes tying him to the bed and then, with hands and feet still tied, managed to get a kitchen knife. He released Felix from his bed, and the two men stood back to back and cut the ropes from around their wrists.

The French police, American MPs, and the Criminal Investigative Division of the U.S. Army were notified. To make things more interesting, we had to take the French police wherever they wanted to go, or else wait for them to use a trolley, walk, or ride a bicycle. They had no motorized equipment.

The French immediately took the two watchmen in for questioning. Felix was given the "third degree," and his son was put through fourteen hours of grilling. Felix's son was more at ease than he had been in the morning; he said he had done nothing wrong, and he knew we had confidence in him. We hope the police are now looking in other directions to find the missing goods.

Shortly after noon, we received a call; one abandoned truck had been located. It was empty but not damaged, and everything was intact except that there were no keys. My truck was located near where the other truck had been abandoned. Although it had been driven only nine miles, all the gas was gone, as well as a battery, spare tire, medical kit, tools, driving glasses, and gloves.

Munsey and I were talking this afternoon and comparing Marseille with Chicago during the Prohibition era. John said that, in Chicago, one was not much endangered unless he was handling illegal liquor or narcotics. Here, however, we are handling the very goods that gangs are most anxious to get. In fact, this robbery was one of the biggest hauls the black market has made in some time. It brings back to me what Barclay Jones said after being in Europe for several months: "If Quakers want to work in and take goods into certain areas of Europe, they will have to mount machine guns on their trucks." This hits deep into the heart of pacifism.

I missed you more today than any day since you left. Why is it that when one is deeply hurt or exceedingly happy, he wants to be with the person closest to him?

May 9, 1946 ~ Madeleine in Paris to Red in Marseille

Just two lines, maybe three, before I leave for Saint-Nazaire. If you do come to Paris this weekend, I'll be terribly sorry to have missed you, but like you, I can't let personal desires enter into the job.

I was startled to hear of the theft. This must have been a bad week for you people in Marseille. It's good to know that the trucks were found, but the food is a great loss.

May 9, 1946 ~ Red in Marseille to Madeleine in Paris

Dammit, I wish you were here! This morning John Munsey said to me, "If you had a choice of staying here a couple of extra weeks or going to Paris, which would you choose?" Immediately, I confessed I would choose Paris. John has been talking with Tom Bodine in Paris; they have promised more food. Just to distribute what we have will take longer than this month, so the thinking is that John Jones and I should stay longer or that John, with the two trucks, should stay.

At dinner time, I told Munsey that I was selfish in saying I would prefer to go back to Paris; if ETU sees fit to keep us here, I would not feel right about leaving. This may mean that the team leaves for Poland immediately after I return to Paris. I still have my fingers crossed that you and I shall have a couple of weeks together before we have to part for too long a time. It hurt to commit myself to staying here, but neither of us would feel right if I left a job unfinished just so that we could be near each other. Agreed?

Please don't worry about me. We are still eating at the army mess, and now I am eating my PX candy between meals. Before I was giving it away. I think that I shall start taking vitamins again.

May 18, 1946 ~ Madeleine to AFSC in Philadelphia

(This is a report on the work by the ETU in Saint-Nazaire in Brittany)
"American" is a name not well-loved in Saint-Nazaire. It means bombings—the bombings that have practically razed the city and made homeless some 25,000 people. It means the terrible night of February 28, 1943, the night that Saint-Nazairiens tell you of as if it were the end of the world, as indeed it was for a large part of the city. The American bombers aimed for the huge German submarine pens, but they destroyed instead hospitals, churches, schools, and blocks and blocks of workers' homes.

But in the last few weeks, "American" is coming to represent something else. Word has gone around that an American transport unit is here with big trucks to move bombed-out people back to their homes—free. In the shipyard, where most of Saint-Nazaire works, hangs this sign:

> *Some generous Americans, the "Quakers of Philadelphia," are putting trucks at the disposal of bombed-out Saint-Nazairiens in order to move.*

Newspapers carry advertisements; one bombed-out family tells another; word is spread by chance conversations with the ETU drivers.

It's hard for the French to understand why these men want to do hard, dirty work just to render a service, to enjoy a day spent working with them, to have the satisfying feeling of seeing a family in its own home after years of repeatedly moving, uncertainty, and danger and destruction. It's especially hard to believe that they are Americans. Americans, to too many Frenchmen, are always rich, with their pockets full of chocolate and chewing gum. But these Americans, though they do give candy to the children, seem not to be rich; they work hard, and they eat in the restaurant of Entr'Aide—a national relief organization.

By ones and twos, the bombed-out find their way to the office of Quaker Transport. Workmen, young mothers, patient old peasants, the story is always the same: bombing, terror, evacuation, bombing, evacuation again. "Half our house was destroyed the night of February 28. We moved what we could to the country, where we have one room for the whole family. Now we'd like to go back to Saint-Nazaire, but there is no way to move our furniture."

"Our house was burned during the bombing. We have found a little house in the village, but what furniture we have is at my mother's home, a long way from here. I don't even have a bed for the baby, and I have to borrow dishes from the neighbors. The moving company wants 10,000 francs to bring our things down here, and with three children, we can't possibly pay that."

Some of the people who come have been bombed out and moved as many as five times. After all that, they haven't much left. Their one desire is to go back home and start rebuilding. Transport is very scarce, and when it can be found, the cost is prohibitive. One woman who came to the office told us of the donkey and cart she had hired to move a table and six chairs back to her house. The load was too much for the little beast and for the old woman who drove him; the whole lot ended up in a ditch. In despair, she came to the Americans.

Sometimes the story of a home destroyed is the smallest part of the tragedy—an only child killed; a father shot as a hostage; a family deported and only a few members returned. The French speak of these things simply and quietly; we can only listen in silence, knowing how little we can enter into their suffering. It is good to be able to offer them even the small service of moving.

Mme. Bottini's move was a typical one. We started off early, taking with us a chunk of French bread and a can of sardines in case no other lunch was forthcoming. The way led through Saint-Nazaire, as it often does. It's a good way to start a trip; you see vividly why the transport team is here.

The few buildings are surrounded by blocks of open space, now cleared of debris. Only neat piles of stone show where houses once stood. Other houses, still standing, have been gutted by fire; you see the sky through them as you pass. Piles of stone, shells of buildings wait to be rebuilt.

There is a plan for a new Saint-Nazaire, but it will take ten or twenty years to complete. Meanwhile it waits on building materials, the complexities of government offices, and the energies of a people just beginning to recover from disaster. About one-third of the population has moved back; some people live in wooden barracks erected by the government, some in partially-repaired houses. Little shops have been set up in homes. People pick their way on bicycles through the shell-holed streets. Men are still tearing down damaged buildings and piling up stone to be reused. Life goes on in the slow, painful, half-hopeless way so characteristic of war-hurt countries. It's a relief to come to the open countryside and see oxen plowing in the fields, hawthorn blooming in the hedges.

The village of Saint-Joachim, to which Mme. Bottini was evacuated, looks like something out of the Middle Ages: mud roads, ancient stone houses, thatched roofs. It would be drab without the window boxes of geraniums and daisies and the calla lilies in the dooryards of the humblest homes.

The Bottinis and their two small children have lived for three years in one small, dark room on the second floor of an ancient cottage. The furniture had to be carried down a half-rotted stairway or lowered through the window. It was modest: two beds, cupboards, half a dozen chairs, a stove, the children's toys, some trunks and boxes. Because these people have so little, they are careful to save everything; this load, like most of the others, consisted partly of moldy boards for firewood, old bicycle tires, rusty pipe, and the spare wheel of a Ford (all that remained of a car taken by the Germans). Knowing how much such things mean, the drivers are patient and considerate about loading on as much of this apparently useless collection as they can.

It was a three-hour job to load the truck. By the time we finished, the weather was threatening, and we didn't dare to stop for lunch. Halfway to Saint-Nazaire, it poured. Mme. Bottini was beside herself. "To think," she moaned, "that we saved these things from bombardment only to have them perish in this disaster!" We reassured her as best we could and drove as fast as we dared. At the new house, neighbors turned out to help, and the load was off the truck in one-quarter the time it had taken to put it on. By then the sun was shining, Mme. Bottini had recovered her good spirits, and Quaker Transport had recovered its good name.

On the way home from a job, the transport trucks always stop at the square in Saint-Nazaire to pick up the passengers who can't crowd on the bus. "Pornichet, La Baule, Le Pouliguen, and all points west," or its French equivalent. Workmen come running from every side, hailing their friends along the way. Some of them are amputees, hopping agilely on a peg leg. Usually there is standing room only. As they get off by twos or threes, they always walk past the cab to say, "Thanks, buddy, that was a big lift." And they use the familiar tu, which—in a country that has lived for five years under a conquering army—is a real sign of equality and good comradeship.

May 18, 1946 ~ Madeleine in Paris to Red in Marseille

Back in Paris again after driving in one day from Saint-Nazaire with George Loveland in the command car. It doesn't "march" very well, so we had to come the whole way at 25 m.p.h., an awful strain when you have miles of empty, straight, fairly good road in front of you!

The lovely, peaceful, fertile countryside is wilder than the neat farms south of Paris. Statues and crucifixes at every crossroad; châteaux on the hills; a tapestry-like field of glorious color: crimson clover, red poppies, and blue bachelor buttons. Half a dozen interesting hitchhikers— some old and pathetic, one drunk, all friendly. I do like France! Every time I go off on a long trip or unroll my sleeping bag, I think of our Marseille trip. Those few days are like a little lifetime, complete and beautiful in themselves.

Of course you must stay in Marseille if that's where you're needed now, but I'll be heartsick if we don't get a little time together before you go to Poland. Maybe it's just because I'm done in after a long, cold ride yesterday, but the thought of not having a little more time of shared experiences and understanding is very hard to take at the moment. After all my friends' talk about the "sacrifices" of relief work—none of which have materialized so far—I feel suddenly that not seeing you for a long time is the first real sacrifice I must make. Of course, if it weren't for relief work, I might never have known you at all, but that's not much comfort at the moment.

Don't mind me, Red; I'll be OK tomorrow. Right now I'm obsessed with the problem of how people stay close in understanding when they're far away and long away from each other. It can be done, I'm sure, and has been, but I'm not sure I know yet the "pattern for apartness." It's partly, I think, being aware and happy in knowing the other person's inner self—his earnestness and honesty and good faith and affection—even if one can't know for the time being, much of his outer self: what he's doing and thinking and feeling.

I wonder if you can make anything out of this muddle beyond the fact that I miss you very much.

Speaking of Poland, there's something I want to ask you about, Red. Be as frank as you can. This is just a supposition, but if there is a chance for women to go there, and if I were available—as I think I shall be—what would you think of my asking for the job? I think it's honest to say that I'd go first of all because I was interested. I'd be as willing to go to Germany or Austria. The fact that you'd be in Poland carries a weight that I can't deny. I wouldn't let it be the deciding factor, but I can't help knowing that it's there. Would it be a good idea or not, assuming that other things were equal? I guess the question I want to ask is: if it didn't make any difference to the work or to anyone else, what would you think of our being in the same area? This is all hypothetical, as you well know.

May 18, 1946 ~ Red in Marseille to Madeleine in Paris

Today is my fifteenth straight day of work. Never a dull moment at the Marseille delegation! We have been informed that more than 50 percent of the stolen food has been found! Now they are trying to get it hauled back to our warehouse.

May 19, 1946 ~ Madeleine in Paris to Herb Hauck in Philadelphia

I dunno what kind of letter this will turn out to be. I'm bursting with things I want to say to you; last night during a wonderful violin concert I wrote you a long spiel—in my head, of course. I feel as if beginning this is like opening a floodgate. I'm terribly confused: first, from the over-wealth of impressions and sensations of the last weeks; second, from my own natural bewilderment; and third, because the very welcome bundle of stuff I found here when I came back from Brittany (those letters may have seemed dead to you but they were very quick to me) was confusing, too. You and I, in our different ways, mon ami, seem to have come to a very bewildering place in our lives. I wonder at it, but with more acceptance, I think, than I'd have had a few months ago.

That's probably as good a place as any to start—the acceptance. Strangely, the last few weeks—in the midst of new places, new facts, new people, great delight, and great wondering—I've seemed to find, with a kind of surprise, a willingness to wait, belief, calm—what you will. Maybe it's the "trust thyself" you eternally preach. I can't see that I've got anything to do with it, it's just sort of there. Conflicts, contradictions, unclearness—sure; but at the bottom somewhere a half-felt knowledge that these are necessary and resolvable, and that in the end I'll make out.

Lately, too, going pretty much my own way, on a job I know little about, stumbling along with almost no direction, and without the concentration of will that some people can substitute for talent or skill, I've found a kind of stubborn humility in my own way and my own integrity, the feeling that I may and do make mistakes and blunders, and that I'm sorry if I do, but that's the best I know how at the moment. If anyone wants to tell me about them, OK, but he doesn't have any business being sore.

Gosh Herb, in the past few weeks, seeing what I've seen, knowing how few people at home can know what I know, I've practically prayed for the gift of tongues, and I'm becoming more and more convinced that I haven't got 'em. That's a bitter pill for someone who's always been told and always thought that she had a "flair for words." When I think of the voices that have been raised in the last ten years in a desperate attempt to rouse the world to its sins against the spirit of man, I quail. Hemingway couldn't cause more than a ripple of sentiment for the Loyalists, and I should try to describe the wretched, passionate, still-believing Spanish refugees I saw at Toulouse?

The men I've seen in political concentration camps—some still clear-eyed and patient, some dull and staring—held there for lack of a piece of paper, or for having been born on the wrong side of a border. Men of talent, intelligence, kindliness; men who want to plow a field or hold a surgeon's knife or kiss a woman or write a constitution. Sure, it sounds dramatic, melodramatic—but life is that when it's reduced to its essentials. So they sit in filthy barracks and starve on thin soup.

The French Red Cross worker who visits them took us around to see them. We're always the good Americans who bring food—of course there's no rationing at home, and the wheat farmers are waiting for the price ceilings to break. God, in this work you get down on your knees mentally twenty times a day and ask these people to forgive you. We went on May Day, which is a big holiday here. Everybody wears lilies-of-the-valley and nobody works, not even the streetcar conductors. Three of us drove out from Toulouse to a POW camp and then to the political prisoners' camp. The Red Cross woman told the men that, although it was May Day, "La charité ne chôme pas." "Charity doesn't go on strike." She's a wonderful woman, a devoted woman, but I thought that was about the stinkiest remark I'd ever heard. What the hell—charity! These men had the right to arraign us—all society—for denying them the right to be men. To offer them charity!

The camp I visited was a sorry affair—poor barracks, no beds, no books, no medical supplies. The little French officer in charge was awfully anxious that we think well of the camp and realize that what was lacking just couldn't be supplied—which, for present-day France, is pretty nearly true. He asked me what I thought of the camp, and the only thing I could say in French that sounded much like what I felt was that it wasn't "digne"—worthy or dignified. He agreed, and told me about his experience as a German POW, and then that inevitable and all-inclusive French remark that explains everything: "C'est la guerre." If the French could forget those words, they might get somewhere.

One of the POWs was a doctor, a very nice guy, trying to preserve some of what he called "civilization." He had almost nothing to work with, and what most of the men need is better food anyway. He told me about operating during the war for three or four days at a stretch without stopping, drinking wine because he couldn't stand food, not daring to lie down to sleep because there were always new cases coming in from the front.

That's something else that strikes me here—naively, I suppose. Hearing people tell stories like those we've read in the newspapers or in war books—stories of deportation, hostages, the Resistance, bombing, liberation. Here every day you sit and listen to tales of suffering that in America would be simply appalling. Here, because it is universal, suffering is expected and undramatic. You don't say you're sorry to people who have lost their only child in a raid, or to old people who have seen their whole family wiped out by the Germans, or to men who've spent five years behind barbed wire. It would sound silly, so you don't say anything.

Suffering seems to be such a universal element here that it has no connotation of good or bad except as it affects people. Everybody knows about it and expects it—everybody except most Americans (or was I such a sheltered child?).

My dear, my dear, to have to try to think our relationship out while we are apart is almost agonizing sometimes. If you do propose, I don't know what I can answer, or when. I have no wish to make you hurt or wonder or wait. The longer I'm away from you, the closer you seem—and the less I understand your hesitancy.

Whatever you decide, I believe—in a dim and half-understood way—will be all right. I hope that whatever I decide will be, too. It will be good to know. I don't wait breathlessly or painfully—partly, I must confess, because I am now so very unsure. Partly because the world's so big, and people in general so much more important than people in particular. By the same token, your unsureness hurts, since against so much suffering and struggling, it seems to me so good and necessary that people be close and generous and sharing when they can be.

Forgive what is not understood. You are very true and warm and dear.

May 1946 ~ Red in Marseille to friends in America

Early this month, John Jones and Winslow Ames went with one truck to Vence, Cannes, and Saint-Paul, arriving in Nice in time to eat supper and get some sleep. Marcel Drot, a French mechanic with us, went with me to Nice, Cap d'Ails, and Menton, then back to Nice to meet the other fellows for the night. At Menton, in fact all along the coast, we could see where bombs had done devastating work. Each time, upon inquiry, we were told that the Americans had done it. All the main bridges are out; quite naturally, air bombing is not accurate, so many other places were hit also.

We arrived at an orphanage at Cap d'Ails at noon. We couldn't get our big truck up the drive, so the woman in charge invited us to have lunch while we waited for reinforcements. We were delighted.

It was a beautiful location overlooking the sea. Small children swarmed around us, and a boy of eleven gave us a recital of piano works by Mozart and Chopin. It was cool and relaxing to sit in the large front room sipping wine with wonderful music, pleasant people, lots of kids, a beautiful view, and time to waste!

The director took us through the nursery and pointed out babies who had German, Italian, American, and French fathers. In addition to providing a home for orphans, she also takes in unwanted children until she can get them adopted to suitable families. The director has not been able to find proper homes for some of the children, so she has adopted them herself.

Unmarried mothers-to-be come and work and are paid 2,000 francs a month. After the baby arrives, the mother may leave if she wishes; then she has six months to decide whether she wants to keep the child.

It is pretty definite that I shall stay in Marseille until the trucks which go to Poland are ready to be delivered to Paris. Then I go there to help service them and wait for traveling orders. About eight of us are going to Poland. From what we can learn, living there will be rough: barracks with potbellied stoves, field rations, no PX, no army mess, no army garages. In fact, none of the extras that are offered in France.

This has been the hardest week since landing here. Monday we loaded two trucks, and on Tuesday, John Jones and I left at 5:30 a.m. He had several deliveries to make; I had one in Saint-Raphael and one in Nice, so I was trying to do it in one day. If you know anything about truck driving, you know that driving with six tons over mountains, hills, and valleys for 130 miles, unloading, and driving a bumping empty truck back is real work. At Saint-Raphael, I was informed that the lady to whom the delivery was to be made was in the hospital. They tried to get me to unload at another warehouse, but since one never knows about the integrity of people until an investigation can be made, I had to keep insisting that unloading was impossible. Finally, I was able to get to the hospital and get directions from the lady herself.

This delay caused me to get to Nice a few minutes past twelve, so I had to wait until two o'clock to start unloading. Everyone takes two hours for lunch; even most of the stores close. I tried to buy gas while I was waiting and could not find a station open. Then I discovered that the transmission was dry, but I had no tickets for oil, and the army is no longer in Nice, and I do not speak French! Some kind soul finally realized my plight and was able to get the transmission filled at the city garage. When I finally arrived back in Marseille, I was so tired that I had to force a bowl of soup down.

Wednesday we loaded again, and on Friday Louise Tibbetts from the Marseille team went with me in a smaller truck to Nice, Cap d'Ails, and Menton. There were walls of beautiful flowers, roses of all colors, and the blue sea.

In several of the small villages, we saw women at the public stone tubs doing the family wash. In late evening, men and women sat along the streets sewing, reading, talking. We had the feeling that these were the real people; here they continue with the daily routine of tending to the fields, feeding their stock, getting married, having babies, regardless of what government is in power. Even a German occupation had little effect. Yet it was in quiet villages like these that the strongest Resistance movements were sometimes found.

Recently, several of us drove to Avignon to visit a school at Saint-Rémy. The children are perfect darlings. They must have excellent leaders; they had such perfect manners. Their work was exceptional: paintings, essays, crafts. The teacher in charge invited us into a large room, and the children came in with their shoes off. He sat to one side playing a guitar while they performed some of the best dances and sang some of the loveliest songs we have seen and heard in many a day.

Unfortunately, I was so tired that I went and slept in the car until Johnny could not bear my missing so much and came out and woke me up. Then, at the insistence of the kids, Louise, who has visited there before, took the guitar and played and sang a couple of American songs for them. When we left, they gave us a huge bouquet of flowers that made a sweet fragrance in the car the entire trip home.

A couple of weeks ago, I drove Louise around visiting goûters before breakfast, since there are some goûters which operate at seven or seven-thirty in the morning.

Food ration cards are given on the basis of various grades or classes. J-3 designates the oldest group of children, the late teenagers. Today, many French families find themselves being supported entirely by a J-3 because the other family members were disabled during the war or have just disappeared.

Louise found that most of the factories employ these kids as apprentices. Some are very much undernourished; none of them receive proper food. Louise chose the factories where the employment of J-3s was large enough to justify goûters. She arranged that goûters be set up where the kids could sit down to eat and had all the apprentices examined by a doctor. Children who were very much underweight or were potential TB cases were admitted to the goûters. The kids organized themselves and looked after the food and the distribution. The goûter consists of hot malted chocolate milk, cheese, chocolate, margarine, or sardines. The kids furnish their own bread.

In addition to J-3s in the factories, Louise also helps some students. One of the places we visited yesterday morning was a Catholic boarding school.

Sometimes I am disgusted with myself for not being able to speak more French. Then I decide that maybe it is a good thing, since I am one to pick up an argument too quickly. So far, the students in Marseille have proved themselves to be rather conservative; each time a student who can speak English and I get together, we have a warm time.

It is not the place of Quakers to be selling any doctrine, but it seems that we have an excellent opportunity to help people understand one another's problems and to be more tolerant and understanding of one another. This is very important in France.

You can give people food, clothing, and medicine until you have exhausted your supplies, and if they think you are doing it to advertise Quaker Oats, your efforts may be in vain, except that a well-fed person is more likely to be at ease than a hungry one. The fact that we say little about the motivation behind our work has been a real criticism of Quaker Relief in Europe.

I have been wanting to tell you about the street cars in Marseille. Most of the cars have come from Switzerland where they were used until they were worn out. Now they have seen five years of war and are beyond repair, but that does not bother the people here. They take one car that has power, hook one or two others to it, and keep them rolling. Still there are not enough; at rush hours there is nothing like the street cars of Marseille. Not even the crowds in New York subways compare.

The cars have no doors and sometimes few windows, so men, women, and children hold on wherever they can. Half the people are on the outside of the cars; the conductors cannot possibly collect all the fares. The back is the favorite spot when there is no place to put a foot on a step.

From the back, the passengers can climb higher and hold on to the openings that were once windows, or stand on the rod that connects one car to another. It's not uncommon to see a fellow running down the street for several blocks trying to catch a car and hop on, on the run. Of course, running in the street holds no hazard from cars here; there are more people in the streets than on the sidewalks. You would have fits trying to drive these streets.

May 19, 1946 ~ Madeleine in Paris to Red in Marseille

I took a sentimental journey this evening to the Seine, across

Pont Neuf and Pont Alexandre III, and stood for awhile looking down to the towers of Notre Dame, watching the sunset fade and the lights come on along the banks and on the bridges. Paris is beautiful, all leafed out now, but you know, it's amazing how much of its

THIS IS A POSTCARD FROM PARIS WHICH WE HAD SAVED. WE SPENT MANY HOURS WALKING ALONG THE BANKS OF THE SEINE.

charm is in association and remembering. I guess maybe I don't love it for its own sake alone.

Your letters make me envious. You are seeing the country these days!

I saw Steve Cary at the Canteen yesterday, and he regaled us with tales of the cops-and-robbers business in Marseille. Sorry, I know it's damned serious, but the thought of dignified Quaker workers (no, not you!) engaged in such Dick Tracy escapades does have its funny side. Sometime I want to hear it all first hand, in one piece, from you. In fact, if and when we ever get together for a few days, I should think we could talk steadily, twenty-four hours a day, just catching up.

The question I asked about transferring to Poland is pretty much passé now, at least for a long while. Everything is changed yet again!

The latest idea is that I go to Toulouse in a month or two and be assistant to the director of the refugee program there. Most of the work in France will be concentrated in the southwest and will deal with refugees, mostly Spanish. It's a job that had never entered my head, and I had a rather uncertain couple of days getting used to the idea. My heart's been set on going east, but there seems little chance of that opening up for a long time, especially for women, so I guess I'd better put down my German grammar and take up my Spanish one.

From the little I saw of the Spaniards while I was in Toulouse, I liked them a lot. They're a proud, passionate, poetic people devoted to a democratic ideal in a dramatic way, and they've gone through hell in the last ten years. There's a possibility that while we're down there, things in Spain may turn upside down, and we'd be in the midst of a mass exodus of Loyalists and an influx of Falangists. This would put a strain on Quaker impartiality but would certainly be exciting!

Mine would be pretty much an office job, keeping in touch with the refugee work in Montauban and Perpignan, and with the Inter-governmental Committee on Refugees. This doesn't thrill me to bits, but if that's where someone is needed and if that's what I can do best, I'll go. I am pretty good at being extra hands and brains for someone else. That's not meant to be bragging, but a fact, just like the fact that you're a

FEEDING CENTER FOR SPANISH REFUGEE CHILDREN IN TOULOUSE. 1946
-PHOTOGRAPH BY MADELEINE

fine truck driver, and it would be stupid if you didn't know it.

I think I'll take the job on a six-month basis, subject to review. Who will do the publicity I've been doing, I don't know. It seems to be the fate of that job that whenever anything more immediate and urgent comes along, publicity goes begging. Maybe I can scrape some time off the job to keep on doing a little, at least on what happens in the south. You guys are going to have to hold your end up alone—and it's the most interesting and important end! The reports we've been getting here about Poland and Germany make me want to pack up and go tomorrow. I'm glad YOU can go. I'll feel as if I'm there by proxy.

Toulouse is a hell of a long way from Poland but not so far from Marseille. Maybe each of us could go half way. Or don't you ever have any free time? They've certainly been working you hard.

I've been forgetting for the past two weeks to tell you—I saw the Folies Bergères. Red, when you come through Paris, try to see that above all else! It's stupendous: the sets, colors, lighting, imagination, wit, beauty. There's nothing in all the American theater to compare with it. To see it is to know why the French are known as the nation with a flair for theater. I could try to describe some of the scenes for you, but words just won't do it. You must go!

May 19, 1946 ~ Madeleine's journal, Paris

This morning I went early to the American Church in Paris. A student of English was wandering around waiting, too, so we talked. He used to come here seven years ago and wondered how much it had changed. Having been in the army sixteen years, he wasn't sure he could ever settle down again. He'd seen Italy and was surprised how lovely it was. Now he guessed there was as much more to see in all the other countries of the world. England wouldn't be enough any more. It came to me that all of us will have to learn to live in the whole world. The awareness of France presses in upon the comfortable knowledge of America, and the nearness of Italy and Switzerland and Germany and England demand part of one's thought and feeling, too. It's harder to live that way; there's no small, comforting part of a country that seems especially one's own. To try to live in the whole world is big and lonely, but it will have to come.

May 20, 1946 ~ Red in Marseille to Madeleine in Paris

Yours was a most wonderful letter. Already it is looking worn from being carried all day, folded and unfolded each chance there is time to read and reread parts of it. As yet I am not over the shock of our finding each other, and when a letter comes like the one today, the closeness seems more a reality than a dream. Thanks for that one, and please send more.

For several years, there were excellent reasons for my being skeptical about maintaining a close understanding when two people were apart. Now my faith is overcoming my reasoning, and I find myself throwing caution out the window.

As for Poland, you know there is nothing I would like better than to have you near me. But first, both of us are going to think of the job to be done. In your case, it should be in terms of what a job for a woman would be. Most likely, it would be as an administrative assistant.

There would be many drawbacks for both of us, not the least being the effect of our relationship on the other men. Both of us are mature enough and are interested enough in the purpose of our being here that the advantages we would receive from being close to each other should be more than enough to overcome the disadvantages. As for the effect on the other men, we would be facing the same problem of any girl who might fall for one of the men.

My status at present is to remain here until the job is finished or until the trucks going to Poland are ready to be serviced in Paris, at which time I return to Paris to help with that. I have, however, given Winslow notice that I expect some vacation when this job is finished. He understands and thinks we are due some time off.

1993 ~ Madeleine from Monan's Rill

However generous the relief supplies of food and clothing, there was never enough to fill the need, even within the limited categories we were trying to serve. Especially, there was little possibility of filling special needs: medicines, medical instruments, and supplies. My family and friends were impressive in their help. When the Army Post Office (APO) mail bags came in, there were often three sacks of packages for me. These I would lug home one at a time, opening them with the help of the other workers. It was such fun for the British especially, just to handle food and clothing the likes of which they had not seen for many years.

Most of the gifts were added to the stores set aside for the workers who were dealing with individual cases. A few treats that were marked for me were shared with the team on special occasions.

The greatest contributor, a one-woman relief operation, was Dr. Lydia Hauck, the mother of my dear friend Herb Hauck. Not only did she ship medicines, food, medical instruments, and clothing on her own, she enlisted the help of the Essex County Medical Auxiliary, as well as that of her daughters Louella and Janice.

May 22, 1946 ~ Madeleine in Paris to Lydia Hauck in New Jersey

Dear Dr. Lydia, This afternoon I carried your biggest package home with me and unwrapped it, and truly, I've never opened a package— not even a Christmas present—with more pleasure! The things you sent were a wonderful delight.

Sugar's rare and wonderful to have, so are all sorts of pills and salves. Rice is a treasure because when one's insides go on the blink from too coarse food or dysentery, it's all one can eat. And then everything was in cans, with covers on—you can't know how prized they are! And in another box was that beautiful apron (if you don't mind, it will probably make a gift to some French girl on a special occasion, and she'll think she's been given the world); and the cheesecloth, and a wash cloth, and tea. Good heavens, one would think you'd been in France in the last few weeks and knew what is hardest to find here!

The pabulum and canned milk I took to a girl who works in the Secours Quaker office; she has a thirteen-month-old child who hasn't eaten solid food yet, and the pabulum may start her off. Francine was pathetically grateful. I tried to tell her a little about you and why you'd sent the things. So little means so much here; it's an old story, but always a humbling one. These people have gone through so much.

Francine's had a hard time. She fell in love with a very fine German boy who escaped from the army, and she had a child. Now she's moving heaven and earth to get a passport to Germany, so they can be married and be together with their baby. She may be able to go soon, but it will be a terribly difficult life.

Please don't send money; there is almost literally nothing to buy in France these days, certainly not in the way of food. Jelly, jam, and peanut butter are always swell to have. Bread is a staple here far more than at home, and very often there's not anything to put on it. That sounds pathetic, doesn't it? It's not meant to, it's just a fact. Nobody thinks anything of walking along the street, breaking off a piece of his baguette—a long, thin loaf about the size of a rolled-up umbrella— and eating it dry. I've made more than one meal on bread; it's better tasting, crustier stuff than we have at home, and wonderful when it comes fresh from the baker.

There are still two of your packages unopened. (I'm famous around the office for having so many!) I can carry only one or two home at a time. But until I get them unwrapped and get another letter written, let me thank you for them, too. Now that I'm back in Paris for a month or so, I hope to get to know more French people, find out what they need most, and distribute your things as I think you'd want them used. (I'll use some of them myself, too, never fear.) As for what I'd especially like, chocolate bars with nuts are about the most valuable thing we have; they're nourishing, don't take up much room, and are good for trips. You see, my perambulating job is affecting me—I always think in terms of trucks and trains.

May 28, 1946 ~ Madeleine in Paris to Red in Marseille

> *I haven't lately been to Cannes,*
> *To Avignon or Nice;*
> *But there are still some lovely sights*
> *To see within Par-is!*

I can't go on in doggerel. Much as I love the Côte d'Azur, I almost didn't envy you your trips last night. Nine of us were invited to dinner at Quai St. Michel, a beautiful apartment with big, bare rooms, huge French windows, and a view of Notre Dame and five bridges across the Seine. There was a fine rain just before sunset, and over Notre Dame appeared a double rainbow! From that height (fourth floor French style), one can see the delicate tracery and columns of the façade of the cathedral. Then we went up on the roof, from where one can see all over Paris: chimney pots and tile roofs glistening in the rain; Arc de Triomphe against the sky; the sunset colors in the green Seine; and the arches reflecting great white circles in the water. I wished, how I wished that you'd been there.

I'm having a pleasant day at home in bed with all the symptoms of measles except the spots. "Pop" Wilmot Jones and Lucy have ordered me to stay in until we see what gives. Irksome, because I was going to a play tonight and to the country tomorrow. Ah well, I can read and write and sleep—all pleasant things.

The Refugee Conference is scheduled tentatively from June 13 through 15, somewhere in the south. Whether I return to Paris afterwards, I don't know. At this point, it does look as if we would pass in the night, but you know how little plans mean here. We'll surely work out some way of meeting. Be sure to let me know all possible info on your coming and going, and I'll do the same.

I've been especially glad for your letters the last week or so, even though I've not answered very well. Truth to tell, I've been rather down, and I don't like to write that way. I want a job, something to sink my teeth in.

I wish I could share some of your weariness, and you could share some of my frustration! There's so much to be done, and I sit around reading files and wait for the refugee program to get started!

It can't be helped, I guess. But I do begin to appreciate what CPS meant to you all! I chafe after two weeks of inaction, and you had four years! The reports come through from Poland and Germany, and they're heartbreaking. Meanwhile we sit in Paris with a huge office staff and diddle for days over the phrasing of a policy report!

I wish I were a man. At least I could drive a truck and have the satisfaction of knowing that the stuff I was carrying would get in some little kid's stomach.

This is Yaude caught on the horns of a dilemma again. When I'm working with individuals I think: "This isn't enough. The forces that create the problems of these people are social, political, economic; they can't be touched by individual action." When I'm into planning and administration, I gripe because we're too removed from people as human beings. Not being smart enough to resolve the problem, I just yell about it, which gets nobody anywhere, including me. Sorry.

Incidentally, did you see this sentence at the end of a report? I thought at once, and enviously, of you. "The rebuilding of Poland is a heartbreaking task, but it would appear that Polish hearts are not easily broken." Magnificent, that.

Red, I'm glad you're as forthright as you are; it makes things so easy and natural. Like you, I want very much some time together for more knowing before we both leave Paris. I'd like to have a weekend in some quiet place, maybe a cathedral town near here. First, because for a couple days anyway, I'd like not to share you with everybody else around, and second, because you sound as if you could use a rest. How possible this is I don't know. I don't want to raise a scandal around Secours Quaker. As far as I'm personally concerned, it's perfectly all right. What do you think?

You once raised the question of premarital relationships. That needs talking over more than writing over, I expect. For several reasons, I doubt that it's a good idea now, but I wonder if that would make it difficult to be together and alone somewhere? Again, what do you think?

If we stayed here, there are scads of things you've not yet seen: concerts at the Palais de Chaillot, which is a French Radio City; countryside around Paris; a wonderful tea shop; and the Sugar Bowl, I've finally been there, and it's a piece of home—an American snack bar with hamburgers and milkshakes. There's the Bois de Boulogne and maybe a boat ride on the Seine. Right now I have an idée fixe: lying in a field in the sunshine, talking and reading and maybe falling asleep. I don't much care where the picture is, so long as you're in it.

May 29, 1946 ~ Red in Marseille to Madeleine in Paris

The sweetest letter of all came from you today. There has been spring in my steps ever since reading it. Then tonight I did something of which you may disapprove. If you go to Toulouse before I come to Paris, we probably won't see each other.

The best thing seems to be to get a replacement for me down here pronto, so that I shall be free to go to Paris before you leave there. I called George Loveland, therefore, and asked what could be done. You may not like my publicizing the fact that I am anxious to see you, because I frankly told George why I wanted to get back to Paris sometime before June 15.

Unfortunately, my replacement has not been chosen yet, and then he has to be here possibly a week or nearly so before I can leave. But George promises to take it up with Winslow when he returns.

Is there any chance of your postponing your trip a few days? True, this is rather selfish of us, but if we can have another few days that are as wonderful as those last two weeks together, going to Poland would be easier—and yet harder. I want to reassure myself that it was not all a dream, and that the Madeleine who sends these letters really exists.

Your frankness astonishes me but pleases me even more. Never have I corresponded with anyone with whom I felt so free and easy. You once mentioned how to develop the technique of "knowing the innermost though apart." Is not your expression without inhibition part of the secret? You know that I have real reason to distrust correspondence as a means of maintaining the knowingness of the inner self, yet each time I read a letter from you, there is a feeling of confidence that one does not usually have until after a long acquaintanceship.

At times the trip to Menton, Nice, Eze, and Saint-Jeanet was awfully hard, because the more I saw of the beauty and romance of the country, the more I wanted to talk about you. Instead, I forcibly withheld myself; in my opinion, Louise has not yet fully recovered from a recent break with her fiancé. We had a couple of long talks about that and about relationships in general.

Although there were times when I felt like holding her in my arms as we sat on the side of the mountain, overlooking the river and valleys as they lost themselves in the sea, I never could bring myself to do it. Mostly because it would have hurt too much to have touched her and found out that it was not Madeleine. I hope that I am not often thrown into such situations with interesting and attractive girls because I do not trust myself. I am not sure just how well the situation between Louise and me is expressed here. Have no fears, however. The strained feeling I had then has disappeared since returning to Marseille. The two-day trip made me realize how much you really mean to me.

I'm sorry that you are feeling frustrated about your work. Nevertheless, it may give you more patience when you get on the job and realize that even there, much waiting has to be done and often impossible barriers arise. Agreed that often the "forces that create problems for these people are social economic and political," more basic is the human relationship.

Regardless of what kind of system there is, there must be a feeling for the other person and a concern for human rights and liberties. To me, some systems are more conducive to this than others. There may be basically less selfishness in a given system, yet each of us is innately selfish. In trying to change a system, we must continually strive not to forget the human touch for the sake of the system. You should have ample opportunity to help those who are oppressed to have some understanding of those who resort to ruthless tactics. Some day the oppressed may be in power and have the opportunity either to use similar tactics or try a more Quakerly manner.

Although it would be nice to see Paris and do things with you again, the most important thing is that we get a chance to know each other better. The highlight of being in Paris will be to be with you, at one moment to be thrilled by some scene we are sharing together, and again just to lie with you in my arms while we whisper sweet nothings.

John Munsey and I have of late shared some inner secrets; he takes great delight in telling me about Eunice, his fiancée, and he in turn listens to the concerns of Red for Madeleine. Today I told him about our wishing to share a weekend together. He understands; his only answer is that it has been done before. I still desire it. Are you acquainted with anyone well enough who might be able to advise us?

As for a premarital relationship, that is only a physical expression of our inner selves. The most important thing is to have knowledge of and confidence in each other. If physical expression is not desired, that is of small importance.

'Tis true that it is difficult to write about something about which one has for years been hesitant to speak.

June 1, 1946 ~ Madeleine in Paris to Red in Marseille

I got your long letter today, and already I'd heard that a replacement was to be sent to Marseille. Yes, I was a bit startled at first and—shall I admit it—a little embarrassed. Quaker gossip goes around here like wildfire. Long before I knew your urgent reasons, however, I was glad you'd asked for the replacement, and I've been whiling away the time with the fond hope that one of the knocks on my door would usher in a tall redheaded guy whom I haven't seen for more than a month. Maybe being ill has sapped my guts, but at the moment I don't care what anybody thinks or says. I'd just like to see you!

Damn the unmeasly measles anyway! If I don't watch out, this letter is going to sound cranky, and I don't mean it to be that. In case you're worried, don't be. I'm hardly sick at all. It's measles that didn't turn out to be, if you get what I mean. I'm supposed to stay in bed three more days to see if anything happens, and I've been examined and prescribed for by a timid, nice French doctor.

This being honest is a two-edged business, isn't it? I'm glad and proud of your telling me about Louise. I think I know what you mean, and yet I felt a twinge—and why should I, when you're so like me?

Lately, for example, I've had several wonderful letters from Herb Hauck, the man at home about whom I've told you a little, and I thought impetuously, "How I'd like to read this to Red; it's so clear-sighted and honest and good. I'd like him to know this guy." There's a sense in which all people of goodwill and sensitivity have affection for one another, and that sense lies so close to the kind of affection we tradition-ally think of as being for two people only. What's the relationship? I don't know. Maybe it's something we haven't even guessed at yet. I've been reading brave words about awareness being the condition of survival and growth; I've written some like that myself. It sounds great, but it's hard to do. Sometimes it takes a little helping by somebody else.

I'm glad our weekend together isn't absolutely a precedent-shattering idea! It would be good to ask someone older, but I don't know who. My guess is that during Yearly Meeting time everything will be in such a stir that one or two absences won't be greatly noticed. I don't mind anyone knowing, if they understand, but I do hate feeling I have to justify myself to anyone. I don't think I have to, except to myself.

June 1, 1946 ~ Red in Marseille to Madeleine in Paris

A carload of milk arrived today. It seems strange that Marseille was unable to get food for so long, and now as they are trying to close the program, we get more than we can handle. John is rather disgusted, and I don't blame him. There has not been the best planning at this end, but most of that can be blamed on the uncertainty of when shipments would arrive and what would be in them. Of course the robbery threw us off, too.

Yesterday, John worked most of the day making out orders for delivery. We had plans of hitting them hard today and tomorrow when word came that the carload of milk had arrived. In addition, Jim and I spent all morning searching through the motor pool trying to find spare parts. Such is life at Marseille. Did you say something about being frus-trated? If we do not move over fifteen tons of food next week, I shall be very much upset.

This afternoon we know our fate with the army—whether we can stay here or not. This may be the last letter I shall write from this room. Things are really getting tough. We can no longer use the motor pool. Last night we were asked out of Special Service. Incidentally, the lady there seemed to take great delight in so doing. By contrast, Captain Fleharty is doing all he can to keep not only John and me here at the mess but also the rest of the American delegation. He said the army was in a position to see who did the work around here, and I was pleased to know that some of them thought we did a little work.

1993 ~ Red from Monan's Rill

The night before I left Marseille, I was rather late getting to bed, so I did not leave Marseille until 7:30 a.m., hoping that I could make the Dijon gas dump by 9 p.m. that night. There I could get food and a bed. I was driving my old GMC, with a Chevrolet sedan in the back. At Cavaillon, the truck started giving trouble but kept rolling. At Saint-Rambert, I stopped to clean the gas filter, but nothing was open for food or gas. At Lyon, I bought some good gas and made it to Dijon by 6 p.m.

Thinking that this was too early to stop, I kept on toward Paris, knowing that I had a sleeping bag if I got too tired. But about 10 o'clock, it started raining, and since trying to sleep in the rain would be miserable, I kept on driving. At 12:30 a.m. I arrived in Paris, exactly seventeen hours from Marseille, well over 500 miles. In those days, given the poor conditions of the roads and of our trucks, we figured that the trip took three days.

When I drove up to the ETU garage at 2 rue de Civry and honked my horn, the night watchman came out to see who was disturbing the peace at that hour. When he saw me, he turned pale. "You left Marseille this morning," he stammered; "You can't be here yet!"

Actually, I probably shouldn't have arrived at all. Later, when we started to repair that truck to go to Poland, we found a front spring broken, two valves sticking, three spark plugs broken, rear brake linings worn, rings needing replacing, and connecting rod bearings pitted. The only way we can figure that I was able to get the truck to Paris is that once the engine got hot, I never allowed it to cool down. I seldom drove over forty-five miles per hour, and never over fifty. I had planned to make an easier trip of it, but I did want to get to Paris. Madeleine was there! And as long as the truck was threatening to go en panne, I couldn't see myself stopping.

1993 ~ Madeleine from Monan's Rill

Red had called me from Marseille, so I knew when he was starting, but he couldn't tell me when he expected to arrive. Sunday was highly unlikely, but all the same, I stayed at the apartment in the rue de Varenne, although everybody else had gone off to enjoy a day in the country. Late in the morning there was a knock at the door; there stood Le Grand Rouge. I made him a lunch of dried soup and tinned cheese. I imagine we went out walking. It was a beautiful day, but nothing that we did or said was as important as the wonderful fact that we were together!

Horse chestnuts were in bloom along the boulevards, flowers were bright in public gardens, and one could buy paper twists of ripe cherries, a marvelous treat after the long winter. We walked the quays of the Seine, returning often to our beloved view of Notre Dame across the river. We spent very little money—we had very little, but that mattered not a whit. We were in love and we were in Paris, and Paris is kind to lovers.

The prospect of a separation of many months, perhaps a year, was hard. No question of our not accepting it. All of us who had been chosen for overseas service felt singularly fortunate, and we were committed to do the job wherever we were sent. But Red and I desperately wanted a little time, even just a weekend, alone, to sort out our thoughts and feelings. Although the mores of relationships between women and men were far more traditional then than now, there was a degree of tolerance and understanding for the emotional constraints imposed by relief work. It was, in fact, the head of the ETU who suggested to Red a modest inn outside Paris where we might go for a few days.

We arrived on a Saturday afternoon and asked the innkeeper for two rooms. A Frenchman, a realist in matters of romance, he clearly thought these two Americans were crazy! But he gave us two rooms—adjoining. We did spend part of our time in one room, but although we were intimate, we did not make love. In today's world that is hard to believe. We were constrained by several factors: the prohibition against premarital sex was still strong; and we were not certain of the efficacy of the contraceptives available to us. If a pregnancy were to result, we would have felt that we had let down the organization that had invested a great deal of time, money, and faith in us.

So we walked and talked and were quiet together. This was another time when I do not remember a single sentence we spoke. But the weekend became like a rock to which our thoughts and emotions were moored during the long separation that lay ahead.

Besides the inexplicable behavior of a pair of lovers who would not share a room, our host was disappointed in another way; we insisted on his prix-fixe menus, modest meals which obviously did not bring him the profit that his off-the-menu suggestions would have done.

In part we did this because our funds were very low. Relief workers had their food, clothing, and job-related transportation supplied; medical attention was provided as needed. "Squander money" of $2.50 per month covered stamps, toilet articles, movies, or concert tickets, and any other extras we could squeeze out. We were also allowed a modest sum for leaves, which were taken, if possible, every six months. We also refused the tantalizing lobster or beef steaks because we could not indulge in black market delicacies in a country suffering from severe food shortages.

June 3, 1946 ~ Red in Paris to friends back home

There are five of us here in Paris getting ready for Poland. Since you will be hearing more about the fellows going to Poland in the coming months, I shall give you a short description of each.

Van Cleve Geiger, from Florida, is the most able man of the unit and will take much of the leadership. In my opinion, he has a deeper spiritual motivation than any other member of ETU—slow and deliberate, but sure of himself when he does act. Reed Smith, from Washington, has little mechanical knowledge but is inquisitive and is learning. He likes people and is very sensitive. Extroverts find it difficult to work with him at times, but all of us have been in CPS long enough to know how to give and take. Both Reed and Van Cleve came over on the *SS Brazil* with me.

Ralph Durgin cooked for the Young Men's Christian Association (YMCA) before CPS and cooked for about three years during his stay in Friends camps. That experience helps us now; we can turn all the responsibility for ordering kitchen equipment and packing food over to Ralph. He has a wonderful sense of humor and keeps us roaring with laughter at his attempts to speak French. He has the ability to see humor in tragic things, a talent that should be a help to us in Poland.

Henry Dasenbrock, from Idaho and Oregon, was with the Brethren Service Committee in Oregon and then in Puerto Rico (also CPS). His hobby as well as his vocation is photography. He hopes to do a job of photography in Poland and then get assigned full-time to that work. He is by far our best mechanic, and we rely upon him for many decisions about the condition of the trucks.

At first we thought we would try for the boat that leaves Antwerp on June 25; but now the departure date has been moved to July 1. We had planned to drive the five trucks loaded with our stuff, plus three small trailers and one jeep, to Antwerp, then take the boat to Gdynia, Poland. Now with the delay in sailing, they are trying to get air transportation for me to fly to Warsaw on Tuesday, so I can get in ahead of the group and start making arrangements.

The boat trip sounds fascinating; there are no messing facilities or bunks for us, which means that we shall eat and sleep on the trucks as we sail through the North and Baltic seas. If I should go by plane, someone would drive my truck to Antwerp and then I would meet the boat at Gdynia.

THE EUROPEAN TRANSPORT UNIT BEFORE LEAVING PARIS. 1946
-PHOTOGRAPH BY JOHN ROBBINS

In addition to the five of us, there is another man already in France who is to join us as soon as he finishes the job on which he is working now. He is John Robbins, who also came over on the *SS Brazil* with us. Two men from England are to join us, too, and I understand about three more are coming from America or England later. We are to live in a barrack and eat food furnished by the Polish government.

June 10, 1946 ~ Madeleine in Paris to Dr. Hauck in New Jersey

Dear Dr. Lydia, Your letter filled with good news—for it's wonderfully heartening to hear of all the interest in our work in America—came on the same day as some bad news: the closing of the Army Post Office. It was a shock for us, and means some adjustment on both sides of the ocean. I have been very happy to get all your packages—I'm afraid at this point I can't remember the number, but it must be about sixteen by now!

A large one has already arrived for Dr. van Huybers, and she picked it up on Friday. By the way, I saw her the day she got your first letter, and she was so touched she almost wept. Between French and German, she told me how close the letter made her feel to you, as if you had been her mother. I think that is a triumph of both feeling and expressing. She needs very much understanding and affection, more than the food and clothes. You need have no fear that her packages won't be shared; she's the kind of person who gives the shirt off her back.

I wish there were some way I could tell you of the great fun it is to open these parcels! Everyone who has been abroad will tell you the same thing. It's the sort of gift that is doubly precious, first for its value here, and second for the thought and affection that have been packed with it.

Yesterday morning I splurged and opened a tin of bacon, beautiful meat full of flavor, with clear sweet fat. And those little tins of dried soup have made more than one Sunday supper. I don't mean to be extravagant in my thanks, because I know the spirit in which you send, and I know from my own experience how one dislikes here to be thanked for only sharing what should not, after all, be ours alone. All the same, I don't think you can quite know what a double glow comes out of those jars and packages!

If you can, share with your friends the meaningfulness of their gifts to the French people, who feel more than I can express the wonder at someone's far away thinking of them, and who know so intimately the privation that makes the smallest thing precious. This giver-receiver relationship is a difficult one to maintain, and one that should not have to exist in a well-ordered society. But what is given and accepted in good spirit does doubly bless.

The names, especially of children, will follow as soon as possible. I'm on the track now of some children's homes and orphanages which can use American contacts. Incidentally, bright cards and pictures can surely be used there; schools and nurseries are opening up, but they have so little to do with.

For myself, I've noticed that a good thing to have would be a supply of food for a semi-invalid diet. No, I'm not a semi-invalid. What I mean is that, on the occasions when one isn't feeling very well, the coarse bread and heavy food we generally have are extremely unappetizing; in fact, one just doesn't eat for awhile. Your soups and tea have come in wonderfully handy. Things like noodles with chicken or bland prepared foods of any kind would be welcome. Fruit and vegetable juices are price-less here, but they're bulky and expensive to send.

There's a very interesting school project in a tiny, isolated village called Le Chambon which needs help. When the AFSC man who is directing it comes through Paris, I shall ask him for more information and send names to you. I should think that would be a wonderful place for the knitted caps.

I don't know how you and your friends feel about Germany and Germans. For people who are interested in democratizing Germany, one of the most needed things is books in German. They're wanted in that country, but for the time being, our channels for getting in supplies of any kind are very small and restricted. But there are thousands of German POWs held in French camps, used as slave labor or just waiting around, sick, often near starvation, hoping to go home.

I don't believe it's wise or realistic to expect these men to learn the ways of democracy without any teaching. These men know there was something wrong with their country, and they're feeling after a new conception of government and morals, but so far there's been nothing to help them. The camps are absolutely devoid of literature of any kind; there are no classes, nothing. German classics or technical books, Bibles, and above all, translations of modern works on politics, international relations, philosophy, and so on, would be worth a regiment of occupying troops.

If you think any of your friends would be interested in collecting books of this kind, I know they would be easily distributed and read and reread hundreds of times.

June 10, 1946 ~ Madeleine in Toulouse to Herb in Philadelphia

Quite arbitrarily, it seems to me, I have been assigned as Assistant to the Director of the Spanish refugee work in Toulouse in the south of France. Publicity is traditionally the spot from which people can be pulled with the greatest ease. It may be because I haven't done the kind of job they wanted, but I don't think so. At any rate, I don't think they could tell in so short a time. As far as I know, my old job just goes uncovered.

The most interesting part of relief work goes on in Poland, Austria, and Germany (if and when we can get in). There is a possibility that later I may get attached to the commissioner's office and go trailing around countries to get stories, but at the moment that's no go.

I liked the Spanish very much when I was in Toulouse before, and I'm glad the Intergovernmental Committee on Refugees (IGC) and some French agencies are at last getting on the ball for them. But "assistant" means administration, and I dislike that and distrust its efficacy anyhow. Also, the Toulouse delegation—being old, established, and sufficient unto itself during the harrowing days of the Occupation—is a formidable hierarchy. The strong souls who tried to democratize it seem to have been quietly shunted elsewhere.

But why should I bore you with intrigue and hearsay? It's probably not a candle to what you already know too well. It will do me good to cut my teeth on a situation like this. But for the moment I do nothing very much: read files, do odd jobs, study a little Spanish, and fret at the endless and time-consuming routine of office and committees. Another post-CPS revelation—army, too, for that matter—I felt "wasted" for two weeks, and what did men do who were wasted for four years!

This feeling wasted is a subtle problem. You grouse, first, because what you're doing isn't up to your capabilities and your idea of your own worth and, second, because it doesn't seem to have any bearing on the big problem you thought you were going to tackle. The two can get awfully intertwined.

What a ponderous letter this has come to be! I should write you another about some of the lighter things here: the wit, subtlety, and taste of the French theater: it's so typically and revealingly French. And the courageous and charming people: yes, they are both, in an astounding mixture. And the almost alarming understanding some of these kids— refugees and deportees—have of events and people. And how beautiful Paris is, especially after a rain.

June 14, 1946 ~ Madeleine in Toulouse to Red in Paris

It's quiet in the office for an amazing change. Everybody's on holiday, and I'm doing the monthly report to the Home Committees on the work of the Refugee Program. Tiens! I, who hate detail, am sitting here doing little charts and things. Hugh's taken Juanita [Hugh Jenkins, the head of the Toulouse delegation, and his wife] off for a rest, so I'm carrying the office alone again. Oh well, next week I shall pick myself a nice day and go lie under a tree or go to a quiet hotel for one night's sleep undisturbed by the neighbor's kid practicing his music or the cats squalling or the garbage men playing with the cans at six in the morning—I'm getting to like this place in a perverse way.

But that wasn't what I started to tell you. Sitting here this afternoon working, I thought how pleasant and quiet-feeling it would be if you were working in the next room. No, I wouldn't insist that you be working, too; I'd let you read or nap if you wanted, but just to know that you were there. And maybe I'd have you check my columns of figures at the end to see if the francs came out right.

I hope we both always have our jobs, Red, whatever they may be, but I hope they can be near together. There are many pitfalls in this business of people working separately; it seems as if even the best will in the world doesn't keep people from drifting apart. I'm willing to try and hoping to be convinced, but I've seen a couple of cases where people started out and then their paths got further and further apart; it's made me a little doubtful. One thing that makes it hard is that this is a whole new pattern for living (as I've probably said before ad infinitum), especially as far as the woman's part goes, and most people have enough old-fashioned ideas somewhere in their subconscious to make difficulties crop up somewhere. I think you'd be a good man to try with, my dear. I wish the trying could begin this moment.

Just had a letter from Joe Howell, who writes pathetically about his wife and two little kids. I think she's having a hard time, and he must be, too. I'm not sure the Service Committee is right in sending men with families off for so long. Everyone wants to do his share, I know, but sometimes it seems as though one doesn't know what a separation is going to cost until it's well under way. I'm glad we're having a chance to do something while we are both free.

June 19, 1946 ~ Madeleine in Toulouse to Red in Paris

We've been committee-ing solidly all day long, and it's now 9 o'clock. I'd love to take a quiet walk along the Seine and see the arches gleaming in the water. But Toulouse is a noisy, crowded southern town, and there's no place around here to be alone or quiet, which is what I want most now, to think of you.

Someone brought your letter in this morning in the middle of the conference, and it was like sunshine! Awfully good to have. Childishly, I hadn't felt you were as close the night I left as on Sunday. I should have known that you were preoccupied with something else and not minded so much, but I've so much to learn! I wonder if you can know how strange it is to me, Red, to feel young and inexperienced after several years of feeling pretty adequate and knowing? It must be good for me to have to start learning over again, even though it's somewhat painful. But I marvel again at your patience and understanding, and thank you for it. I think I must trust you even more than I'm aware of, to have let you see the nakedness of my spirit these past days. With most people, one's impulse is to hide one's inadequacies and save one's pride. With you, I've let myself be seen as "poor in spirit" as much as with anyone I know.

June 20, 1946 ~ Madeleine in Toulouse to Red in Paris

I'm going to apply for recognition as a CPS—or rather, an ETU—cook. Do you think I can pass on this: dinner for ten cooked over two burners with low gas pressure? First there was soup concocted out of spider crabs, a little eel, and other unwary shellfish that René found on the beach. Then potatoes served up in a big tin can, beef and gravy, a salad, and coffee. I didn't do it alone; there were so many cooks, it's surprising the meal turned out as well as it did! Coffee we made by dunking a perforated can containing the coffee up and down in a pan of boiling water. It works!

There are fresh eggs here and wonderful sweetened cream cheese and twice the usual bread ration. It's wonderful, after Marseille and Nice, to see food stores with something to sell, and people looking not quite so pinched. Yesterday I even saw a couple of kids with cookies in their hands.

June 23, 1946 ~ Red in Paris to Madeleine in Toulouse

Last night Boyd France and I met for the first time; he is the fellow working in Paris whose parents I know in Winter Park, Florida. He believes that the *Herald Tribune* is good on foreign news. It seems that a subscription to the *Tribune* would keep you pretty well posted. It should get to you no more than a day late from Paris. Or there may be an English paper in the south which is sufficient. Already I feel as though I am losing contact with what is happening. In Marseille we had the *Stars and Stripes* plus the *Times*. Once we get to Poland, I shall insist that we be kept adequately informed. The fellows here do not seem to mind living in a little world of their own, and that's what we are doing, since we seldom make contacts outside.

Boyd said there is a big battle raging within the Peace Conference here about whether they will continue the daily press conferences. [Britain's Foreign Secretary Ernest] Bevin is insisting that they dispense with them, but the *Tribune* informed [US Senator Arthur] Vandenberg that it would mean political suicide for Byrnes if he ever agreed to closed conferences with no leaks to the press. So [US Secretary of State James F.] Byrnes is holding out and letting the American delegates have a press conference after each meeting. It is unfortunate that Byrnes is agreeing to keep things open on the basis of political expediency. By Jove, I would like to see a man so strong in his beliefs that he could forget about himself. President Wilson must have been such a man. Now we have no Wilson.

Boyd comes from a family that for several decades has been well-versed in Russian history. He tells me that many of the stories he hears coming from Russia are very disturbing; the Russian distrust and suspicion of the Anglo-Americans has gone so far that it has become childish. He is rather pessimistic about preventing another war.

Darling, it is after midnight, and tomorrow will be far different from last Sunday morning when there was a soft knock on my door and a lovely girl appeared. Today I knew what you meant about having a secret ache inside. When Dasenbrock and I took my truck out for a test run and found ourselves in the park where a few evenings ago you and I had walked and talked, I am afraid I was not observing the truck as closely as I should have been.

Yes, it is quite true that I was preoccupied with something the night you left. I kept refusing to think of our parting as long as possible. It was one of those times when I refuse to be a realist. Even yet, I have not felt the full impact of your leaving. Each time I stop work long enough to relax, I hurt, but I cannot let it become too strong, because I may do things that are irrational, like staying up too late to write letters. I wish I had the capacity to cry. I feel all tied up inside and nowhere to go. For too long I have depended upon the woods and trees, the lakes and streams, the stars and sky for spiritual elevation. Now I feel lost. Trucks, boats, air trip, Poland, administration, all put together give me little comfort at the moment.

June 24, 1946 ~ Red in Paris to Madeleine in Toulouse

One of the first things I thought of this morning was that today I would get a letter from Madeleine, and I was happy. Tonight I am still happy, but my heart sank twice during the day when the mail came in and no word from Toulouse.

We are having difficulty with the Polish visas. Today Steve Cary called UNRRA (United Nations Relief and Rehabilitation Association) and was told that the Polish Embassy refused to give permission until they had heard directly from the office in Warsaw. So cables are being sent to UNRRA-Warsaw asking them to contact the proper officials there to wire the Polish Embassy here. This means that it would take a miracle for me to fly this week; the only plane leaves Berlin Wednesday afternoon.

EUROPEAN TRANSPORT UNIT PREPARING TO LEAVE PARIS TO DRIVE TO POLAND. 1946   -PHOTOGRAPH BY JOHN ROBBINS

Now we are hoping that we can obtain permission in time to make the boat. More worries and anxieties. I am learning, however, to take them in my stride. If we make it, good. If we don't, we can find something to do here. Nevertheless, I am anxious to get on a real job. I feel as though I have been marking time in comparison to the job that awaits us in Poland.

Several times you have mentioned how patient I have been with you. This has been rather surprising, since patience is not usually accorded me as one of my attributes. Both of us seem to have pierced through to some of the inadequacies of the other and felt a certain joy in knowing that the other is aware of our inadequacies and still cares. Both of us are interested in growing, and we find satisfaction in growing with the other.

Remember when we read from Corinthians about charity? Never has that passage had so much meaning as on that day. "And though I bestow all my goods to feed the poor, and give my body to be burned, and have not charity, it profiteth me nothing." (I Corinthians 13:3) Then it listed the various virtues of charity, and I thought, "What a wretched soul I am!" It is a great comfort to know someone to whom you can express your shortcomings, knowing that she cares and desires most of all that you have charity.

Remember what Charles Morgan said in *The Flashing Stream* about absolutism? "My Absolutism is a faith in Man, not in any particular individual, but in something greater than ourselves, a part of which is in each person." Whenever I lose that, I shall become very cynical. The Peace Conference is faring badly; the Iron Curtain is getting tighter; the fate of the masses is decided by the whim of individual or national loyalties. In Europe there is a return to the Dark Ages; in America people are living in material luxury but spiritual poverty.

It seems as though the whole world is ready, not for a revolution but for something positive for which to live. So often when one speaks in terms of ideals, he is reproached with the impracticality of the ideals. Both of us have experienced that. Can it be that the atom bomb will show us how fruitless those things are which are only practical? Although it is late for scientists to become concerned about more than pure science, they may start a concern that will encircle the globe.

June 26, 1946 ~ Madeleine in Toulouse to Red in Paris

I'm rich—two letters in two days! I hope very much this gets to you before you leave. But your leaving is so indefinite, and your letters come in such odd order.

Like you, I'm never alone or quiet long enough to write the kind of letter I want you to have, my dear, and sometimes that means I don't write at all. Like last night. We went out for a walk and found a church with a beautiful porcelain door and then turned down to the river and wandered back through the twisted streets, smelling the "bouquet" of Toulouse. (Next time I go out walking it will be with a perfumed handkerchief.)

Hugh and Juanita chased each other like kids and squealed at the rats. It was fun, and very English. Dick Sherrington, a gentle, charming Britisher, was along, too.

I'm learning more at this point about the British than about the French. It's good, Red. Evidently you have to be with them a longish time before they open up, and they don't get excited and enthused over things and ideas as we do, but what a lot there is there!

We were talking politics last night, and they were telling me with delight how flabbergasted the French were over the fact that the English would get behind Churchill during the war, all the time intending to kick him out afterwards—a kind of political wisdom the French could well do with. When it was time to go to bed, and I'd carried my "bang"—Toulousain for "bain"—which is about a pint of hot water—to my bedroom and closed the windows against the bugs, there was no place to write and only a ten-watt bulb high up in a twelve-foot ceiling for light.

I hate to present you with scraps and tatters of thinking, yet that's all there is time for these days. Just so you know how it is, and I know how it is with you. I feel now as if a weekend alone would be almost like one with you, if it would give me a chance to think a little about you and about us.

Like you, I'm learning to wait. I'm learning, too, what you already know, I think: how infinitely much work and pains must go into the mechanics of living and working. This starting from scratch is a revelation to me. Somehow one must achieve the miracle of keeping long ends in view while filing dossiers and fussing about paint and desks. I've been sheltered from a lot of such detail or managed to escape it, but I think now that one must know the whole of a job, being careful not to accept routine from habit but being willing to accept the tediousness that is inevitable. Such an obvious thing to be learning at my age!

Although this job's not really opened up yet, I'm beginning to have an inkling of what administration means. I still don't like it; I don't like the necessity for it. If it's done with humility and equality and understanding, it can be all right. Certainly I see more clearly than ever before the need for it. (This place looks at the moment as if nobody had ever heard of administration!)

Administration also means being willing to step out when one isn't needed any more or when somebody else can be found to take over a job—especially in this setup, where the whole next year's work is devoted to making Secours Quaker unnecessary!

I have what Berger (the psychologist who was on the *SS Brazil* with us) meant by a wide span of attention. Too wide. You, mon ami, have the power of exclusion, which makes you a more effective worker than I. One ought to know at twenty-eight what one's going to do in the world, but I still don't and it doesn't greatly trouble me any more. I think our closed concepts of professions have narrowed our interests and understanding dangerously sometimes, especially among Americans. So I grope along, as I guess you do, too.

June 26, 1946 ~ Red in Paris to Madeleine in Toulouse

Poland, Poland, where art thou? Our visas are in the Polish Embassy, and we are in Paris. No visas, no travel orders, no food, no gas, no parts, no beds, no stoves. Just a lot of goodwill, and that is wearing thin.

Don't get excited, it is not as bad as that. Steve Cary is sure that he can get the visas tomorrow and then the UNRRA travel orders. We shall try to get rations from them, too. If we do not, Ralph has scrounged enough food from the stocks here to carry us for a while. In addition, we hope to buy some food in Belgium. Yesterday we were informed that we should bring containers enough to hold one month's supply of gas, between 5,000 and 7,000 liters. I have been looking and so far have about 2,000 liters. The parts are to come from Italy, but we don't expect them yet. We have not received any of the equipment which we ordered. If they have as much trouble in Sweden trying to get our supplies as we have had here, we are going to be in a real pinch.

Willis Weatherford has returned from his trip to Poland. He visited the province where we expect to be working and describes a wonderful chance to do a real job. Homes will be built in three areas from which we shall choose.

In two areas—one in the north and one in the south—the homes will be built of fireproof material. There are nearly 10,000 tons of cement and lime to be hauled, as well as some hardware. The cement will have to be hauled twice, once to the factory to be made into blocks and then hauled to the home sites. In the third area in mid-Poland, there is wood available to build the homes.

It's not really homes they are building now; plans call only for cattle barns to be built this season. Families will live in one room of the barn until a house can be built another season.

There is little community planning or cooperative spirit within the villages. Each man looks after his own place, hires his own help, and

so on. The engineers are anxious that the ETU unit have enough imagination and initiative to help establish community projects and ways for
people to help each other. UNRRA is willing to send in some tractors for
the farms if people are taught how to use them properly.

Some government officials are really anxious to see us get
started. They are building us a huge barrack in which to live and keep our
work shop. They are furnishing our food, gas, and oils, as well as financing any major repairs on the trucks which we are not able to do ourselves.
From what we can learn, it is going to be rough and primitive, rather like
pioneering, but also with all the old customs and traditions to overcome. We
are to be assigned one interpreter, but already we're hoping for one interpreter
per truck who would also serve as a helper. That would be wonderful!

Sweetheart, the past two days have made me wonder where
that patience of mine has gone. I need you to talk to, to have you reassure
me that one plan or another is the right one. There are some strains among
the men in the team, and it is really hard for me to keep relationships on
an even keel.

June 30, 1946 ~ Red in Paris to Madeleine in Toulouse

Madeleine, it was a wonderful weekend, just like a gift from heaven
to have you here. Nevertheless, I am disappointed that I did not get to come
to you in Toulouse to see where you are working and meet some of the people
with whom you will work and live for the next few months.

Were I sure that I would be here tomorrow night, I would
dispense with this letter. It would not be right, however, for me to leave
Paris tomorrow, not knowing when a letter could get back to you. I am
the most comfortable I have been in weeks. There is a satisfied feeling
very deep inside. Sweetheart, you are showing me how much there is to
life. Two weeks ago I said I loved you, and it was sincere, yet today when
I say I love you, it is much richer and means much more.

July 1, 1946 ~ Madeleine in Toulouse to Red in Paris

Yes, I got here all right. But why was everybody so surprised
that I should turn up this morning? Hugh was gratified to see me, but
didn't expect me. Darling, your charm isn't what Toulouse cracks it up to

be! I'm afraid I didn't dream of staying over, much as I'd have loved it.

It was a fairly good trip when I stopped wishing I had a bed. Remember the hotel in Digoin where John and I stayed on the way to Marseille? When I'm on a train all night, I always remember that clean room, the soft bed, the lilies of the valley on the bedside table, the stars, and your kissing me goodnight.

There were six of us in the compartment on the train and a pleasant lot they were. We all woke at two in the morning, switched on the light and talked until four, mostly about the Germans. Dear God, what bitter hatred these people have, and it seems so terribly justified.

One of the younger boys had been in the French army, and all of them had suffered directly or indirectly through the Occupation. The horrible stories went on interminably, and there I sat, trying to argue that in spite of all that, we couldn't starve or shoot all the Germans. And try to tell the French that the Germans are starving! They want them all destroyed, all—even the children. Sometimes the best I can muster is a stubborn humility that, as just as their claims may be, there has to be a better way than retaliation.

Beautiful countryside this morning: sunshine, wheat fields twined with flowers, and spired churches against the sky. Somehow I was terribly glad to be back here, Red. My job's here, there's much to do, and I do love this gang. Someone met me at the station, which was touching, since I hadn't said when I'd come. It's blistering here today and confusion still reigns, but Hugh fixed up a little office over the weekend where we sort of muddle along, and tonight we go to the reception that the Prefecture is giving for us.

I remember all the weekend with sunshine and starlight. Did you see the wisp of a thought of a moon that came out last night in the green and rose sunset? I am glad of thee. There's more I would say, but since I'm writing this while everyone is having tea around me, it's not a good time. I hope you got off to Poland at last, but if not, I'm glad you have this.

July 2, 1946 ~ Red in Paris to Madeleine in Toulouse

We have a plane booked for tomorrow at 11:45 a.m. for Berlin via Bremen.

I feel more and more drawn to Poland and the people there. The more I read, the more I realize how tough the going will be. We will have times, as we do now, when the boys will be very discouraged. This morning we received word that the boat leaves on the tenth. Durgin is nearly ready to call it quits and start elsewhere. It hurts for them to see me off, not knowing if they really sail on the tenth or not. The British have been through this before and are wondering if they will have the same experience again.

Your conversation with the French is so typical! Reports of the treatment of Germans by the Poles are so awful! How can we ever get across the idea of a better world when there is so much hatred? We need so much hope and faith, "but the greatest of these is charity." The job is huge, and sometimes I become scared.

Then I realize I must carry my end as well as I can. Your job is in southern France, and you will do it as best you can, each of us in our own way striving for better human relations. We are so small compared to the job to be done, still we must go on; the whole is made up of so many parts, of which we are but a fragment.

I was talking with Willis Weatherford this evening. He believes that our mail will be censored. If so, I may not be able to write as freely as I would like.

July 3, 1946 ~ Red in Paris to Madeleine in Toulouse

I did not make the plane this morning. Missed by thirty minutes! Had the official thought to bring the passport with her to the place we first met this morning, I would be in Berlin tonight and Warsaw tomorrow night. However, here I sit, hoping that I may leave here next Wednesday and take a British plane out of Berlin on Saturday.

July 5, 1946 ~ Madeleine in Toulouse to Red in Paris

(Red left for Poland before the letter arrived)

Shall I never be rid of you? Are you going to Poland or not? What a heartbreaking miss—half an hour!

It's hot as Hades here—that is, hot as Philadelphia—though after two summers there I must say this heat doesn't hit me as hard as it does the English, who fold up at 80 degrees F.

Work sort of ambles on. Our transport has a jinx on it; only one truck works out of all our equipment. Reorganization goes slowly, and I'm beginning to get that feeling again of wondering what I'm doing here anyway. But after all, it is just the beginning, and the fact that I came here already edgy to get started is nobody's fault.

You'd chuckle to see me trying to sort out insurance policies in French! They all have to be changed or modified, and tomorrow I talk with the agent—I, who have never read my own policy through! What you don't learn on a relief job.

One thing pleases me: Already I feel as if I'm breaking into the French community. Last night the man across the street came over to invite us all for glace at his house. Very informal, for a Frenchman! So we trooped over, thinking to find something like ice cream. Instead it was a sweet liqueur, with ice, very good.

There we sat in a formal drawing room, sprawled around, swapping jokes and languages, just as at home in the summer people sit on their front porches having ice cream and ginger ale. Tomorrow I go to tea with a lady I have not yet met; tomorrow night we have students here. Saturday we will hear records at the home of a French teacher, and Sunday go on a hike with the student group.

QUAKER SERVICE DELEGATION IN TOULOUSE. 1946
- PHOTOGRAPHER UNKNOWN

The idea of censorship burns me, but I guess having someone read personal details in our letters is no different from kissing on the Metro! Actually, I care much more about being able to get the straight story from Poland.

Hugh is wonderfully pleasant to work with, and together we're planning to change some of the authoritarian, class-strata concepts of the old regime. I like it!

This reminds me that the May issue of *Politics* came today, a fine issue. When and if you get it, read "The Independent Woman." It says a lot of things I've fumed and fretted over for years. With your approach, Red, you're a good man to help a woman be significantly (and not just rebelliously) independent. And it takes help, believe me. We're still fettered by custom, upbringing, and education. Sometimes I think I've started too late to make the whole transition from Victorian helpmate or Hausfrau to a woman who's a complete and valuable person in her own right. But it's got to be done. When one group suffers from inequality, everybody suffers.

July 7, 1946 ~ Madeleine in Toulouse to Dr. Hauck in New Jersey

Dearest Dr. Lydia, If my requests get too many or too burdensome, you are to let me know straight off, just as you would want me to.

If you or your friends would be interested in helping Francine further, she would be overjoyed to have some warm winter clothing for her little girl, Christine. The baby is sixteen months old now, and Francine has enough for her for this winter, but she's already thinking of next winter. She will be living in Germany then, you see, and after her short visit there she is appalled at the prospect of there being absolutely nothing to buy. Everything the child needs for the next two years at least she will have to take with her.

Francine insisted that if anyone would be kind enough to send her things, she wanted to pay for them. I didn't think you would hear of that and told her so. Anything that comes should be sent to her directly in Paris, where she is working.

Incidentally, it seems to me that Francine herself could well use some pretty, warm clothes, although she wouldn't ask for anything for herself. She's a pretty little mite of a thing, smaller than I am, with dark hair and eyes and a young, sweet face. She's overcome at the idea that anyone as far away as America would be interested in helping her out.

Dr. van Huybers has a spot on her lung and has been sent to a sanitarium in the Alps. I had a note from her just the other day. She is very happy there and sounds more cheerful than I have known her to be before.

There's much I'd like to tell you about Toulouse and the group of people here. It's a small delegation, about eight people, most of them British. I feel as if I'm getting to know more about the British than the French at this point, but that's all to the good. We have more to learn about one another than I imagined.

We have chosen to work this area
because it is one of the worst hit by the
war...more than twenty five villages with
only one house left

-Red

Painful Separation

July 27, 1946

Dear My Red,

If anyone noticed a wide grin on me
this week, it's because I got a letter!
A wonderful one it was, Red. I feel close
all the time to what you are doing,
perhaps because I'm doing more myself. I could have wept that none of
mine arrived on that plane; further
on in this letter I'll give you a list of
R.M.'s and numbers. Perhaps I'd
better begin making carbons in case
several numbers get lost. Darn.
One really does feel isolated if the
mails don't function. I'm proudly
glad, my dear, that you do so well
and so cheerfully in spite of loneliness.
I hope to do better on that score in
the future.

I half hope some of my letters
didn't get to you, they're that full of

July 8, 1946 ~ Madeleine in Toulouse to Red in transit

It's a bright day here but it would be brighter if there were a letter from you. Sorry, but it's hard not to be disappointed. If you're off to Poland, I can only guess at how desperately busy you must be. Even here, where things sort of amble along, I've found myself working long, indefinite hours, and it's hard to get a corner of the table under the one light that's bright enough to see by, to get letters written. So I've skipped you for several days but not in my thoughts.

Toulouse is an ancient, filthy, surprisingly lovely city. We have open drains, fleas (I sleep swathed in DDT), dirt, and smells. These I find depressing, especially on dark days. I've always believed that one's surroundings shouldn't make so much difference as mine seem to for me. I've got over a lot of my extreme sensitivity, but since coming here I find I have a lot more to get over. Suddenly, now that we're parted, there are so many little things I want you to know. It will take months and months, maybe years, to get said all the little things that were passed over in the rush of big things these past months.

Yesterday for the first time, I found myself liking Toulouse. Some of us went up the tower of a thirteenth-century church. There, high up in the sun and wind, we looked through tiny brick arches at the rosy-red roofs and bricks of Toulouse, set in a circle of green hills. The winding Garonne flashed in the light, little towers rose all over the city. We hung over the edge to see gargoyles and gardens, and the air was clean and fresh. Then we walked around the top of the church, behind the walls, under the roof! Red, if only you'd been there! We could see the top of the vaulting, the tremendous beams supporting the roof, and in two places tiny windows opened into the church itself. It was tremendously old and strong, and strange to us who are not used to living familiarly with long past centuries.

About the job, I can tell you little for the moment. We are disorganized in a grand and glorious way! The old staff hasn't yet left, and the new hasn't yet got going. All sorts of projects are in the air, but none have foundations under them. A fascinating one has to do with establishing a woodworking school in Puycelci, an old walled village near Toulouse. It's practically abandoned, very primitive, and very beautiful. Getting a project going there would be a huge amount of work but wouldn't cost very much. It's good, working with a delegation. You get to know people intimately, and as almost always happens, you can't know people well without liking them.

Just what I do isn't awfully clear either. Hugh says I am to have a French secretary and not do the detailed work myself. It's a waste, he says, with which I feelingly agree. Hugh is a swell sort. Having him and Juanita here is wonderful. Sometimes in the first days, when everything seemed confused and ugly, I thought that they were the only beautiful things here. It was beautiful, seeing them together. You have not known me long, Red, or my years of tirades against the littleness and misunderstandings that make up so many marriages. To say so much about the Jenkins is, for me, special.

I've finally written to Herb but haven't brought myself as yet to send the letter. If I have to wound people, I'd rather do it face to face than at a distance. Do you know the saying: "Faithful are the wounds of a friend"? A strange saying, and one whose meaning I discovered once in pain and wonder.

The world seems wonderful and petty by turns. I wonder what part of it you are seeing now and how it seems to you. Do write, my dear. If it's as hard to get two minutes together there in which to write undisturbed as it is here, I'll understand. I'm strangely content to have you away, even not knowing where you are or what you're doing for the moment, knowing it's somehow good. But I'm terribly impatient to get on with our knowing one another and growing together. Perhaps if we both do as well as we can while we're apart, the knowing and growing will somehow go on just the same.

July 8, 1946 ~ Red in Warsaw to Madeleine in Toulouse

Warsaw, at last! So much has happened, so much territory has been covered since you last left Paris on that night train. It seems weeks or even months since that kiss on the quay.

I should warn you now about wide circulation of anything I may say in my letters. Sometimes the most innocent story can have terrific repercussions. One human interest story told by one of the relief team and circulated in the States has caused Bill Edgerton and Philip Zealey headaches, worrying about what might happen. The whole situation here is rather precarious. They feel we are very fortunate to be working here, and they do not want to jeopardize our work by giving ourselves publicity in the States.

Bill is full of stories he has picked up here during the past four months as he and Philip were establishing the mission, and he is now faced with the problem of accepting or rejecting the chance to make radio talks when he returns home. Even the Polish Embassy would like him to do it, but it is so hard to say in a few words anything that people at home would not misinterpret without much detailed background.

Bill is the same fellow I knew several years ago, young in spirit; he would not look a day older had he not grown a mustache. He is keen, observant, and understanding. He says that were it not that he is anxious to be with his family, he would join the transport team as a regular member. His family needs him, however; he has been away for two years.

Twelve noon. I wish you could hear the call that is now being played on the radio. There is a legend about it. In Krakow in 1241, a village was being invaded by the Tartars. A man in the church steeple was sounding a warning to the countryside on a trumpet; he had given the call from three sides and was giving it from the fourth when a Tartar arrow killed him, breaking off the call abruptly. That is the way the call is played now; it is beautiful, but ends suddenly.

BOMBED OUT BUILDINGS IN WARSAW. AT NIGHT SOMETIMES A LIGHT COULD BE SEEN WITHIN THESE RUINS WHERE SOMEONE HAD CREATED HOUSING. 1946   -PHOTOGRAPH BY RED

Philip Zealey, our mission director, is a tall, lanky, soft-spoken Englishman. He knows a great deal about Poland, having been here before the war. He does not speak Polish as well as Bill, however. It is going to be easy working with him. Both Bill and Philip are glad that I know Al Johnson; they have known him only through correspondence. There is still some doubt as to whether Al is the man to take Bill's place; Al himself is not sure that he should. He'll start and see what happens.

Friday evening while I was in Berlin, Claude Shotts took us for a ride through what was once a beautiful city. Today it is dead! Berlin is a city of rubble. The beautiful Tiergarten has lost all of its trees; we understand that Germans cut them for fuel last winter. Now huge statues mostly of lions and antelope remain standing alone. There are some dug-outs with grass roofs, as though people had lived in underground rooms. Most of the garden is now planted in vegetables. For blocks there was not a single building undamaged; most were totally abandoned.

Really, darling, you can see movies and pictures and read about the effects of war, but one must see the effects before he can have a real feeling of what took place. I wonder about the people, and the horrors of those nights when the planes came.

Claude says there is only one undamaged church in all Berlin. Huge libraries stand as shells. I am told that Warsaw is even worse. That is hard to believe.

When I left Saturday, I flew out of the Russian airport outside Berlin. I was the only passenger. The country we flew over was beautiful, similar to other farming areas, yet with a character of its own. It did not take us long to reach Poznan, the frontier stop where the airfield had been bombed. We taxied up to a wooden shed on the side of the field; here many people stood in the rain. After customs was through with me, the crew brought in four chairs and placed them in front of the regular seats.

As quickly as it takes to load a bus, the plane was full, but that did not stop the Poles from coming aboard. The aisle was packed with people standing. I was amazed, but to them it was just another ride, and they seemed no more concerned about a crowded plane than we are about crowded busses. Everyone seemed to have baggage, and I wondered if the pilots could get that load off the ground. After a long run, we were off; I was greatly relieved when we cleared the trees at the end of the runway.

Soon we were in Warsaw. At the airport, we boarded a crowded Dodge army truck with wooden seats for the ride into the city.

It was rather late before we got around to eating. There was so much to discuss with Bill and Philip. They were most interested in the latest news from Paris, and I was eager to know what is going on here. Finally we decided to have a snack; it consisted of one-half a baked chicken divided between three of us!

Meals have been like that ever since. Prices are out of this world. At the present rate of exchange, it costs from $3 to $5 per meal on the free market. Of course I was concerned about the amount of food we will be getting as a team and was informed that it will include fifteen eggs per week per person, plus ten pounds of potatoes. Now I am wondering how long our consciences can let us eat like that in a starving country.

As yet I have not been in the worst part of the city, but the area around here was practically destroyed. In fact, the city was so devastated that the government thought of abandoning it and building elsewhere, but the people started coming back to Warsaw, and the government followed. Now there are shops along the streets with high, naked walls behind them; sometimes it is dangerous when the winds blow. Bill showed me this morning where a wall fell on a building and killed three people. Everywhere people are cleaning bricks and walls, hauling, painting, rebuilding, working like so many ants.

It is a huge job, but they are determined to keep at it. I would be discouraged at the very thought. Take the little job we are to do: hauling stone for homes. It will take our eight trucks more than two years just to haul the stone, yet here the Poles are starting with only two trucks. This is happening all over Poland where more than 5,000 villages were destroyed!

Madeleine, often I wish you could be with me, yet I am satisfied as long as both of us have a job to do and are looking to the time when those jobs can come closer together geographically. You have awakened something in me that has quieted my spirit.

July 9, 1946 ~ Madeleine in Toulouse to Red in Warsaw

We went to Carcasonne for a Sunday outing, through fields of wheat being harvested, golden in the sun, and vines beginning to cover the ground. The city sits on top of a hill, and the first sight of it from the valley is like looking at an illustration for Grimm's fairy tales. There should be a sleeping princess there and a knight to waken her. Instead, it's two-thirds restored, very new looking, and automobiles drive over the drawbridge. From the crenellated walls and towers there are beautiful views of the countryside. The new town hasn't been built quite up to the old walled one; a broad strip of grass and wild flowers still surrounds the wall, and we picnicked there in the sunshine. I'd love to see Carcasonne at night, when the old magic of medieval days could creep back into it.

This is a beautiful region, Red, rich in history and antiquities. The Romans fortified Carcasonne first; later builders just added on. But for all that France is so lovely, I look at it with reservations. All its beauty and interest bespeak the past, and I look in vain for the future. The student groups we have here argue hotly about Gothic style, but they don't know parliamentary procedure.

The French seem to bury themselves in culture and history, so they don't have to look at the awful present. I thought as I looked over the battlements of Carcasonne at the ancient church lying outside the walls, that maybe the decay of Western civilization really started centuries ago, when men first built these fortifications.

They put far more labor and ingenuity into their fortresses than into their homes. They knew more about fighting with each other than about living with each other—which is still true of us. What we see now is perhaps only the long culmination of a mistake as old as man: the mistake of individualism and force. I remember what one of the Friends Relief Service (FRS) men said about Germany, and I suppose the same thing is more vividly true of Poland than of France. He said that Germany was always intensely interesting, but one can't ever be really happy there.

You remember, Red, once in Marseille you said I belonged with flowers, or something like that? I was troubled, because that didn't seem to me to be enough. It's like the lovely landscape and ancient buildings here; they're lovely but they aren't enough either. There has to be a kind of sternness at the heart of everything lovely—call it truth or virtue or duty. It's that sternness that seems to me to be lacking now in the French as a whole. The English seem to have it, whatever their faults. And I'd put my bet, if there were any takers, on the nation with that moral toughness.

Oh Red, I wonder how long it will be before these letters get to you. And selfish though it is, I wonder how long before yours get to me?

I'm so terribly eager to know what you're doing, the more so as your activity is a sort of vicarious work for me. I hesitate to tell you of my work, it's still so little. Don't worry about it; if you do, I won't be able to bitch to you any longer. Often I feel that CPS must have been a little like this; you went in wanting to make a contribution, to do something useful, and you were told to sit down and wait for a matter of a few years. This is probably a good experience for me to have, but I sure do chafe under it.

Why all this inactivity? First, the program is very new. Some of the branch offices don't welcome the idea of an administrative center; they'd prefer to be strictly on their own. Second, the Toulouse branch had an almost 100 percent turnover in personnel, which has set the work and the planning back months. Third, the program which looked so beautiful on paper has already fallen apart in several respects.

I looked in awe at the great ones in Paris who proposed and disposed. I thought they knew all the answers; they could create a program where none existed before. But they made a lot of mistakes and wrong guesses, and there is some putting on a good front with not too much behind. I'll do my part of the job as well as I can, but I will not put up with circumlocutions and the appearance of being all-wise. Neither will Hugh. He shoots straight from the shoulder and is democratic in his approach to people. Never have I appreciated that as much as now. The world is already complicated and troublesome enough without people botching things up worse by not saying what they think, and working to opposite purposes.

There! Sorry to have unloaded on you, but now I feel better. You are to take these accumulated gripes with about a peck of salt. As an official program, we are still only a week old, still having growing pains. Next time I write it will probably be to complain because I am too busy!

Please, please, let me know how it is with you. Every time I eat a peach, I wonder if you have any fruit. Every time I get a hollow feeling before lunch (and we do have excellent food here), I wonder if you're getting enough to eat. And every time I look around for something to do next, I wonder if you're driven past capacity.

It's hard to think of you in context, as it were. I just know that somewhere north and east of here that bright head of yours shows against the sky, your hands hold tools or a pen, and your jaw sets as you try to break through some of the red tape that surely surrounds your work. Oh damn, I do miss you.

July 10, 1946 ~ Red in Warsaw to Madeleine in Toulouse

We must accept the fact that we can receive letters only once a week, but that's hard to take now. When a plane comes in and there is no mail, it's even worse. That was the case yesterday. I am anxious to know if you are getting my letters, as mail is often lost. I shall have a letter to you on the plane each week.

Today Philip and I have been to see a vice-minister and a couple of other officials. They seem anxious for the team to start working. One man said he wanted to see what western efficiency is. Evidently they think we can move heaven and earth in a short time, but they are aware of the extent of this job.

We lunched today with a woman who worked with Quakers in Poland after World War I, when they tried to control the typhus epidemic caused by the people coming back from Russia. She was here during the Insurrection and, like anyone who was here during that time, has some pretty horrible stories to tell. Some of the things we hear are too much for the imagination. Philip has a friend who was in a concentration

camp for several years. One night the man began relating stories about the camp and went on for three hours. I commented to our luncheon guest on the spirit with which the Poles are going about rebuilding Warsaw. She said that instead of pitying themselves for all that they have suffered, they often laugh at some of the things that were most horrifying a few years ago. This was even truer during the Occupation; sometimes, even when hostages were being killed, someone would find some reason for humor and everyone would laugh. Remarkable!

How they have the courage to make anything out of the rubble that is left here is fascinating. One church has only a steeple and a few columns left; I was told they still hold services in the crypt. Bill told me of one building that was ordered to be cleared away; when workmen

CHURCH IN WARSAW. IN SPITE OF THE DESTRUCTION, SERVICES WERE BEING HELD IN THE CRYPT. 1946   -PHOTOGRAPH BY RED

went into the rubble, they discovered that fifty people had found openings underneath in areas that were protected by arches. They were using the cellars and open places for living quarters!

Philip is anxious to have regular meetings in Warsaw of the team leaders to work out mutual problems. We are all to get the same weekly allowance of 500 zloties (zl). Although AFSC may be more liberal in vacation time and allowance, it is desirable for all members in Poland to receive the same. From what I gather, Philip will let the teams in the field decide as much as possible, even though operations might be different from what he would like.

Bill and I were to take the night train for Gdynia to meet the transport team, but we received a cable saying they had not left Paris. Most disappointing. I leave in twenty minutes for Kozienice, where I shall work with the relief team until further word from our fellows. They are hard-pressed for manpower just now.

There is so much to tell you about the past two days and such a short time to do it in that I hardly know where to begin. I have been through some of the worst areas; one was a battle field for six months. Some villages had not one house standing that was not damaged. Some had one or two standing and everything else leveled. We picked up a man who lives in a dugout; the Germans tore down his house and took the timbers to make one room beneath the ground. He has come back to it since they left. In one village there are sixty-five families, fifty of them without a man.

Stories like this are accumulating. The wonderful part is that the stories are told without self-pity. Instead, people accept what has

A TROLLEY PULLING A PASSENGER CAR IN WARSAW. 1946
-PHOTOGRAPH BY RED

happened and are trying now to make the best of it. Bill was very much impressed with the amount of work that has been accomplished in some of the villages since he was there last. Yet they have no trucks or heavy equipment. You see wagons carrying one or two long logs or two men sawing logs by hand.

July 10, 1946 ~ Madeleine in Toulouse to Herb in Philadelphia

The May issue of *Politics* came a few days ago, and a part of you seemed to come with it. I wonder if you can understand how all ideas of liberal thought and generous intent seem to shine with a special light here. The city of Toulouse feels like a desert. France as a whole is sunk in apathy and hopelessness, the reports from the east are still more deadening, and sometimes I feel as if I too were dry as dust, with no more vision than a stone.

Contact with the outside world (I'm just beginning to guess what the five years of Occupation must have been like) is much harder here than in Paris. The radio doesn't work, English newspapers are hard to come by, and our best American news comes by way of English weeklies. I think I have never been so spiritually lonely in my life.

Your books have been wonderful. Imagine me walking down one of the narrow, stinking, sunlit streets of Toulouse reading *The Devil and Dan'l Webster*! I do, sometimes, on the way to work, to gather courage, and I think of your reading *Winnie the Pooh* when Staten Island got too much. I marvel at how many things you told me of then that I haven't understood until now.

This sounds much worse than it is, actually. The real reason for the griping is that I'm just not busy enough. I came down here steamed up to do a new job, and I've been sitting for the last three weeks. So has Hugh Jenkins, the director. The Refugee Program looked lovely on paper, but circumstances, poor planning, and change of personnel have shot it as full of holes as a sieve.

I waver between appreciating this experience as an example of the army (that's the isolation in a cultural desert) and CPS (that's the waiting and wasting of willingness). Presumably the situation won't go on forever; if things don't shape up here in Toulouse, they'll close the delegation, redistribute the personnel, and call it quits. I hope that doesn't happen.

There's a lot to do here, but it's not the usual relief pattern of handing out food and clothing. It's much more a problem of retraining people and helping them integrate into a community and plan for a future in either France or Spain. It's a kind of work that ought to involve an understanding of the economic, social, and political problems of a community and its country. That understanding ought to be followed by definite ideas on the working out of the problems, but not in a paternalistic or authoritarian sense. One can't move into a community, enter into its life, and try to help people find their place in it without a pretty definite goal in mind; otherwise your efforts will be sabotaged or perverted to ends you never dreamed of.

What I've been trying to say is that, although I believe this is what is needed here, I'm not sure that Quakers have the background or the vision to do that kind of job. Toulouse is an old delegation, as relief work goes. It came through the heroic (I mean that literally) days of the Resistance in grand style. It is, in a way, an epitome of France: doing splendidly during the war but unable to rethink and re-imagine a world where the Old Order is giving way. My God! I think I've never been so frustrated in my life! Here I am—a healthy, intelligent, educated, some-what-experienced woman of the most favored country on Earth—plunked down in the midst of a situation crying for understanding, direction, imagination, and plain hard work, who is seemingly unable to supply any of those desperately needed things.

The greener pastures are to the east, of course. There you could either be so busy that you'd be too dog tired to introspect, or you dream fondly (but probably vainly) that in such a country, still suffering openly from war, conditions would be fluid enough so that you could do some-thing new and creative. Here the situation has jelled enough so that it's hard to turn things into a new course.

Well, I've learned at least two things since being here. First, to like and appreciate the British. Their calmness and just plain integrity and morality are as fine gold compared with the shabbiness of much French dealing. This sounds terribly anti-French, I'm afraid. I've grown to like individual French people very much but the French collectively, less. There's nothing that can't be "arranged." You can even barter on insurance rates and policies. You have to know somebody to get anything, even what's legally your right. The country is being strangled by its bureaucracy, and its politics look just hopeless. The really fine French people I've met are so fine that you wonder if, for ten of them, the city won't be saved.

Second, I'm learning a bit about the administrative game. I suppose that's what you call it when you set up an office, try to make policies work, and dictate dozens of letters every day. I'd give my shirt to be out doing a hard job of almost any other kind, but remembering the coming managerial revolution, I think I ought to find out something about this mysterious process.

You'd like the room in which I work. The Canal du Midi and the tramline pass in front of my window, and slow barges and Tooterville trolleys go by constantly. I'll try to get some pictures of Toulouse trans-port for you and, if I can, a conductor's whistle, which blows at each stop and sounds like a kid's Halloween horn.

I feel better now, having blown off and having written you. What would fulfill me would be a letter from you. I've almost never waited so patiently and impatiently to hear from anyone. By now I wonder if a letter will come at all. I couldn't imagine that being true. There are good reasons for your silence, and I try not to pry into it. Herb, Herb, the thought of your hurt lies like a stone on my mind. Tell me how it is with you, and if you can, how it is with me. This time I am in suspension—completely—in an alien country with work, affections, ideas, all in abeyance.

It's curious to think of you, not knowing where you are or what you are doing. Not knowing matters far less than it would have a few months ago. Over here you take seriously the fine words about space and time not making a real difference or you go nuts. Everything is in hiatus at the moment and somehow unreal. I feel as if I were a cocoon, waiting to come to life.

Your Navy summer uniform is now the happy possession of Hugh Jenkins. I was going to send your two boxes of clothes to a little isolated town where Congregationalists are working, but when the hot weather came (it was very like Philadelphia for a few days), and Hugh sweltered away in his heavy English tweeds on formal occasions (and nobody can be formal like the French), I dug around in your boxes.

How is Louie? I'd like to hear from her sometime. And from you.

July 11, 1946 ~ Madeleine in Toulouse to Red in Warsaw

It's one in the morning, I can't sleep. I've been thinking about you, so I might better write than toss. Outside the stars shine around the little brick tower that we think of as "ours." Inside, in the kitchen, I'm having a bowl of cocoa. Join me?

You seemed very near today; I imagined walking upstairs to the Caveau apartment with you. One reason for your being so vivid was a wonderful letter from my roommate and her husband, Janice and Mario Levi. They told me a little of what a "wonderful and awe-ing thing it is to come to know another person closely." And as I was lying awake tonight, I thought how utterly fantastic that I should think of Red, whom I've known so little a time, in that connection. But it didn't feel fantastic at all. In any situation that I imagine being in with you, there's nothing strange or strained.

All of us here at the Caveau are rather on edge right now. Secours Quaker is the scene of a tragedy that none of us can do much to relieve.

The German wife of one of our employees has come here to see her husband. She was a political prisoner for four years before the war, lived through the war, and now lives in Berlin (and you know what that means), trying to re-educate German youth. Her husband hadn't known during the war whether or not she was alive; in sympathy and loneliness he has turned to a Polish woman (also working at Secours Quaker) who lost all her family through deportation and in labor camps.

The three people involved are all fine people; they've suffered intensely, and through little fault of their own, continue to suffer. The German woman, who was distraught and irrational, is with us at the apartment for the moment. She has found a home and a haven here, though we have so little to offer. Tonight, as Dick and I made up a bed for her, I felt as if for the first time I had a reason for being here.

A clean bed, a sleeping pill, and a goodnight kiss are not much for someone who has gone through hell. But as she said goodnight, she told us, "The knowledge came to imprint itself on my mind that one could trust no one, that all men were evil. But there you were, standing about me like angels, and I could no longer believe that. I found again the old me who believed in mankind."

Oh God, Red, it seems as if the past ten years demand of us that we be superhuman. Even the closest ties of affection and understanding are not enough; they have to be rooted in universality to withstand the terrible stresses of these times. Pathetically, people have held during the bitter years to the memories and affections of the past, and too often that past has been destroyed by what has intervened. This kind of tragedy must be repeated thousands of times over Europe these days.

Do you ever have the feeling, in the midst of all the sorrow, hate, destruction, uncertainty, and ugliness (and you must see them there more vividly than we do here) that the present is unreal, a dream from which you will wake up? The last five or eight or ten years must have seemed like that to people in the prison of Europe. For us, it's not even that many months.

But as circumstances are more difficult, people are more beautiful. I think I've never felt so close to people as I do to the Anglo-American group here. We turn to each other because there's not much else to turn to, and in the uncertainty and sadness, more laughter and loveliness comes out than I'd have thought possible. It's quite wonderful. I wonder if you find something like that in Poland.

July 14, 1946 ~ Red in Kozienice to Madeleine in Toulouse

Albert and I took turns driving the Ford truck from Warsaw. It would have done you good to have been with us for those two days, not to mention what it would have done for me! In areas of nearly total destruction, houses and barns are rising, fields of wheat are being harvested, grass is

green, and there are many signs of activity. This is all the more remarkable since seldom do you see machinery in the fields. If you do, it's an ancient model of a reaper.

All the officials with whom we talked Thursday and Friday were very excited about our coming with the trucks and men. They are very much concerned about their people living

RED AND ALBERT CLAYTON, MEMBER OF THE FOOD AND
CLOTHING DISTRIBUTION TEAM AT KOZIENICE
-PHOTOGRAPH BY AN ETU MEMBER

another winter underground. I told Bill that it would be easy for us to come in and take much of the credit for rapid rehabilitation if we are not careful. It is important that we talk little about what we are doing and try to encourage the Poles who are doing a good job, although they need little encouragement.

I suggested that we not start hauling immediately but work on some of the roads first, since we expect to be traveling over some of the roads as much as twenty-five times a day. Wherever we could work for a few hours and save several minutes per trip would be well worthwhile. The officials told us that they had already informed the people of the village that we were coming, and that they should start on the roads themselves. They are anxious that we drive trucks and not be bothered too much with other things. Bill was jubilant because so many had at first accepted the idea only with a great deal of skepticism.

I wish you were here; we might go walking in the moonlight where I went this afternoon before dinner. These quarters are in the grounds of what used to be a castle; the grounds are still surrounded by a high wall but the castle was destroyed early in the war. We live in one wing that was repaired. In back are beautiful woods with a stream running through. It's so quiet and peaceful there, with an occasional passerby or a cow grazing across the way.

Tuesday night now, and how wonderful it is to have a letter from you! It seems strange that you should envy other people for the "feeling of being alive" when most people would envy you for your talent of giving so much of yourself to others. Often you are able to give because of the impression that you are getting so much from life yourself. That is one thing that struck me about you, that you get so much out of beauty, people, new things, and even the small daily things of life.

July 15, 1946 ~ Madeleine in Toulouse to Red in Poland

Dear my Red, I'm in a flower-filled field overlooking a valley of farms. Hot in the sun and watching the clouds, I wish terribly you were here.

The whole Toulouse delegation fled to the country and moved in on Montauban. It's been heaven—green trees and sweet air and quiet. I feel still and sure inside for the first time in weeks. Last night I slept out on an open porch with honeysuckle climbing over it and a full moon shining through the trees, and remembered you, Red, and how you look in the moonlight. Strange days, these are; I seem just to be waiting.

I wish I knew where you are and how. I fear always being selfish in my pleasure, wondering if your surroundings aren't much more ugly and disheartening than those I complain about.

We've been swimming, once in the Garonne, once in the Tarn. It's good, this feeling of being washed and sunned and rested. We'll need it for the coming weeks.

All the questionings and uneasiness I've had about this job, Hugh has had, too. In a way I'm glad; it shows I'd sized up the situation fairly well. We are not at all sure there's really a place for us here. As things are set up, there's too much administration for so small a program. We're going to thrash the whole thing out here and in Paris and try to make a good decision. Neither of us wants to be on a 'paper' job when there are such crying needs to the east. Red, tell me as frankly and as quickly as you can what the possibilities of work are for a woman in the areas you've seen. I don't know at all what the future will be, but for my own thinking and perhaps for future planning, I'd like the information.

I'm not greatly disturbed over this, Red, and don't you be. There's been some blundering, but I don't see that it was mine. A lot of relief work is waiting, and I'll do my share of that if I must. Only I hope I get to do one real job while I'm overseas.

July 17, 1946 ~ Red in Kozienice to Madeleine in Toulouse

Why couldn't you have been with us today? It's been a lovely day.

JACK GRIST, A MEMBER OF THE FOOD AND CLOTHING DISTRIBUTION TEAM IN KOZIENICE, WITH FAMILY IN FRONT OF THEIR BUNKER-HOME
-PHOTOGRAPH BY BETH CLARKSON DEARDON

After raining all day yesterday (and since the station wagon turned over it has no windshield), it turned beautiful and warm. Dorothy Abbott and I went to two villages in a section where twenty-five villages were completely destroyed. Only one house and a church remain standing!

We stayed until near lunch time and then came back to the stream. Here we stopped and went swimming—if you can call it swimming; the river looked nice and wide, with little current, but it was so shallow that we had to look to find a place that was over my knees. We did have the advantage of a sandy beach where we sat in the sun and ate lunch. Relief workers have a hard time!

At the next village we saw people threshing wheat by hand. Have you ever seen that done? The wheat is laid out very carefully in a big box with a cement floor; then two men, each with two sticks attached by means of a leather thong, begin to beat the wheat. This knocks the kernels loose. The kernels are raked up, and then the hay that is left. I was disturbed about such crude methods, since this country lives on its wheat production, plus potatoes, milk, and eggs, but Dorothy soon found out that there are three threshing machines in the area. Peasants hire the use of a thresher by the hour, but some people are so short of bread that they have to do the threshing by hand until the machines arrive. They need the hay for making the roofs of barns and houses.

Two of the fellows here are married. Often, when they speak of their wives, I wonder what marriage really is aside from announcing to society that two are becoming man and wife. Does it change the inward feeling of either? Does it limit the friendship and affection each of them may have for other people? Wouldn't one's affection for other people enrich the bonds of an ideal marriage?

I'm reading *The Story of Poland* by Bernard Newman. If you

MOTHER AND DAUGHTER INSIDE A POLISH BUNKER-HOME NEAR KOZIENICE
-PHOTOGRAPH BY DICKIE AND TONY CHAPELLE

can get this, you might get a better picture of Poland than I can give you with limited observation and time. It reads as easily as a novel and certainly is as exciting.

There are so many things I have failed to tell you about: the women policemen; long narrow wagons with rubber tires; trucks used as busses; the thatched roofs which make each village a real fire trap; sandy roads or no roads at all; beautiful flowers and small fields; the sunburned and shapeless peasant women who are yet attractive; the pathetic stories of aged couples too feeble to work and whose children are missing; land mines exploding still (we heard an explosion today); new stores that are appearing along the streets of Warsaw; the many wagons hauling debris out of the city; men and women cleaning bricks by hand and piling them up; how clean the streets are—women come along every day with brooms and sweep; the engine held together with split pins used too many times; women selling milk and bread; windows still boarded up because there is no glass; continual changes in schedules as transport becomes more efficient. This isn't satisfying, but it gives you some idea of how wonderful it will be when we can share our experiences; it will take us a lifetime to catch up!

July 22, 1946 ~ Madeleine in Toulouse to Red in Kozienice

Another beautiful weekend missing you. I saw another place I'd like to share with you, the Pyrenees, barren and beautiful. We were only twenty-six kilometers from Spain, bathing off the coast near a little fishing village. Back through the mountains on a road that nearly lost itself, beside great gorges, flower-bright pastures, terraces of vines, and gray mists that caught on the sharp peaks. Lovely, lonely country.

All of the Toulouse and Montauban delegations went to Perpignan for the opening of the community center and some of us to work—eleven hours of conferencing. The democratic processes are wonderful but hard on the tailbone. The aftereffects of one-sided, authoritarian planning have made the whole Refugee Program black and blue, but by dint of open covenants openly arrived at, Hugh is winning his way. He and I went down prepared to throw up the Siege (central office) and look for another job. The delegations begged us to stay, said it was the first time they hadn't felt the central office was trying to force something on them. So we're sticking it out, Hugh with half his time in Paris, and I with more Siege responsibility and some delegation work on the side.

What a mess of a letter this is, Red, like a little kid's, all folded and smudged. I've been at it half a dozen times today, always being interrupted. I'm becoming a poor correspondent, I fear. I haven't written much the past weeks because I've been quite unhappy and the words just wouldn't come out. I've told you about it, but it's not the sort of thing I want to pour out to you every day. And now that things, having hit rock bottom, seem to be looking up, I'm getting too busy!

The more I see of groups trying to work together and making such a hash of it, even with the best intentions, the more I come to think of our long meetings as exciting experiments—people, trying to work with one another. It's like putting chemicals and catalysts in a test tube.

It's the thing we know least about and need most to know. Reading of what has happened in Poland the last two weeks, and the civil war that's threatened in China, and how Talmadge is running ahead in the Georgia election, I'm almost glad that I'm not a highly trained mathematician or musician. Because if I were, it would be too easy to bury myself in a complex, absorbing job and forget about the rest of the problems. The catch is, of course, that if I am occupying myself with the great Human Experiment, my contribution is so tiny that I can't see it and neither can anybody else.

One thing I don't worry over any longer—your food. What an everlasting problem food is! I believe firmly in taking care of oneself in order to do a good job, but every once in a while I ask myself what peculiar combination of circumstance or providence ordained for me to have the food instead of one of the people I'm trying to help. I haven't seen an egg since our weekend in June, and Hugh brought some back one day from the British Council. We all gathered round the stove in an admiring circle while they were fried. The next day I had a drink of milk, my first since the *SS Brazil*. Do you know, I had forgotten how it tastes; the first swallow was a distinct surprise.

Red, I do miss you. I must find you now, and for a long time to come, in all the things I've experienced with you. In the first stars coming out, in sun and wind and beautiful scenery, in all people of courage and goodwill.

July 20, 1946 ~ Madeleine to AFSC on a visit to Perpignan

This is the country where fairy tales are made: ruined castles on hillsides; gray mountains catching mists on jagged peaks that stretch off to mysterious distances; wrinkled, brown old women dressed all in peasant black, driving hissing geese along the road. Into this picturesque but poor part of France came the Spanish refugees, beginning in 1939. Men and women crossed the Pyrenees on foot. Along with soldiers who had lost an arm or a leg in the Civil War or a foot or hand from frostbite in the bitter crossing came families who panicked and blindly made for France as the armies advanced.

In a country that has never been rich, where a living is scratched from dry hillsides, growing vines and a few olive trees, hurt by war and occupation, refugees have a hard time. Quakers moved in; they have been in Perpignan since 1939-40, feeding Spanish children, distributing clothing, retraining amputees, and educating teenage boys who have never had a chance to learn a trade.

The Quaker Center really "belongs" in Perpignan. All sorts of people bring their problems in perfect confidence to its door. Both the French and the Spanish communities gather there to study, to read, to dance, and just to sit and talk. On Friday night, July 19, in honor of the opening of the Spanish foyer, the Casa del Catalunya, the Spaniards held a Sardane in the street in front of the center. There was a grand, formal opening in the afternoon; Pablo Casals made a speech, and there were toasts and other speeches and a crush of people. One woman, pushing through the crowd, asked a Quaker worker what the Quakers were distributing. "Today, nothing but goodwill."

When it grew dark, a Spanish orchestra climbed up on the narrow platform outside the center and struck up the foot-lifting music of the Sardane. The dance was on. Circles of dancers formed along the street, then circles within circles: tiny children still absorbed in watching their feet, grandmothers and white-bearded old men who lifted their knees more nimbly than anyone else. Everyone wore a nosegay of yellow broom tied with red ribbon, the flower and colors of Catalonia. The music shrilled through the narrow street, the dancers turned in steps now stately, now sprightly. But it was much more than the Sardane that they were dancing. They were dancing their hope for their homeland that lies just over the mountains, they were dancing the long years of exile and their faith in Spain and in freedom.

July 22, 1946 ~ Red in Kozienice to Madeleine in Toulouse

Ever since arriving here and seeing how these people are working to rebuild their country, I have marveled at their spirit. For more than one hundred years Poland had no body, but her soul lived in the hearts of her people. It is heartening and satisfying to see how rapidly the body is being rebuilt because the heart beats so strong. It came as rather a shock to me that perhaps it is this very spirit, this extreme patriotism, this strong loyalty, that caused people to work up their emotions to the point that they would fight with their fellow man. Is it possible to transfer this enthusiasm for Poland to enthusiasm for rebuilding a world?

There was a time when I strongly favored a United States of Europe, but it is only since coming here that I have felt the need of an attempt to so unify Europe that borders between countries mean no more than divisions between provinces in France or powiats here. At one time there was a movement in England to unite the countries of Western Europe; the main purpose, however, was to organize for a defense, which might seem offensive to others. The plan included free trade between countries and easy crossing of borders. It seems to me that if a few countries who could work together would start implementing this plan, carry on with pragmatic principles, and change them as necessary for easy operation rather than holding fast to rules because of their political concepts, other

TRANSPORT TEAM AT THE CROSSING FROM GERMANY INTO CZECHOSLAVAKIA WHILE IN TRANSIT TO POLAND. 1946
-PHOTOGRAPH BY ONE OF THE ETU MEMBERS

countries might see that it would be an advantage to join the group. Modern transport is such that Europe could become an economic whole. The resources of the various countries complement each other, and it would be much better if there were contributions by each for the benefit of all rather than big countries arguing over the markets of the smaller ones.

Perhaps this is not realistic considering the differences in political and economic ideologies that exist in Europe today, but I feel sure that boundaries can never be settled satisfactorily until they mean less than they do today. Boundaries have been pushed around so much during the last thousand years that it is impossible to decide them on an economic basis; it is even harder to decide on ethnic standards. In many areas, those living in the cities feel loyal to one country while those living in rural areas feel strongly toward another. Even in the cities, there are large differences in loyalty. The best thing would seem to be to give people something greater to relate to, something which would incorporate all loyalties.

You can imagine how disturbed some men are when part of their coal mine lies in another country. Sometimes the office is in one country and the mine in another. When can we break through these

barriers to the place where it makes little difference where the boundaries are? We would then be nearer to eliminating many occasions for war, provided changes are carried out with regard to the human element involved. What I am thinking of are working agreements, which a country would feel free to join and would be anxious to join, not as a mea-

FAMILY IN FRONT OF THEIR PRE-WORLD WAR II HOME, NEAR KOZIENICE, POLAND. 1946
-PHOTOGRAPH BY AN ETU MEMBER

sure for military defense but as a positive step toward solving some of its internal problems.

Today is cold and rainy, far different from the last four days. Tomorrow Wojtek Jankowski, our Polish interpreter, and I go to Gora Pulawska to wait for the team's arrival. They are due here Tuesday or Wednesday. Unfortunately the barrack is still not ready for us. The boys will be disappointed but there is nothing we can do except pitch in and help them finish it for us. In the meantime, we shall be living in the schoolhouse.

Wojtek is proving to be a good teacher—if only he had a good pupil! When we go to the market, he tells me what to say and then insists that I say it. Of course, I cannot understand the answer, but then he takes over. Last night a peasant talked to me for more than fifteen minutes after I used a couple of words which Wojtek had taught me!

At present, as I sit in the sun typing, three little fellows are looking on with a great deal of curiosity. They are all handsome: blond with blue eyes. One has his head clipped except for a few locks in front that are combed forward. Maybe I shall take a picture of him and send it to you. They just now observed your picture and were making exclamations about it. When I understood "Anglais," I said "America," and they repeated in chorus "America!" with a great deal of pleasure. I haven't learned what they think of your grin, but the score is even: they don't know what I am writing to you.

People are very friendly and, you can imagine, very curious. Wojtek cannot understand why I say "Dziendobry" (Good morning) to nearly everyone we meet. He is from the city of Gdynia and has much to learn about the ways of peasants.

I am certainly thankful for the week I have been able to spend with the relief team here in Kozienice; it gives me a better understanding of their problems and gets me better acquainted with the team. Bill was very glad that I could lend them a hand; all of them had been overworked and the trucks needed repairing. Beth becomes more charming as one gets to know her; she is considerate as well as very capable of leading the team. She has delegated responsibility so much that you would not think she is the leader. Beth and I have started talking about ways in which members of the teams can get together. They are distributing food in our area, so I have suggested that we might arrange for them to eat lunch with us once or twice a week.

July 27, 1946 ~ Red In Gora Pulawska to Madeleine in Toulouse

Hurrah and hallelujah! The boys are here! Arrived shortly after dark, tired, hungry, and dirty. More flat tires than you can count. Now they are off eating supper while I sit and watch the trucks. I haven't yet found out whether they have a letter from you.

As long as the weather stays nice, we can manage without the barrack, but once it starts to rain, we shall run into trouble. The boys tell me there are several days of mechanical work to do. The truck that will come to me is the truck we drove going to Marseille. Remember? How can we forget? I was happy to know that they had put it together.

Why is it that I find it strange to be starting a new adventure without you? I was glad to stay behind when the men went out to eat; I wanted to rush in and tell you the glad tidings. Now I would like to have you here so that you, too, could help plan and direct the work for the next few weeks or months. The next year should be one of the most interesting that I have yet experienced.

July 27, 1946 ~ Madeleine in Toulouse to Red in Gora Pulawska

If anyone noticed a wide grin on me this week, it's because I got a letter! A wonderful one it was, Red. I feel closer all the time to what you are doing, perhaps because I'm doing more myself. I could have wept that none of my letters arrived on that plane; perhaps I'd better begin making carbons in case several get lost. One really does feel isolated if the mails don't function. I'm proudly glad, my dear, that you do so well and so cheerfully in spite of loneliness. I hope to do better on that score in the future.

I half hope some of my letters didn't get to you, they're that full of gripes. We've learned a good deal from the situation here:

Don't use authoritarian methods; they always backfire.

Don't shove personnel around; they lose 75% of their effectiveness.

Don't try to do everything yourself; share responsibility and credit.

Don't be "diplomatic"; lay your cards out and insist that others do the same. Sorry! You know all this already. I've learned by watching it work.

Our offices are being repainted and repaired, and though the whole place is ready to fall down, it's beginning to look more cheerful. We swank with a Rose Room, Green Room, and so on. Fine as long as the plaster doesn't come down! One of the things the old delegation said we didn't need is a Community Center. We're finding we do. The first thing people, most especially refugees, need after food and shelter is companionship and intellectual interests. So in the midst of the lumber and paint pots, we are starting classes. I have two English classes for French and refugees. Never taught in my life, but last night you should have heard my Spanish-Russian-Polish-French class (only six of us in all) singing lustily, although with outlandish accents, "She'll be comin' 'round the mountain when she comes."

There's more administrative work now, but the delegations have confidence in us, so even the details seem to be building up to something. Sometimes (don't laugh) I think of the framing of the Constitution, and I wonder if the men who drew it up had as much trouble as we sometimes do over a single minute or decision! I hope to get an Information Service letter started round to the delegations, with refugee news, maybe UNO (United Nations Organization) information, and anything else they'd like to have included. Beside that, I'm doing some case work visiting.

Red, when I get back to the States, I'm going to be a housing fiend. I have never seen such slums. I wonder if it's worse to see people living in such rat holes (literally) or to see them without houses at all. It would almost seem better to have to start from scratch.

Next week I hope to go on a publicity trip to a camp for French political prisoners.

I wish you could look in for just a moment to see the place where I'm spending the weekend. There's a tiny house in Montauban where we come sometimes to get away from the noise and smells of Toulouse. It's like a play house: two rooms—a white-washed kitchen with red-and-white tiled floor and a bedroom. That's all, but it's sweet and clean, and the green shutters open out on the little garden and the sky, and you can hear birds and crickets. Being here is like a picnic; we have very little to cook with, and we empty one dish to use it for the next course. I'm using my mess kit, we have a couple of bowls, three plates, and some tin cups. I keep thinking what it would be like to have you here. You'd practically fill the room, Red, but you'd find it charming. The French owners hid Jews here during the Occupation; a risky business at best, and where you'd "hide" anyone in this tiny place, I can't imagine, but they did.

One thing I sometimes find oppressive about things French is the littleness. Tiny houses, tiny rooms, tiny cafés, tiny street cars, often tiny landscape. Everything orderly and neat and charming, but what I'd give for a hundred miles of prairie, or the Rockies, or a road in the desert where you don't see a house or a person for hours. For the first time since I've come here, I'm beginning to think I'll be glad to go home. Not that I want to go now, or for a long while, but I'm getting the sense of what it may be like to get back. There'll be some things that it will be so good to have again: wide spaces and clean cities and people who look healthy and well-fed and who talk straight from the shoulder. There'll be a lot of things there, too, that we'll want to scream about.

Like everything else I've ever done, it seems to me I'm getting much more out of this than I'm giving. The ways I can pay back seem so small. Maybe one never knows the ways in which she passes on what's come to her. Perhaps all our contacts and dealings with people involve a passing-on. That's what troubles me so much about my hour-to-hour inadequacies. It's as if one had to do one's job, the job of living, twenty-four hours a day. And, oh Red, I don't! It's easy to get frayed, living and working with people, sometimes under difficult conditions, never being alone or still. Right now I'm writing while Juanita plays the recorder in one ear and Connie talks about accounts in the other. Of course my typing adds to the general clatter. I don't get irritable very often, but inside I feel like yelling, "Shut up!" Sometimes, dreaming of the end of that mythical six months when we'll see each other again, I think I'd like to be on top of a mountain with you, saying nothing for days on end.

As to food, the French breakfast doesn't seem quite so impossible now, but I have a lot more sympathy for the slow, dull way in which many Frenchmen work. I feel like doing the same when my

LOADING ROCK TO BE USED IN BUILDING NEW HOMES IN
LUCIMA, POLAND   -PHOTOGRAPH BY AN ETU MEMBER

stomach's empty. One thing I'm sure of—our American standards of food, hygiene, and comfort seem rather ridiculous in contrast to what people manage with here. Better food and housing are meaningful, it seems to me, only if they allow people to live better. As ends in themselves, they're sadly inadequate. The French who think of their glorious past in terms of the good food they used to have are pretty discouraging folks. And my American friends who spend all their time taking care of a suburban home aren't contributing much to the world.

Red, I'm dreaming of a house that's big and plain, open to sunshine, with a green space around it, and your fresh water spring, if that's possible. And something like it for everyone else. So many people ask so little: their own vine and fig tree, I guess. That expression seems very vivid here, where most farm houses have a grapevine trained across the doorway and where there are fig trees in many gardens. But one doesn't have that humble measure of security without having asked for a lot more: liberty and self-dependence and responsibility.

Have you read the accounts of the Bikini experiments? Awesome things, they are, so tremendous that it's impossible to be frightened. It looks as if the military is not going to have the Atomic Energy Commission as their pigeon, as the English say. But it's hard to get a good feel of Americans' public reaction to the bomb when one is over here.

Frogs are croaking in the garden, and the first stars are coming out, making me remember all the evening stars we've watched lighting up together. This is a wonderful place to sleep. I hope that wherever you find yourself this evening, it is as pleasant a place as this. Tiens, but we're rich.

July 31, 1946 ~ Red in Gora Pulawska to Madeleine in Toulouse

Today we hauled our first load of rock, and we have loaded our first load of lime. Tomorrow we have three trucks on the road; next week, we are hoping to increase this to at least six.

Tonight more than ever I would like to have you here. You have said that you want to be someone by yourself and not just with me. That is my wish for both of us, too. But now I know that I shall never be complete without you.

If you keep up with me, you will have to add to your cuisine. These Poles know how to cook. The main things that impress me are the number of interesting ways they can prepare beets, the way they prepare chicken rolled with butter inside and only one bone, and the wonderful borscht. Philip has promised to buy me a cookbook of Polish dishes when he goes to England.

OUR TRUCKS WERE OFTENTIMES USED AS BUSSES. ASIDE FROM THE QUAKER VEHICLES, THERE WERE ONLY SIX TRUCKS IN THE KIELCE DISTRICT IN 1946.
-PHOTOGRAPH BY AN ETU MEMBER

Incidentally, you need have no fears about us as long as UNRRA is providing the government with food. We are supposed to get 120 eggs per week! They are so expensive, however, that the fellows are reluctant to purchase them. At the present time, there are enough cheap vegetables to keep us going for many a week. That suits me just fine, as potatoes are cheap, and I can have all I want. We get groats for breakfast; this morning they tasted raw, so Ralph has been cooking all day to see if it is possible to cook the stuff. The secretary of the town has promised to find us a cook who is clean, honest, and capable.

How are you? Are you eating breakfast as you should? Today I cooked lunch and supper wearing a long raincoat and hat while rain fell on the pots.

There is so much I want to tell you that I hardly know where to start. You mentioned that my first letter from Warsaw had come through unmolested. I am very glad; it means that I can be freer about writing to you about what we hear and see.

The last Sunday in Kozienice, four of us had gone swimming at the local pond where a dance and social were being held. Wojtek decided to return to the castle and started out of the park riding the bicycle. This is forbidden inside the enclosure, and also he nearly hit a small boy. The police (the secret police, not the town police) stopped him and asked for the bicycle. Naturally, he refused to give it up. This irritated the police, but they came back with him to me. Now we have the culprit acting as the interpreter, and he has a quick temper to boot!

SUNDAY AFTERNOON DANCE AT A LAKE NEAR KOZIENICE   -PHOTOGRAPH BY RED

We had failed to register him at the local town, and since we are under suspicion, he has been watched because he lives with us. Even a local girl who speaks English has been questioned because she came and visited the team. I asked the police to wait until Rudi—a member of the Kozienice team who speaks Polish—returned from dressing; they would not, so I started to go along with them. We had not gone one hundred yards from the park when the chief ordered me to turn back. I tried to object, but once again, had to talk through Wojtek, the interpreter and the culprit. Finally, I returned and fetched Rudi.

We tried to learn what we could from some Poles Rudi knew, but many people were scared. We returned to the castle and talked it over with Beth, who suggested we wait for a few minutes to see if Wojtek returned. He did not, so we went to see the police.

They were a tough looking bunch of young chaps. The chief seemed hard and sour; he was bigger than the others and had a loud voice that put fear into your soul even if you could not understand him. Then he smiled at the two Quaker ladies, and after that the going was easier. Wojtek was brought out and released to us on condition that the father of the child did not complain about the boy's being hurt.

Wojtek came back very much upset about the whole affair. He had been placed in a room where he saw the condition of the prisoners, and he kept saying that they did not have good American or English friends to help them out. You can rest assured that we have now made proper registrations for all of us here. We have also talked to the Russians about our crossing the bridge after ten o'clock at night. They were very decent about allowing it.

The Russians, "our friends from the east," as we often refer to them, guard the bridge here across the Vistula. It is one they built during the war; now this is one of the main roads going eastward and the Russians pass fairly regularly with convoys of secondhand trucks from Germany and many, many horses. They have made camp across the river from us, and on beautiful days, they take their horses into the river.

A VIEW FROM THE HILL ON WHICH OUR BARRACKS WERE BUILT LOOKING ACROSS THE VISTULA RIVER. AS THE GERMANS WERE DRIVEN BACK ACROSS POLAND FROM RUSSIA, THEY MADE A STAND ON THE WEST SIDE OF THE VISTULA RIVER. AT ONE POINT THE GERMANS REMOVED THE TIMBERS FROM THE FARM HOUSES AND USED THE BASEMENTS AS BUNKERS. IN THE AREA WHERE WE HAULED BUILDING MATERIALS, ONLY ONE HOUSE WAS LEFT STANDING IN ALL OF TWENTY-FIVE VILLAGES. 1946
-PHOTOGRAPH BY JOHN ROBBINS

Sometimes you hear stories about atrocities committed by the Russian soldiers as they travel through. Some of these can be discounted. Others are caused by fellows who have no more moral integrity than some soldiers from any other army. It is, however, impossible to say that some stories are not true. In a village nearby, for instance, soldiers started pilfering. When the villagers objected, several homes were burned.

If you think the young people in France are discouraged and want to go elsewhere, you should be here for a while. Young Poles feel that there is no escape. Everyone wishes to leave, yet cannot say aloud that they are discouraged. These people have a long history of oppression; this is another such period. One fellow said he would like to go to America with me, but if this becomes known he would have to go in the opposite

BEFORE THE BARRACKS WERE FINISHED, THE ETU TEAM CAMPED OUTSIDE. THERE WERE ALWAYS POLISH VISITORS AT MEAL TIMES. 1946
-PHOTOGRAPH BY RED

direction (to a Russian prison). This may not be strictly true, but it suggests the fear that some people have.

Four of us are still sitting around this one light, each with a heavy coat on as it is rather chilly tonight, trying to get letters ready for Philip to take tomorrow. We certainly hope that we are in the barrack by this time next week. The roof is on but it has no windows, and the inside walls are still to be whitewashed.

We have been hauling three loads of lime each day for three days, and hauled one load of stone the day before that. We had figured on our hauling two loads of stone per day, but we have not been able to do that since it takes about two hours each way and over an hour to load. We are hoping that each truck may haul three loads every two days once we get started.

Right now, though, we are keeping five men in camp. One man has spent nearly full time cooking, while one has been sick and another has helped nurse the sick. Reed Smith had diarrhea and fever. At night he slept in a truck under a canvas, but in the daytime we moved his cot under a tree.

We are engaging a language teacher from the Institute in Pulawy and think that we shall be able to take lessons twice a week. I am very anxious to learn enough Polish to benefit from the contacts we have with the people. The truck drivers have been invited to have milk, vodka, and bread; today one was given some chicken. One day Henry refused some eggs he was offered. It is going to be difficult to decide what to do about people's hospitality; we do not want to offend them, yet we know they need the food as much, if not more, than we do.

Today, Wojtek and I were in the local office to ask about a cook and a woman to wash our clothes. A boy and girl we had visited before the team arrived wanted to know if we have time for more visits. They had heard about little boys and girls playing with our volleyball on the hill and wanted to know if they could come and play, too. I was more than pleased and feel confident that we can get some social activity going here without too much difficulty.

After reading your last letter, I talked with Philip about the possibility of new personnel coming to Poland. AFSC is to send more people, but both the relief teams are overloaded with women in comparison to men. There has been talk among the fellows about a girl joining this team, but I am sure it would be Lois; she speaks Polish and has asked to come here. That, too, is far in the future, as we are committed only through the building season.

We are thinking in terms of a wider program for next spring, but many people who know Poland are surprised that we have been allowed to do the type of work we are doing where we are.

August 4, 1946 ~ Madeleine in Toulouse to Red in Gora Pulawska

I've thought about what you wrote about me, Red: that I have a place in the world but it seems not to be among the headlines and bright lights. I guess that's true; it's easier for other people to see my place than for me to see it. Herb said something rather like that once: "You may not get written up in the history books, but you'll certainly get written up in people's hearts." It's partly egotism that makes me look to the headlines and partly the feeling that sympathy and understanding and affection aren't enough to help cure the things that are so desperately wrong with the world. And whatever I do, wherever I live or work, I've got to feel that in some way I'm contributing to a cure. This isn't an era for people just to look after themselves and their comfort. For the nth time, I tell you and anybody who will listen that this is a lot of what is wrong with France today. I am going to put a copy of Emerson and one of Whitman in our reading room here (when we have one) and hope that their doctrines of self-reliance and the morality of the universe will penetrate a few European heads.

It seems to me that the basis of a lot of Quaker work is old-fashioned, Lady Charity stuff. We're trying to change that in the south of France with a program of personal service, but the changing is hard, and I think many people, even the most devoted workers, don't understand the basic problem. Neither do I, and I make myself a lot of bad blood, as they say here, puzzling over it. That's when I miss you most—no, not most, but one of the times. I'd like to talk it out, fight it out.

Your remark about encouraging the people in Poland who were already in there working and not taking the glory of a quick relief job made me want to cheer. That's something like what I'm driving at. To give people food, clothing, and shelter if they need it is nothing; they have an elemental human right to that, at least when we have it to give so easily. What they do need, and mostly we don't know how to give them, is our respect for their spiritual dignity, and for their capacities as men and women of equal worth with ourselves. That, I submit, we often miss out on.

We went out to dinner tonight, being too tired to cook it ourselves and not having much around the Caveau anyway. To pay you back for your many Warsaw menus, read this: hors d'œuvres, beefsteak (small but good), fried tomatoes covered with garlic, fried potatoes, salad, cold red wine, and chilled fresh peaches! All for about 100 francs. The summer is making a difference in the food production of the Midi, but the tragic thing is that ordinary people can't afford the fresh stuff, and it won't be canned for winter because they have no facilities for that. It strikes me that one reason the war has hit France so hard, and probably other countries, too, is that many things—transportation, public utilities, care of food, internal organization, and so on—were in a bad shape before the war started, and the real hardships of war accentuated the already existing conditions. That's one reason why it seems to me that basic relief work can't stop at feeding and clothing people in an emergency. In most cases, the emergencies are only a temporarily vivid exposé of already difficult conditions.

Of course, if you apply the same reasoning to political and economic conditions, the consequences and the work are simply endless.

I'm still toying with the thought of working with you after my six months here. It's an awfully discouraging place—and that's honestly not just me, Red. Hugh feels the same. We've been left an inheritance of misunderstanding and ill-will from the old delegation that's formidable. It's as if our hands are tied by the past.

August 7, 1946 ~ Red in Gora Pulawska to Madeleine

We are still eating out under the stars, except sometimes we cannot see the stars for the clouds and rain. It is not pleasant to sit down at the table and have the roof leak. There is little use in wiping dishes; they get wet all over again. You either stand washing dishes in a raincoat or with no shirt at all. Noon is the only time when it is warm enough to be without a shirt, and even then you have to be hardy to take it.

Yesterday, Wojtek and I went into the village and asked Pan Mazur, the secretary of this gemina (township), if we could borrow a cross-cut saw. He informed me that he was sending some men up to cut wood; I insisted, however, that we take the saw and cut wood for ourselves. Back at the camp, before we could get started, three men, three women, and one wagon arrived. One man was to work with the foreman on the barracks using the wagon; two were to cut wood, and three to dig a hole for our privy. Two of the men were soon sawing wood, leaving the three women to dig a hole! I was very much embarrassed, so I kept them waiting until I was free to work with them. Soon I was picking the ground and the women were throwing the loose dirt out. We had loads of fun, but by noon I was completely exhausted.

Last night we had a first lesson in Polish. Today we hauled five loads of lime, Leslie hauling two loads. Once we can get inside and not spend so much time just trying to live, we might really help these people.

August 8, 1946 ~ Madeleine in Toulouse to Red in Gora Pulawska

I missed you sorely yesterday. The Refugee Program seems to be coming down around our ears. Hugh, I think, is leaving. For the moment, I am in charge of the south, which is in one hell of a mess. The job's too big for me. Much of the information and many agreements have been communicated verbally, the result of Hugh's conversations in Paris, and I'm trying to patch together something to present at our monthly meeting on Monday.

We still have no house, no barracks for the Toulouse projects; we are losing the heads of the Toulouse and Montauban delegations. Delegates here are going stale. I'll do my darndest and try to hold things together until another head comes down. Haven't any notion who or when that can be. Wish me well, Red. There's no one here strong enough to lean on for a bit, no one with whom I can share this.

I know I shouldn't be writing you just now. Things may change; I'm not even sure at the moment that Hugh has gone. It's just part of sharing things with you, and I did so awfully want to talk. Well, I shall sharpen my pencil and carry on.

In spite of all my griping, the effort is good. But it's hard for me to get used to so much effort for so little result. All part of what I need to learn.

Consider your hair pulled! Also consider yourself kissed. You amiable dope—of course I don't want your letters shorter! Ramble all you like, only tell me how you are and what you're thinking. When I first get a letter, I tear it open, gallop through it and peek at the end to see if you still love me. Then I read it more slowly. Then I carry it around in my pocket or purse for a week, looking at it in odd moments, mulling over what you've said.

I think perhaps we shall dance well together. This evening after the conference, seven of us went to an open dance floor in the Parc Toulousain, the only park in the city where you can walk on the grass. The floor is surrounded by tiny tables and chairs, like a café; there are palms and chestnut trees lit by Hollywood-like indirect lighting. It was another beautiful night: full moon, luminous sky, warm, and fresh. The music was soft; we laughed a great deal and danced with each other. I got on well with Charles Thum, who is over six feet, so I figure I should do the same with you. I did so wish you there! It was one of the rare times when Toulouse seems bearable. You'd have loved the soft music and soft lights and the moon on the Garonne, romantic soul that you are!

PS: I know I should have waited! Hugh's staying on, at least for awhile. We may get some new personnel. Plans for the barracks have arrived. Now all we need is the barracks!

August 10, 1946 ~ Red in Gora Pulawska to Madeleine in Toulouse

It seems strange to sit here writing you, not knowing when or where you will be reading this. Often you seem much nearer when I am alone somewhere, just thinking. There are times when I have to wrestle with myself to remain satisfied here with you there. It has been a long time since I have wanted something so badly. As you know, I was never excited about coming to Europe; it just seemed to fit into the pattern. I was being tossed by various circumstances, not putting too much effort into diverting the stream one way or another. I had a concern to do something constructive where there had been war, and the rest followed naturally.

Now I find myself wanting to arrange events in such a way that our relationship might continue growing. I want to know you better. Each day I am more anxious than ever to know you, and each day I realize how much living we must do in order to become acquainted. Already, when people ask me what I shall be doing when I return to the States, my thinking is in terms of we instead of I.

Leslie, Albert, and I went to a dance in Pulawy with three Polish soldiers; one was our French-speaking friend. The soldiers had to get permission, but that was not difficult. We asked the Russian guards at the bridge whether we could come back across after ten o'clock, and they said that would be OK as long as we stayed only two or three hours.

The dance proved more interesting than we had expected. Leslie met a nice looking girl, and she sat or danced with us most of the evening. About 1:30 a.m. we decided to leave. As we started out, Leslie invited the girl to walk with us as she lived on our way home. All of us were aware of the fact that she was scared. So there we were: three Polish guards, one American, two British, and one Polish girl.

MARY ESTER WILLIAMS WASHING DISHES OUTSIDE AT GORA PULAWSKA. LATER BARRACKS WITH KITCHEN WERE COMPLETED.
–PHOTOGRAPH BY AN ETU MEMBER

We came to one Russian sentry and passed on the other side of the street. In the semidarkness, there was another soldier in a long cape, carrying a gun, but none of us paid any attention to him. Evidently he said something, but we paid no heed. Then: Clink Clank! An international sound that is unmistakable; if you do mistake it, it's only once. The guard was throwing off the safety catch to his gun. The girl shrank back, and for a moment I thought she would run, but Leslie was calm. One of the Polish guards spoke to the Russian soldier, who told him to come forward and be recognized. He told the Russians who was in our party. We were then ordered in no uncertain terms to cross the street and pass on the other side. The girl was really trembling; when we passed the little store where her family lives and works, she was happy enough to bid us farewell and run inside.

The six of us continued on to the bridge. There we were met out of the darkness (I never saw anyone) with a gruff "Stoy! Stoy!" That's Russian for "Stop!" Once again the Polish guard went forward and told who was in the party, but this Russian would not let us pass. The guard had changed since we'd crossed before. The Polish guard came back, but before he could translate what the Russian had said, the Russian hollered, "Get off this bridge or I shall fire!" We didn't have to know Russian to know what he meant! Well, it was nearly two o'clock in the morning, and we were tired, knowing too that we had to work the next day. One of the Polish guards with us was supposed to go on duty at 2:00 a.m., but we went back to the dance and either danced or sat around until four o'clock, when we went home. After four o'clock, no one seemed to mind our walking about. It was frightening. (Please keep this story confidential!)

Today, Wojtek and I visited Czarnecki's home. They were having a birthday dinner for his twenty-second birthday. Czarnecki is the Polish chap who works so closely with us. We expected a small tea party, but instead we found a table laden with chicken, roast pork, smoked ham, and a meatloaf. The only vegetables were salads. First we were served an orangeade which they called an American drink. Then came vodka and more vodka and more vodka. More toasts, and then just one more. Of course, vodka came with the dessert. Afterwards, Czarnecki announced his engagement, and then we did drink vodka! Finally the table was pushed back and we danced. Already we were late getting back, but as we said good-bye, I was informed that it isn't proper to leave without a final drink!

The most enjoyable thing this week was a letter from you waiting for me at Kozienice. Madeleine, dear, please do not spare me your trying days. I do not remember a single important job that has not caused me some concern about why I was doing it, and if there was a need for the job. Often this is when new ideas appear and new direction is found. The important thing is that you are developing democratic practices. Are people convinced that this slow, inefficient method is better than the autocratic way? If one takes into account human values, a great deal of patience is needed. As you say, it is a field in which we have not gone far enough to be sure of ourselves.

August 11, 1946 ~ Madeleine in Toulouse to Red in Gora Pulawska

Seven of us spent the weekend in the tiny house in Montauban, went swimming, saw an old walled town, and had a conference this evening. Riding back in the back of Hugh's open camionette, with a warm wind blowing, the full moon making the fields silver and the trees black, you were terribly near. Oh Red, I do want so much to see you, not desperately, you know, but with a deep longing. I can wait, but my dear, I'll be glad when the waiting's over.

Monday night now, nearly midnight. We've had a monthly conference of the delegations today, and it's hard work. But rewarding. It's exciting to me to see people trying to work together. In spite of all the mistakes, I think that is the line of the future. People stumble and make fool mistakes and get in each other's way, but they keep on trying. It's good.

August 14, 1946 ~ Red in Gora Pulawska to Philip Zealey in Warsaw

Yesterday I sent you the following telegram: "Jeep wrecked badly Wojtek slightly hurt Stop obtaining Helen for investigation Stop report to insurance." Maybe I should start at the beginning of the story.

About 4:30 p.m. Tuesday afternoon Wojtek took the jeep to Pulawy to pick up some inner tubes which we were having repaired. When he did not return immediately, we became concerned but decided that he possibly had gone to the library. After supper, we were planning to send someone to look for him when we heard the jeep coming across the bridge, sounding as though it would not make it up the hill. The Polish guards in the village had stopped him when they saw the condition of the jeep, so there were several of them who rode along into camp with him just to learn more about what happened.

Wojtek's story was that a Polish soldier had stopped him in Pulawy and asked his help to start a car which was just at the edge of Pulawy. Wojtek, too eager to drive the jeep, used poor judgment and consented in spite of the fact that he soon realized the soldier had been drinking. As they got to the edge of the town, the soldier wanted to drive but Wojtek refused. Then the soldier drew his pistol and demanded that he drive the jeep. They had gone only a short distance when he ran into a tree. Wojtek was thrown against the windshield, cutting his nose and knocking him unconscious. When he came to, the soldier had disappeared. Wojtek repaired the jeep enough to drive it back across the river.

The frame of the jeep is bent, both front springs are bent, the radiator is banged; in short, the whole front will have to be torn apart and rebuilt. We don't think the motor is damaged.

Our first thought was to use the French-speaking Polish guard and make an immediate investigation. We did not, however, move too quickly in this direction because some of the fellows were rather concerned about our relationship with the police if we started investigating in a case in which one of their men was involved.

Before we were completely satisfied, we realized that Wojtek had not seen a doctor as we had understood him to say, so we took him to the hospital where a clip was put into his nose and he was given an anti-tetanus shot.

THE PULAWY SIDE OF THE VISTULA RIVER. IN THE BACKGROUND IS THE HEAVILY GUARDED BRIDGE WHERE SEVERAL INCIDENTS OCCURRED.   -PHOTOGRAPH BY RED

Two of the Polish guards wanted to go with us and shoot the soldier. We practically had to force them off the truck. I went to Kozienice and asked to borrow Helen (the Polish cook and interpreter for the Kozienice team who speaks pretty good English) for the day.

Since Wojtek had been so upset, I waited until my return from Kozienice to question him about the details. For the first time, I became aware of his fear of the police. He kept insisting that although we might get some satisfaction out of questioning people, and although the police might be pleasant, he was afraid that sooner or later they would take revenge on him. He was afraid they might arrest him on a frivolous charge and then when we went to find him, they would say they knew nothing about him.

Van Cleve Geiger had returned from Lucima by this time, so he and I talked at some length with Helen. At first she thought that Wojtek was unnecessarily scared; she soon decided, however, that the risk to him was too great for us even to question people who might have been near the accident. Since this still did not satisfy us, and since we did not want to do anything that would endanger Wojtek's safety, we went to talk with Pan Mazur. He agreed that no good would ever come from an investigation on our part. Also, he strongly recommended that we never allow Wojtek across the bridge alone.

The details of these discussions have been talked over with the group; they feel it is best to repair the jeep, and the less said the better.

The affair has had a sobering effect upon us. It brings close to home the feelings many Polish people must have today. We hope that we may be able to use this as an opportunity to better understand the Polish people. Not only that, but it brings us into close communion with oppressed people regardless of where they are.

August 21, 1946 ~ Madeleine in Toulouse to Red in Gora Pulawska

It's a bright cool morning. I've just been reading for a moment in a little book of Hugh's, and I came across this phrase: "In the freshness of morning and in the weariness of evening." And I thought how it would be good to be with you at both those times.

At the moment (forgive my being a bit gloomy), though, I don't see when we'll be together again. One of the Refugee Program delegates, an English girl, who has every qualification of experience and language to go to Poland and who has been promised an assignment there, is being put off perhaps until 1947 because there is no opening.

However—first maxim of relief work: always expect the impossible. We'll see. I've asked Hugh to bring me a Polish grammar from Paris. I'll send to London for the Polish history you recommend.

Darling, vacation is just a word for you, n'est-ce pas? I hope to go to Switzerland, perhaps the end of September. One of my cousins is being married then. I'm really eager to see all these hearsay relations, and the idea of a week in a clean, energetic country gets more appealing all the time. For two weeks, I had a mild dysentery—not serious, but sort of a drain, and I lost a little weight. To compensate, though, I have a good tan! How about you?

I send you this quote from H.G. Wells because I think you'll like it, too. He just died this week, you know; this was quoted by J.B. Priestley in a funeral address.

So far and beyond this adventure may continue and our race survive. The impenetrable clouds that bound our life at last in every direction may hide innumerable trials and dangers, but there are no conclusive limitations even in their deepest shadows, and there are times and seasons, there are moments of exaltation—moments, as it were, of revelation—when the whole universe about us seems bright with the promise of as yet unimaginable things.

I have Wells' *History of Mankind* here and sometimes I dip into it. He looks a long way ahead, and it's good to read; between Bikini and the Paris Conference, I've been greatly troubled the last weeks. But there are still the "as yet unimaginable things." Being with you is one of them.

August 1946 ~ Red to AFSC in Philadelphia

(Progress Report of Anglo-American Transport Work at Gora Pulawska)
Although we were given vivid descriptions of the working conditions here, we were not properly impressed and, therefore, are finding the conditions even worse than we had expected. We had planned to haul two loads of lime per day per truck to Lucima, but that is definitely out of the question until something is done about the roads. It is taking us from two and a half to three hours of driving time to do each round trip of thirty-five miles! The best we hope to do is to make three loads every two days with each truck, yet even this is hard on the drivers.

We have broken two front springs already and predict that those are not the last. In addition, some of the fenders are cracking from the vibration, yet neither of these has caused us the headaches nor trouble that flat tires have. The seven trucks had four flats from Paris to Poland and forty-two by the time they reached Gora Pulawska! Now, on each trip to Lucima, it is a common thing to have at least one flat tire.

Still this is not so bad as hauling the lime. For although we do not like to sit and drive and let the Polish men do all the work of loading and unloading, those of us who have been working most in it are acquiring raw places on our skin from the quicklime. It is impossible to dress properly, and what clothes we have and a wet handkerchief do not keep us from breathing the lime into our lungs. We still have not solved the problem. There are four men from the village to load each truck, but often there is only one woman to unload. Even if there is adequate help for both loading and unloading, we would like to help with some of it.

So far we have been obtaining the gas for hauling from the corporation which furnishes the lime. Although they were rather startled at our asking for forty liters per trip, they have kindly consented and promised all the gas, oil, and grease we need for hauling. Supplies for other uses will be obtained from Kielce through the starosta.

Although the garage has a roof, it does not have the cement floor that the starosta promised. So far all our work has been done under the trees on top of the sand and grass. This means that we must be careful about grit getting into the working parts and protecting them from moisture at night. Until we get the floor, this will continue to be a problem.

After living under the trees for three weeks, we have a roof over our heads at last.

Living outside with such disorganization began to pass the point of being fun. At the beginning the cooking was done on two primus stoves, then on the stove sent from Sweden, but as we were always expecting the move inside within three days, we never did fix a proper stovepipe. After it continually came down with the wind, Ralph Durgin finally tied a bucket of water to the smokestack to keep it in place.

BARRACKS AT GORA PULAWSKA BUILT BY THE POLISH GOVERNMENT FOR OUR ETU TEAM. EVEN THOUGH STRAW WAS LATER ATTACHED TO THE OUTSIDE TO PROVIDE INSULATION, WATER SPILT AS CLOSE AS EIGHT FEET FROM THE STOVE WOULD FREEZE TO THE FLOOR.
-PHOTOGRAPH BY JOHN ROBBINS

Even then it was difficult to get the stove hot if there was a wind. These things would often be complicated by rain just as the meal was being prepared.

Several times it rained at night, and the fellows found their cots holding big puddles of water. In the beginning, our only protection was sleeping under a canvas over a truck. Later we could move into the dining room, as it had a roof, but the roof had not been covered with

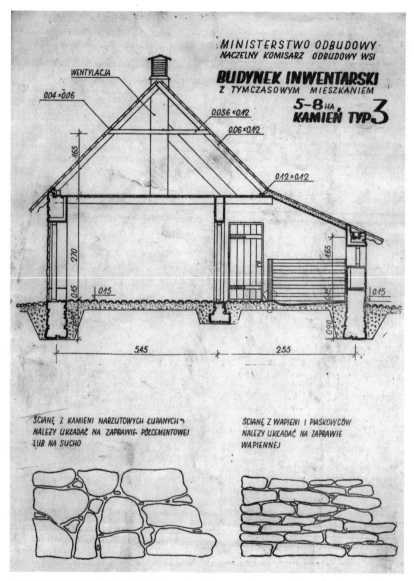

HOUSE PLANS FOR THE HOMES BEING BUILT IN LUCIMA, POLAND, 1946. THE STONES
CAME FROM A LOCAL QUARRY AND LIME WAS USED TO MAKE THE MORTAR. DUE TO THE
LACK OF EQUIPMENT, ALL MATERIAL HAD TO BE LOADED AND UNLOADED BY HAND.

paper, so we had to move out again during the day to give the workmen a chance to finish it. Truck parts were kept on the ground under one canvas while the food and kitchen equipment which we were not using were kept under another. During this time, the men who were working on the building were living underneath some wall partitions placed together with some hay thrown on the ground. In addition to them, there would be eight to twelve men from Lucima spending each night somewhere around Gora Pulawska in order to load the trucks the next day. Since they used our washing facilities, they would lie on the ground nearby while we ate supper and then be here in time to watch us eat breakfast in the morning.

There were two main problems that arose from this: first, we lost three truck wheels complete with tires and tubes (we have not taken inventory yet to determine what else is missing). Secondly, we never felt comfortable eating before these men. It is bad enough to have people watching what you do all through the day, but it is much worse to have hungry men watching you eat when there is not enough to offer them. We had long discussions as to whether we should feed them and would have done so if it had been for only a day or two instead of six nights in every week. We can expect no revision of these plans until the middle of November.

The men from Lucima were not our only spectators, for it seems that we occupy what was once the park for this village, so now we serve as the zoo for them. The first Sunday that we were here, people would sit around in small groups watching everything that happened all through the day; the second Sunday we played some volleyball and counted forty-five Poles here at one time. Mostly these are kids who play with our ball and bring us apples to eat; others are the Polish guards who like to come up and spend a few minutes; some are people just passing through the campgrounds.

To add to the amusement of the villagers, the Polish guards have made a dancing platform on the grounds. Now each Sunday and every holiday there is a dance here. It provides the people not only with a dance but also with another excuse to come see the Americans and Englishmen. A continual stream of people passes the windows and doors. They get hot and ask for water; at night there is a lantern to provide, and of course, our latrine is the only one on the hill. We have enjoyed all this activity as much as the Poles have, since it has provided us with various contacts as well as with an opportunity to dance. Not only that, but the Poles are not the only ones who look at someone else with curiosity.

The highlight of it all was the day Ralph Durgin cooked grilled cheese sandwiches on the range under the trees. Before he had finished, it was hard to find Ralph, surrounded as he was by women and children gazing in amazement.

To complicate things a bit more, we had someone sick nearly every day for the first three weeks. Although we have tried to be careful of the water we drink, several of the fellows have had diarrhea of various degrees.

The immense amount of work to be done here is quite obvious. It was our understanding that this work would stop temporarily during the extremely cold months; however, now we learn that only the lime hauling will be stopped, and we can expect to continue hauling cement and stone. Even now we have to be careful about hauling the lime when it rains, as it is loose. Since the people have to slake it before using, they cannot handle it during the months when the water would freeze. Nevertheless, there is no reason why we should not expect to continue with the stone hauling and build up stockpiles for next spring.

The stockpiles of stone are growing painfully slowly. When we arrived they had piled enough for three barns (it takes about 100 cubic meters per barn), and now there is still not enough for the fourth.

There are some new aspects to our present work. We understand that each barn requires ten cubic meters of lumber, lumber which is to be hauled from the mill at Zwolen. Unless we do it, each peasant must send for it in a wagon. Considering the fact that there are only seven horses in Lucima, it would take several months of hauling for them to obtain enough for their ninety-four barns.

In a recent discussion with Pan Mazur, we learned that they receive an allotment of food for the poor and needy each month from Kozienice; however, the cost of hauling is so much that it is sometimes less expensive to buy the food on the free market. We plan now to pick this food up for them each month. Also they are repairing their church and need some tin from Kielce for the roof, and although we have not investigated the rail shipments from Kielce to Pulawy, it is possible that we shall take this for them also.

The big job that we would like to do here is hauling phosphate from Kozienice for the people here. This past spring, they could not get enough for their fields because they did not have enough horses and wagons to transport it. This fall they should get eighty tons. Of course, we are always faced with the idea that maybe the winter of 1947-48 will arrive with people still living underground if we use our trucks for other purposes. Honestly, the more I see—the overworked horses, the tremendous job of rebuilding, the slow process of traveling—the more I wish we had brought fifty trucks with us plus a road grader.

The next thing needed is farm equipment; however, this is of little use unless someone can come and show these young boys how to maintain and operate the equipment properly. In this gemina alone, there are 3,000 hectares of land unplowed because there are not enough horses and no equipment. This could prove to be a dangerous job, as all the mines have not been cleared from the unplowed fields. The manor system has caused the peasants to have a long history of poor farming methods; therefore, those coming with the machines would have ample opportunity to help the farmers with farming techniques.

Another need is for small portable sawmills with enough trucks to transport the logs and lumber to and from the mill. It is a common thing to see a log

TYPICAL POSTWAR HOME IN LUCIMA. THE CHIMNEY OVER THE ROOF MEANS THIS BUNKER IS BEING USED AS LIVING QUARTERS RATHER THAN POTATO STORAGE.   -PHOTOGRAPH BY RED

resting on a high frame with one man above it and another below sawing the log into lumber. It takes about nine hours to saw a medium-sized log into boards. One of the disadvantages of taking the logs to the mills is that they find so many bullets and shrapnel that it is continually ruining the saw teeth. Also many of the forests cannot be used yet because they still have mines. However, the idea for using the forest by any means faster than the present rate will not be encouraged by those who are anxious to see the forests protected after the great damage done to them during the war.

Although we have been handicapped by not being able to speak Polish and also have had a difficult time because of having only one interpreter, we still find that the morale of the people has been increased just by seeing our trucks hauling materials to rebuild their homes. Pan

Mazur said that because they had only one truck and only the promise of one more, the people had become discouraged and afraid that the reconstruction in this area would stop. Now they are sure that it will continue. It is a heartening sight to see Lucima today; we have hauled the lime for eighty barns out of the ninety-four to be built. Now the village is burning with activity—men digging holes for the lime, women mixing lime and water for slaking, boys and girls driving the wagons to and from the river with barrels of water. It is all as busy as an ant hill. It makes one glad that he is part of this, and yet at the same time, so disappointed that we cannot get the barns built before winter. Without additional help this will not be the last winter that people will be sleeping in the ground.

If only there were some way to express to you the reaction we receive when we do no more than speak to a person pleasantly; then you would have further assurance that our presence here is serving a real purpose. Much of this results just from the fact that we as Americans and English will speak to them personally. We hope that someday they will understand why we are here.

August 23, 1946 ~ Red in Gora Pulawska to Madeleine in Toulouse

Tomorrow, Beth and I are taking the train to Warsaw for a team leaders' meeting. I am hoping that we can make it a delegation meeting instead, so that other members of the unit might be able to attend, rather than just me making the trip every month. Ex (Esther) Williams has been most helpful for the past two days. She sends her very best wishes to you.

Yesterday I received two letters plus a short note written afterwards from you. It was distressing to learn that so many headaches have been thrown your way. Somehow the entire setup does not seem the type of work we should be doing. The work itself is all right, but certainly the spirit in which it is being done makes it lose much of the effectiveness. Gripes and grievances will most assuredly affect the best worker, then this will go on to affect those whom we should be helping. It is the one thing I keep hitting on here: If we cannot learn to be tolerant and pleasant to one another, regardless of differences, we have little to offer these people who have been torn apart for so long. It's no good to say ours is a family quarrel; it will affect us and the way in which we approach the Poles.

Madeleine, I wish it were possible to express to you the quietness of spirit and the relaxation that I feel. This is particularly true when I am thinking of you. The feeling of anxiety and the pain of waiting have been overcome by a much stronger faith and trust in you. 'Tis true that much of you is a mystery to me; that part I accept on faith, and I have no fears. Each of us will always be a mystery to the other because we do not know ourselves fully.

It seems strange that at the end of the two hardest weeks I have experienced since arriving here, I receive letters from you telling about your hardships. I felt closer to you and wanted to be there and share some of our experiences. I was glad that you have beautiful places nearby to which you can retreat for a weekend. Be sure that you continue those trips. I can tell by the letters that they mean much to

RED AND SAM SNIPES, A FRIEND OF RED'S WORKING FOR UNRRA
-PHOTOGRAPH BY JOHN ROBBINS

you. Within three weeks, I shall take a day or two off for myself. Maybe once again I shall be able to write you a letter worthy of the woman that you are.

August 23, 1946 ~ Madeleine in Toulouse to Dr. Hauck in New Jersey

The last time a truck came down from Paris, there were three large mail sacks aboard for me—filled with APO packages, most of them from you! I am getting to be known as the one-person commissary of the south! Whenever anyone has a needy case who has to be depanned—helped over a rough spot—they come to me and I supply them from your abounding store. I try to pick out the neediest cases, and those that we have not the funds or the stock to help ourselves.

The boxes you sent directly to Francine have arrived; by this time perhaps you have heard from her. She wrote me, too, absolutely in raptures over the warm, lovely clothes for the baby. The packages of food addressed to me for Francine have been delivered to her. I should think that by now she was well-stocked for her German adventure.

The box for a children's institution was in the lot that came down from Paris; I am keeping it for the kindergarten nearby that's run by a convent. It's traditionally been a haven for the workers of this delegation. During the terrible days of the Occupation, the sisters sometimes hid people for the Toulouse Quakers. Even now, when one of us needs a rest, we may go there for a weekend of doing nothing. It sounds, after the constant turmoil and crises here, like heaven: one has a room alone, where meals are brought. You needn't talk to anyone if you don't want to, and there is a beautiful park to walk in.

For the other things, I can't begin to enumerate them all or to thank you half properly. The special things like popover mix and the tinned candy and the spices we are saving for our new house—if we ever find one. We have just a month to go on our present lease, and nothing suitable has turned up yet. But when we do settle down, our house will be bright with your contributions! "Thank you" is terribly inadequate for so much thoughtfulness, but all the same we do thank you, very heartily.

The big box with the doctor's bag and the white coats arrived and has been taken this weekend to an isolated prisoner of war camp that is badly in need of medical supplies. The doctor hasn't had a change of white clothing up to now, so you can see how very welcome that package is. You will be hearing from the camp, I expect. The delegate who does the prison work says they have requests all the time for stethoscopes, which can't be had in France. At the moment they need three badly. I should imagine that stethoscopes are rather expensive equipment, and I do not mean this as a request. But if you happen to know anyone who feels a concern for POWs and would like to contribute a stethoscope, I know it would be well used.

I'm afraid you can't feel at all from the words the warm feeling that comes from the things you pack with so much care and affection. I wish I could tell you. The sugar we are saving for Christmas (but with sugar so short in the U.S. you shouldn't deprive yourselves); the Nescafé is so precious here, especially for journeys; the cocoa we stir up on our rickety kitchen table before going to bed (Our apartment is the kind that has decayed petit point chairs but primitive cooking facilities.); the tea towels have been declared too pretty to use as towels but will make gay curtains in the kitchen-that-is-to-be; the boxes of chocolate bars I'm saving against the day when British NAAFI closes down (that's the Navy, Army, Air Force Institute and the British equivalent of the American PX, which ended a month ago).

For future boxes (though I seriously wonder if you can or should consider sending them at the same rate; they are very useful but they represent a great deal of time and expense, I know) little tubes of Vaseline would be good; there won't be much heat this winter, and everybody suffers from chilblains. The small suppositories are very good and thanks for the soft toilet tissue!

Thank you for the newspaper clippings. It's tremendously heartening to read about the interest in the U.S. in helping French families and to know of your work, Dr. Lydia. Sometimes we seem so very far, in distance and time and understanding, from America. Workers in the field here sometimes have gripe sessions over how their home committees seem to have forgotten them. That's inevitable, I guess; the work is spread over such a wide area, communication is slow and uncertain, nobody ever has enough time, and we are all sorely lacking sometimes in understanding. For the moment, the work in the south seems to be stymied by crises both minor and major: the dog has just killed a chicken in the courtyard; the cook is going to quit; we still can't find a house; our transport is out of order so the delegation is totally immobilized; and we may lose our financial support from UNO.

That's not to say that we don't enjoy ourselves. Last night we had a hilarious evening with ten people to dinner, all crowded around a small square table. Our Spanish cook made her national dish—rice cooked with tiny lobsters (head and all) and little clams (shell and all). The lights went out, so we lit a candle in a tin cover and sang French and English and Spanish songs until midnight. It's a good life, whatever the gripes; we are beset with problems and can't solve them all, but we're close to each other, we're absorbing some of the thinking and the problems of other countries, and so we're lucky people in sum.

August 23, 1946 ~ Madeleine in Convent to Red in Gora Pulawska

I've found a quiet place at last. I'm in a convent! No, I haven't taken the veil—a poor nun I'd make! But it seems quite the thing hereabouts to retire for a weekend or even a vacation. Some convents take in people as pensionnaires, almost like a hotel. Others take people in for sweet charity.

I went to mass at 6:30 this morning, not so much from piety as because the bell clanged right outside my window. A sweet-faced Sister just came in to ask why I hadn't eaten breakfast. It seems the Mother Superior noticed I hadn't drunk my café au lait (it's that awful mud-colored stuff) and was inquiète.

There's a huge park here and a wonderful view of the countryside, but the quiet didn't last long. The Mother Superior came to talk to me and then a Mother from Ecuador, a jolly woman who studied in a convent in Michigan and loves New York City! They were so sorry because I'd been alone since last night. Next time I shall go to the other convent where meals are served in your room by a Sister who can't speak! Perhaps I make too much of this being alone, but it's easy for a small delegation to get ingrown and keep "giving each other tastes of that stale cheese we call ourselves."

Red, are you surprised sometimes by the amount of work it takes to get a very little done? Is it the same in other work, too, or just relief work? I begin to see better the need for administrators. But it's such a fallible need, arising from people's inadequacies, largely. So much of our work is making up for our shortcomings, misunderstandings, mistakes, not to mention those of the people with whom we try to work. I'm not discouraged so much as surprised. Tiens! So that is how the world gets on, a halting sort of progress but one which I can have a hand in, too. You see, my dear, however childish this may sound, I've always been in awe of people of affairs. But I'm beginning to see that people do things and make decisions not so much because they know more than others as because they have the courage or the ego to try—or lack the imagination to foresee! Fools rush in....

The Refugee Program moves on from crisis to crisis. The foundations appear to have been faulty and ill-understood. Every time Hugh goes deeply into a question, he reaches a morass of conflicting assumptions. Latest and worst is that the Intergovernmental Committee questions our use of their money! The whole program, to the tune of two million francs, was based on what we supposed was their acceptance of our plans. We may have to retrench, lop the program, let most of our staff go, and pitch in ourselves. That's OK. We have a good group here, and they can lick any problem they're turned loose on, but so far we don't see the problem clearly. Did I hear anything about hauling rocks?

Don't misunderstand, Red. For my part, I feel better about my job than ever since I came. With Hugh away so much, I'm clearly needed, though with a couple of secretaries and accountants at my beck and call, I worry occasionally about getting to be a self-important administrator. Funniest sight of the week is the Spanish bookkeeper consulting me in explosive French about accounting problems! Well, I worry carefully through the figures, only pausing now and then to laugh out loud at myself!

That was a beautiful sentence you wrote: "If this has been a dry time in your life, then you must live a very rich life." No, your good horse-sense about my troubles wasn't exactly a consolation, but it was good for me. I tend to ask too much for consolation. I guess things hurt me easily, and then it's nice to have the hurt made up for—nice, but not very adult. I've a lot of growing up to do; sometimes I wonder if ever I'll finish.

August 27, 1946 ~ Red in Gora Pulawska to Madeleine in Toulouse

This is a letter that should not be written. If your situation has not improved, it will not help you. Yet I do want to share some of my turmoil with you. I am not discouraged, but tonight I am faced with more unsolved problems than at any one time since arriving in Poland. Worst of all are the personality conflicts within the unit. We still have not learned to live and act as a team; rather we are eight individuals—no, nine; the interpreter also has a mind of his own.

Last night I returned from Warsaw after a very pleasant and profitable session with Philip Zealey, Al Johnson, Beth Clarkson, and Peggy Harrison. My greatest dissatisfaction was the decision to cut our unit to eleven men and increase Kozienice. I could have been obstinate about it, but we must attempt to work as a mission rather than as three separate units. We have learned that there is no chance of getting more visas for Poland after the twenty-nine initial visas have been obtained, but we have already started talking about projects for next year that would need additional personnel. Even worse, practically all the jobs need specialists. Then, it was disturbing to stay over for an extra day and not accomplish what I had wanted to do about getting information on supply parts.

When I arrived here last night, I found out that there had been trouble getting the trucks loaded. The village would not send in enough help, and the corporation, the governmental agency that is supplying the lime, would not supply the men. The regular Sunday dance had lasted all afternoon and on until 11:00 p.m., when it was finally dismissed with a hand grenade and several rounds of pistol firing. And there had been more drinking than usual. All this means that we must try to talk with the Polish guards.

There was also friction within the unit which I did not sense until one member refused to eat breakfast this morning because we would not let him invite three women to eat with us. The fellows had also refused to allow him to invite the women to sleep here last night. Honestly, it is tough to bring these people here and then not provide for them. There are no accommodations here, yet we have from five to fifteen people every night except Saturday. Some of the team say that we would not turn them away if we were at home. As for food, I do not feel badly about giving them food now, as there are many fresh vegetables and

eggs, but I dread to see this winter. I remember reports from Bill and Philip telling about wearing heavy coats, woolen caps, warm gloves, and waterproof shoes and seeing kids nearly barefoot. Imagine what winter will do to those of us who are sensitive now about people sleeping in a cold room in the middle of

WARSAW, SPRING OF 1946. AT ONE TIME, THIS STREET WAS COVERED BY SIX FEET OF RUBBLE.   -PHOTOGRAPH TAKEN BY AN ETU MEMBER

August! What about food for the Poles, when the only things they can store over winter are potatoes and wheat? It is already discouraging, and UNRRA closes here in December.

We called a meeting this morning. The first question was whether we should accept money offered us for rides. We have almost a regular bus service. This raises many questions. Some of the men would not accept money, since we are fed in the villages. Others would like to accept, but refuse, since the money is usually given with the idea that we will buy a drink with it. (Money is given rather than inviting us in to have a drink.) The compromise was that each man who wanted some way to explain that he was willing to accept contributions to a relief fund could install a can with a message in Polish on the side of the truck. Anyone wishing to give would be shown the message; he or she would then understand that the driver was not accepting the money as a personal gift. Others will continue as they have been doing—refusing the money.

Next came the problem of hauling people this Sunday to the various villages to solicit money for the rebuilding of the church. We shall do it, but the wrangling about whether we should was worse than a CPS camp meeting.

The worst came when we announced that those of us in Warsaw had accepted the Kozienice team's recommendation of reducing the "squander money" from 500 zl per week to 250 zl per week. This was OK with the men until I said that we would still be allowed expenses for food and lodging for one weekend per month, since it would be hard to do anything on 250 zl. They immediately felt that this was coercing them into spending their money for travel, since in reality, the new proposal would not reduce the amount those who travel would receive. As a matter of fact, this was a compromise with the people in Warsaw; some think that 500 zl is too much! Well it is, unless you wish to visit a city, where you can easily spend 400 zl for one meal.

Later in the day Van Cleve told me that it was a bad time to have had a meeting; everyone was in a bad humor last night, and the incident at breakfast did not help. Today we hauled lime from another stockpile, and the conditions are worse than ever. Tonight three of us did not go to the Polish class; one is too tired, one is feeling sick, and I have too many things on my mind.

One village refuses to send more than three people at one time to load trucks. We need about eight. However, that village receives its last load of lime tomorrow, and we shall have an understanding with the head of the village before we start hauling rock. Today the corporation did furnish some men after we told them we would park the trucks unless they loaded them. The boy (he is only twenty-two) who should coordinate things between us, the corporation, and the villages is a very poor administrator or else they do not have plans well thought through in the corporation office.

Tonight I feel as though I could write on and on. It's just piling up, and I cannot talk with the people. It is maddening! Some of this I had predicted. We knew at the beginning that we had men in our unit who could lay plans for this work and rush it through, but we did not wish to do that. We preferred, as much as possible, to fit into the patterns the people here set up and to give advice only when we see errors being made.

The next morning

On the train I met a girl who had been to Warsaw to carry a package to her father who is in prison there. He was an officer in the army before the war. Two months ago he was arrested; neither she nor her mother has been given any reason why he is being held or for how long. She was going to the university at Lublin, but now she must work to support her mother. Once a month she takes a package of food and cigarettes to Warsaw, but she is not sure that her father receives them. He cannot write to them, and she cannot see him even after making the long trip.

I take it that he sympathized too much with the Anglo-American side. Since she spoke English, many Americans visited their home when there were more Americans here than there are now. She has invited me to visit her and her mother. Now what is one to do? My inclination in places like this is to do the most natural thing, which is to visit them when I am in Lublin. Since I plan to visit Lublin soon, you may hear more of this story.

Have been nursing a cold all day. I stayed in bed most of the morning but feel much better now. Don't be disturbed; I cannot afford to be sick here, so I went to bed before I was forced to do so.

I have not mentioned it to you, but it's possible I could get to Switzerland for my leave. When do you plan to visit there? The chances of my making it are extremely slim, yet I cannot see taking a vacation without you.

Two kids came up and asked if they could have some of the excelsior we have from packing boxes. Their father has died, and they wanted it to make a pillow. I helped the little girl fill her basket with the excelsior and then had Wojtek ask if there was anything else we could do. A neighbor had come with the children; soon the neighbor was back with the widow, their mother.

She wanted to know if she could get a pair of shoes. Her husband had been a prisoner of war and died from injuries or malnutrition or something resulting from his imprisonment. They have no land and have been living off his wages. A pathetic story, but similar to what one hears from nine out of ten people. We have avoided special case work like poison, but this time we felt we could not let it go by.

September 1, 1946 ~ Red in Gora Pulawska to friends back home

Greetings from Poland. No, I have not become lost nor have I forgotten you; 'tis true that this is the first letter I have written all of you since leaving Berlin, but too many things have happened and too many details to attend to—many things which cannot be told yet, many things too boring to even mention.

Gora Pulawska is located on the west bank of the Vistula, and we are on a hill overlooking the village and river with a wonderful view of Pulawy, which is across the river. Pulawy is the market town of this area and was hit hard by the war but is in excellent condition compared to most of the villages. Gora Pulawska is one of the many villages where every home was destroyed; even yet people are living in dugouts, cellars, and old ruins. Reconstruction is a slow process at the best, and they have little equipment and practically no transport. Our barrack is located in a grove which was once the site of a huge manor house, then later a beer brewery, and just before the war, it was an agriculture school. However, there is only one small building standing and only one room of that is habitable. A family lives in the cellar. There are many huge holes, which housed the Germans when they held this hill. Across the road stands what is left of the Catholic church.

We have chosen to work this area because it is one of the worst hit by the war—more than twenty-five villages with only one house left.

Already we have hauled all the lime needed to two of the villages furthest south in this powiat; now we are hauling the stone and soon we start with the cement. There were 10,000 buildings or units of buildings destroyed in this region (if a family had a home and a barn destroyed, they count that as one).

This year they had hopes to rebuild 1,400 barns; now they do not expect to build more than 500. The barns are so designed that they can house the family as well as the stock until a house can be built. Even so, they hope to have a barn for every family within five years. What do they do in the meantime? Your guess is as good as mine. Now the weather is good, and they are cooking outside and sleeping on hay, but this winter is another problem, and I dread to see cold weather come. Clothes are as bad a problem as shelter, and food may be even worse.

If you have heard stories about the horrible conditions in Berlin, let me tell you that Warsaw is far worse. It is impossible to give you a picture of it, and I am told that had I arrived twelve months ago, I would not have recognized it today. I can believe this, as I was up there again a week ago, after only a few weeks in Gora, and could see some great changes in that short time. The insurrection of Warsaw was one of the most dramatic and horrible events during the six years of war. For forty-five days the people lived underground and moved about via the sewers with no outside help; then the town fell again to the Germans, and the Germans retaliated by deliberately blowing the buildings apart. Few buildings remain untouched, and the streets are filled with debris.

When I first arrived, for example, the café where we went frequently could be reached only by following a small path that led through several piles of bricks and mortar.

Now the city is becoming a town of small shops made from the

LOADING ROCK FROM QUARRY NEAR LUCIMA. ONLY TWO OF OUR SEVEN TRUCKS WERE DUMP TRUCKS, FORCING US TO UNLOAD BY HAND.   -PHOTOGRAPH BY HENRY DASENBROCK, ETU MEMBER

hulls of the remaining ruins. This is even more remarkable when you realize that most of the debris is being hauled to the dumping ground by wagons and horses, and oftentimes there is only one horse per wagon. Sometimes you can see a load of wood coming through the streets being pulled by two men with ropes over their shoulders and a third man pushing.

Traffic is becoming greater; there are traffic police at some of the busy corners; many of them are girls. Today there are 27,000 trucks— more motorized equipment than Poland has ever had—but not nearly enough. Streetcars are beginning to run again; trucks used as buses are making scheduled runs within the city as well as to other cities. Train schedules are changing every month and each time they become better.

What was once the ghetto is the worst. The Jews in Warsaw were crowded together in old brick buildings. For a long time it was a prison for them under the Germans. Today it is hard to find a wall standing; we climbed over piles and piles of bricks; sometimes they were twenty and thirty feet high. Buildings that were built over the centuries, destroyed in a few short weeks.

I have been telling you about the buildings, but it is really the story of the people themselves. You never hear anyone say that he regrets the effort that was made to rid their city of their oppressors, but all of them can tell you of any number of close friends who lost their lives in that struggle. One girl was saying that the last time she saw the ghetto was from the window of a home where they were having a party. Everybody was having a wonderful time until someone drew back the curtain, and they looked across at the ghetto and became more sober. A week before the insurrection, she left the city. When she returned, more than half the people at the party were dead!

I wish it were possible for me to give you some idea of the courage that these people have; for more than one hundred years their lands were occupied by three neighbors. In 1918 they were given their country back and for twenty years made tremendous strides in building a nation. In 1920, 70 percent of the people were illiterate; in 1939 only 18 percent were illiterate. Poland spent more money per capita on education than any other nation in the world. Then she lost her country again, and Germany made a deliberate attempt to use her only as a source of labor. Buildings of culture were destroyed; paintings and monuments were removed; administrators and professional men were either deported or killed; machinery and equipment were removed.

Today Poland is burdened with a large population of working men who have few skills but are willing to work. There are only five sanitation engineers in all of Poland; teachers must teach 200 pupils! Where there are not enough school teachers, they have two shifts. The kids are undernourished, not to mention the elders. The hospital at Pulawy cannot even take a simple blood test. Yet there is hope and confidence. It is a struggle for existence, a survival of the fittest. If you had plenty of money (zlotys) and lived in Warsaw, you could believe that there was no food shortage in Poland. The first evening I was here, Bill and Philip said that I might drop in for a cold snack. My snack was half a chicken! The next day we had beautiful steaks, but we were paying 400 to 600 zlotys per meal. At the official rate of exchange, that is a terrific price (100 zlotys per dollar). Compared to what the working man receives, this is outrageous.

The average wage is about 150 to 200 zlotys per day. The best paid salaried mmen get 5,000 to 6,000 zlotys per month ($50 to $60). If a person holds a job where he can obtain a high-category food and cloth-ing card, he can manage, as this permits him to buy limited foods at the official price. Everything else is sold on the "free" market. The only thing that is considered black market is exchanging money for foreign currency. In Warsaw the price of fresh fruit is 80 zlotys per kilo or about 40¢ per pound. It is about half this down in Gora, where we live.

Last Sunday, I went to Lublin for the day. I met a girl, Hanka, on the train from Warsaw who spoke a little English, and she had invited me to Lublin. We walked through the city, and it was unbelievable that this had been the seat of the famous "Lublin Government."

The owner of the club where Hanka works took us on a horse-drawn taxi to Majdanek. It was one of the worst concentration camps. Over two million people met their deaths there. It is a huge camp of barracks surrounded by two layers of fences with high-tension wires in between; high towers stand at each corner and on each side.

As we rode along the opposite hill, I thought of Tule Lake camp in California and the Japanese-Americans interned there and won-dered what differences there were between the two systems except in their relative treatment of the prisoners. One barrack has the interior walls lined with photographs. Most of them were taken shortly after the Germans left, but others were pictures of the previous winter. In one room there were many drawings, and in a corner were two wax figures: one of a man who looked to be no more than skin and bones, another of a little girl. It made me sick to think that there could have been one girl like that, much less hundreds of them. In one barrack, there are 800,000 pairs of shoes that they found when the Germans left. We went to the crematories. At first you think that you are walking into a huge boiler room, but upon closer inspection you find five incinerators with frames built with which to push the cadavers into the furnaces.

Another room was built with heavy brick and cement walls; there were two doors with steel casings for close fitting. On one side were very small windows; the ceiling was less than seven feet high and in the center was an opening with a small door. We were told that this was where people were gassed; this camp had six such rooms. The furnaces were run by coal, and the coal room would hold several boxcar loads of the fuel. It is said that they could cremate up to 5,000 people per day. When the Russians came in, they found 1,300 cubic meters of ashes from cremations.

Remember the days when we were first told of what went on inside Germany, and we would not believe? Even during the war we tried to make light of the stories we heard, placing much of it on propaganda. "I came. I saw. I believe." It may be that my pacifist stand during the war made me want to discount the horror stories of atrocities committed by other nations, but I came away from Majdanek as strong in my pacifist beliefs as I have ever been. As yet I do not know a practical solution to how to obtain the freedom for people going through the torture and agony of places like Majdanek and the ghetto of Warsaw. If as a result of World War II we had peace today, if people were free, if we did not still possess the fears and hatreds that cause the Majdaneks, then the militarists would have a strong point to justify war. But such is not the case; there is still anti-Semitism, anti-Bolshevik, anti-capitalist, hatred for the Germans, distrust of peoples and individuals, great dissatisfaction with the peace conference, insoluble problems that have been made more complex by the war...and now the atom bomb!

This may sound cynical and pessimistic; it is not that but a strong plea for those of us who know nothing about what fear and bitterness can do for masses of people and to be willing to understand what seven years of hell has meant for these people. I wish that we could be so sensitive to the needs of people (not only Poles, but suffering masses the world round) that we would willingly show some Christian principles toward helping them. If ever we needed to substitute a set of principles based on high ethics for the old Hebrew law of "an eye for an eye and a tooth for a tooth," it is today.

September 2, 1946 ~ Madeleine in Toulouse to Red in Gora Pulawska

The geraniums in the window boxes are flourishing in the southern sun (not having been gnawed lately by rats), there are flowers in all the offices, and life seems good.

Not entirely. It's Monday, and that's the day your letters usually come if they're coming at all during the week. This is the third Monday with no post. In spite of the sun, I can't help being a little downcast.

How I do wish you were here! I'm having my vacation the first two weeks of October (barring major crises, of which we seem to have plenty), and of course I shall head straight for Switzerland. One of my cousins is being married, and there's an adorable two-year-old second cousin to meet, besides all the other relations. It should be fun. Someday perhaps you'll go to see them with me. They'd like you, I'm sure, even though you don't speak the best of French, just as they liked my father twenty-six years ago—and his French was simply abominable.

September 5 ~ A letter came this morning with the wonderful reports of your work. My dear, my dear, I wish I could tell you how I feel: glad and proud and humble and very quiet inside. Your work must be very tough and very thrilling. I envy you. I envy the clean-cut job and your energy and ability and penetrating insight. I'm sorry for the difficulty and heartbreak. I'm terribly proud and glad of your spirit.

You seem terribly close today, so close I scarcely mind the waiting. And terribly dear, so dear it hurts in my heart and my eyes sting with tears. You are a big person, so big that I feel small. If you have found quietness in spirit, you have found something of great value. I have not yet, though I am always looking. I suppose I shall find it in good time, but for the moment I feel rather humble before you.

Tomorrow we are going to the Pyrenees to climb a mountain with the Perpignan delegation. Next week I stay in Perpignan, a lovely spot, to do some publicity on their work and help with case work while one of the delegates is on holiday.

One more administrative detail! My commitment to the Refugee Program is up in December; my term of service is up in February. Both can easily be extended. But if I want to change my area of work, I'll have to begin telling Paris soon; three months isn't any too much time to get passports, permissions, and all the rest. One way or another, I plan to stay in Europe as long as you do, but I'd like to know more about your plans before trying to make mine so we can have a chance of coming out somewhere within a thousand miles of each other! So—how far can you see ahead? How long in Poland and where? And what would you suggest I ask for? I'd like to go to Austria or Germany if I can't work with or near you.

September 7, 1946 ~ Red in Gora Pulawska to Madeleine in Toulouse

The post was late coming from Warsaw this week, so I was pretty sure there would be a letter from you waiting when I returned today. I am afraid that I may have driven faster over some of the bumps than I should have done. (Fifteen miles per hour is too much most of the time.) Tonight I feel the best I have felt in several days. Really, I feel jubilant. Maybe it is because of the letter from you, or the fact that I am going to Lublin tomorrow, or possibly that I have done physical work for three straight days.

My happiest moments are when I dream of you, who you are, and what you will be a year from now, another five years, and forever. I have tried to dream of a home or of what we would be doing for work, but that seems so irrelevant that I come back to what we are as individuals and what we are as one. I dream of you as a mother, not just a mother who is proud of a child but rather a mother who is symbolic of our relationship with life and the universe. I dream of the visits with our friends and the richness there will be in sharing our experiences and our thoughts with others, you carrying the theoretical discussions and I trying to make applications of theories. Then I dream of those sweet moments when there are only the two of us and the universe, and time has no meaning.

You wrote, "There are all sorts of strengths and graces and pleasures that only a man and woman by close-living and close-growing can share." I heartily agree with you. But those are not the only strengths we have, and often they are overstressed between two people living together. That is why I hope that each of us can have separate work. Also I hope that each of us will feel free to take a short trip without the other at times. (For heaven's sake and mine too, please don't make a six-month trip without me!)

Thursday three of us were hauling rock to Lucima. On one load there was at first nobody to help me unload, so a pregnant woman climbed on the truck to help. In spite of my insistence that she not do this, she kept saying something about maly, meaning small. It hit me pretty hard because this stone was coming to build her home. She lost a son, a house, and all their livestock during the last stages of the war and has been living in the ground since. Now she must help haul stone in order to build a home for her expected child. What courage these women have! They are rebuilding Poland; they plant the fields, harvest the wheat, tend the cows, dig holes for lime, bear children, and make a home, all in the day's work.

September 11, 1946 ~ Madeleine in Perpignan to Red in Gora Pulawska

I've gone completely Midi! I'm writing from an open-air café under a palm tree, with a glass of beer-and-lemonade in front of me. It's partly work; I'm writing up a report on a family I just visited. The visit was fun because I had to take an open-air tram out into the country where one can see the blue Pyrenees.

I'd like you to see all this: the sea and mountains, the sunny towns, the long, slow days that seem to have no end. I wish I could bring you here for a week and watch you sleep and laze and maybe climb a mountain with you. You sound so tired! It will go by, of course, but I wish I might soothe the tiredness out of you.

What are we going to do about it—your wanting to share Poland with me and my wanting to share France and Switzerland with you? We shall have to stay in Europe years! There is such an infinity of little things: customs and towns and views and cafés that I'd like to have you know. Sometimes the minuteness of this French life frightens me; it's so tiny beside the fact of the atom bomb. (I seem to carry that damn thing around in my brain.) People are so concerned with the amenities and pleasures of life, which is all right, but one wonders how much moral power is in them. It's easy enough to fit into this pattern; it's hard not to, in fact. Climate and custom all incline one to this easy way of living, but can never quite relax enough to stop wondering what it means. A gracious life, but don't we now need a good life in a large and courageous sense of the word?

That there should be trouble within your group is distressing. The group is the source of our strength; the people in it can either reinforce one another mightily or invalidate all but the strongest efforts.

There's another question that bothers me: the fact that as our responsibility and influence increase, our smallest failings have greater importance. Sometimes I am so acutely aware of my shortcomings and their effect on my work that I think I should take myself off to the mountains for a year and work out my own salvation before I try to work out anyone else's. But for most of us, I guess it's a matter of working out among people and problems, not going off alone to perfect ourselves.

I've still not told you of the richness and joy I had this week when four of your letters came. They were full of problems and weariness, and I ached for you, but they were full of affection and resolve, too, and I could have shouted over them. You know how much I'd like long letters, but when you're having crises and can't write them, don't add that to your other worries. Only do send a note to tell me how you are.

The copies of your reports and letters to Paris give a vivid picture of what you're doing. Who said you can't write? And the pictures—thanks for those. They show so much more than words what it's like and what's to be done.

I wonder if it's time that we began thinking about when we can plan to be together, how long and under what circumstances, and how much time we should have before we think of marrying.

Even as I write this, I am a little startled. I wonder if you will be, too. The subject has only just recently entered my mind, and then it's because all our planning must be done so far ahead. It's also a strange— well, unconventional—way to broach a subject about which we've talked much but never quite named. It's a heck of a thing to be trying to decide with so many hundreds of miles between us. But like you, I'm thinking of "we" in the future, and by the time the rest of our work in Europe is settled, the future will not be very distant.

I'd better warn you, that before this is finally settled, I'll probably get very skittish and uncertain, and you'll have to help me get over those feelings. I've never before—well, once, and long ago—come close to making actual plans for living with someone, and in a certain sense, it will be hard to come to the sticking point. I wonder if you can understand? It has nothing to do with you as a person but rather with the idea of a definite and responsible commitment on a matter of lifelong importance, which appalls me when I get close to it. Were you here it would seem more natural, I think.

I almost leapt into the air (another of Hugh's Anglicanisms) when you mentioned Switzerland. By now you know I'm going early in October; that would probably, almost surely, be impossible for you. But if you go later, I wonder if I couldn't get over to see you? Or you come here to see me?

September 14, 1946 ~ Red in Gora Pulawska to Madeleine in Toulouse

Madeleine, is it true that you are studying Polish? Honestly, you have courage, and I love you more each day. Today four pictures of you were pinned to the wall. Mind being a Pin-Up Girl?

Do you ever wonder how we shall be together —how we shall live together? I'm not worrying, but just musing about our likes and dislikes, whether we shall have patience with each other, if we shall have many differences in our preferences, say on style of house, place for a vacation, type of work, friends, and so on. Oh, it's great to meditate on days together, how we might spend the first few hours, and where they might be.

I become more anxious to get on with our life together, to get away from this bachelor's life. No, I am not an escapist. Before meeting you, a bachelor's life seemed pretty good: no ties, freedom, absorption in work. Now there is a freedom I never knew before, another world, full of life, great happiness, and great sorrow.

For a while, you and I were alone. Now there are typewriters going next door and one beside me. Tomorrow you should be here to go with us to Kazimierz; it is on the east side of the Vistula south of us. We are taking a truck with several women from here and Pulawy. We hope some of the Kozienice team will join us for a picnic and sight-seeing tour of the old castle. Wojtek is remaining in camp alone, which means we shall have to resort to German and Polish for communication. It should be fun.

September 19, 1946 ~ Red in Kozienice to Madeleine in Toulouse

Tomorrow David Richie leaves for France, so he will post this letter in Paris. Is there any chance of your visiting with him there before he leaves again for Poland? I hope that it will be possible; he can tell you so much about the work and conditions here that is impossible to record in letters. Incidentally, he is taking some food from here, which means that he will be allowed some extra weight in his baggage when he comes back. Have you by chance any good books that you could send? We are rather short of books for these long winter nights. Some of us will be studying Polish, but it is next to impossible for me to spend all my time on language. I've started reading *Man Against Himself*.

This week we ran out of work! Van Cleve came over to Kozienice yesterday to get gas, food and money. They told him they could use three trucks for three days hauling barracks, so three of us went, only to find that Powinski—our contact—had left town for the day. No one else knew where the barracks were or where they should go. So we helped the relief team with warehousing and mechanics for the rest of the day. It was well worth it, since Albert then had time to make us a wonderful cherry pie, and the Polish cook made some excellent pastries.

You are not the only one who has dubious ideas about administration. I also question the effort we make to have a democracy within our group. It takes so much time, so much talking, and then so often each of us acts according to his own desires. We have little to complain of about people in the peace conference who sit and bicker over small points. More and more I come to realize how important the attitude and motivation of each of us really are. In CPS, we came together because circumstances forced us into association. Here we have much more common ground for action and still it takes the slow process of understanding, discussion, and more understanding. What we really are lacking most is someone with great spiritual leadership. There is so much I want to say about this, about democracy (which I still believe is the best system), about administration, but I cannot write tonight.

Wojtek, Hank, Ex, and many others send their regards.

September 27, 1946 ~ Madeleine in Toulouse to Red in Gora Pulawska

It's a bright blue day, cool in the morning and warm at noon, just like Indian summer at home. And it's my birthday! First thing this morning in the office, the German cook brought me a bunch of zinnias, then two of the delegates brought some more—great, brilliant blooms— and then a lovely potted cyclamen. And Dick Sherrington, who paints, has given me a watercolor of the Pyrenees—which I cherish and shall more in the years to come, because I've grown to love those barren misty mountains. The cook made, at Connie's behest, some cheese and apple kuchen on which I've been stuffing myself.

And what happy chance is it that two letters come from you today? It's what I hoped for but hardly dared.

Why can't you be here this evening when we're all going out for apéritifs and dinner and dancing (if it doesn't get too cool or we too tired). I can't pretend that I don't enjoy myself without you; I do, of course, and so do you without me, but like you I get so tired of waiting. In spite of the irritations and frustrations and misdirections of the work here, it is a wonderful experience, and I regret so greatly that we can't have it together, at the same time regretting that I can't share yours. The mountains, Red, and the little villages and the sun and bright colors and the people here I like so much.

Look, my dear, I bet a new penny I can guess what you're thinking now: "Oh gosh, and I went and forgot it was her birthday!" or "I never knew...."

Any such cracks will be received with great intolerance. That is not the reason this letter was written! It was to tell you how apropos your letters were, whether that was accidental or not. (Knowing the French postal system, I'm sure it was accidental.) You have more than enough on your mind without keeping your eye glued to a calendar. And it was to tell you how much I wish you could be here.

By the way, the Friends Relief Services (British Quakers) Information Bulletin came the other day with a long article on the Polish work and one on the Refugee Program. I saw your name as team leader and swelled with pride. Incidentally, Hugh may leave the program before long, but by staying until Christmas or so, I could provide enough continuity to help a new head of program.

Your words about my studying Polish are heartwarming, my dear, but don't praise me too soon. I asked for a Polish grammar two months ago and only now is one in sight! I hope I can pick it up on my way through Paris. Then I can know what you mean by Kocham pania. Hope it's something nice.

There's a batch of pictures coming soon from our weekends in the Pyrenees. The loveliest picture wasn't taken. During Monthly Meeting (which we held on a green pasture in the shadow of the mountains), the male and female representatives split forces. The girls went upstream and the men down. There, among the mossy rocks and rushing white water, cold and clear and tingly, we went bathing in the nude. It was one of the most beautiful things I have ever seen: sun and water and lovely bodies, like tales of ancient Greece come alive. People naked are so beautiful and so much more a part of the grace and aliveness of a landscape than people bundled into tweed and cotton and shoes. I felt, strangely, as if I knew these people differently, more naturally and easily, than ever before.

September 28, 1946 ~ Red in Sobata to Madeleine in Toulouse

This week has been rather rough—lots of driving, into the night sometimes; rain; frustration; and paperwork. Worst of all, one of the trucks ran over an eighteen-year-old boy. I took him to hospital and was in the operating room when the doctor said he would have to wait until the next day to know if there were any internal injuries and whether the boy had a chance to live.

Never have I experienced anything that made me so sick; the boy seemed very much alive, and to look at him, you could not tell that anything had happened to him except that pain was written all over his face. The next day the x-ray showed a very badly broken pelvic bone. Instead of putting him into a cast, they are keeping him in bed with his legs stretched apart. They are afraid to operate and set the bones properly. The doctor says that he will be able to walk but not run. I still wonder if he will pull through; he was developing a slight cold yesterday. Medical facilities are not what we are accustomed to in America. The wards are as crowded as they can possibly be; even the halls are used as wards.

I am glad to know that you have come to the stage where you can question the value of the details in the work you are doing. Usually it is after periods of slight depression that new ideas and renewed interest come to one's work. You can follow along after others in their patterns until you begin to see that something is not right; then you have the opportunity to make real contributions to the work. This is not to bolster you, it is just reflection on past experience.

How often I wish you were here! Maybe you could help me find my place in this team. It is still not a team but eight individuals driving trucks. Personality conflicts are not as striking as they were, but dissatisfaction and doubts are creeping in, questions about our reasons for being here and the validity of the work. This can be a good sign if properly controlled, but I am not the leader. Sometimes I feel a real need for a leader in this group instead of the shared leadership. Two or three of the fellows have been visiting with Polish girls rather frequently; others are concerned about the reputation we may get. We are due two more men, but already some are questioning what jobs they will have. Some are anxious to get off this rather monotonous job of hauling several times a day over the same roads.

So far I have played the part of an executive secretary. Team meetings have not been too successful; it is difficult to sum up the feelings of the group in such a way that action can be taken which is satisfactory to all concerned. Van Cleve and I get along marvelously. In fact, my relationship with any one individual is OK. It is very important, however, that Van and I work smoothly together; we are beginning to take action without waiting for the group, and they may call our hand on this, but I become impatient. Most of this action relates to which of the two of us should make certain official trips, and the approach we should take with officials. Honestly, after team meetings I sometimes wonder how they ever settle anything on the international level.

Maybe it is time that we had a team meeting to talk about motivation, our work, our relationship with the people and with one another.

Today I used several very simple sentences in Polish. This was my first attempt and it seemed good. Already I can get around and get what I want, but it has to be with the aid of a dictionary. Fortunately, I am able to understand Polish better than I understood French. Frenchmen run all the words together. In Polish, the accent is always (well, nearly always) on the next to the last syllable. Simple. I am not sure that I ever shall be able to pronounce this language properly, though.

Do you know what Gibran says about working with love? To work as if it were for your loved one. You are in my thoughts so much that even while I work, it is as though the work is the combined efforts of both of us. That may not be as Gibran meant it, but that is the way it is with me.

Do you ever get really hungry for good music or beautiful pictures? I feel as though I could sit for a week and listen to records. I actually get hungry for beauty. There is waste and devastation everywhere around; I need something to balance it. Yet people are making their homes here and some never leave. Are they better able to take it by not knowing anything better?

In one sense, it doesn't matter
greatly what we do; it does matter
tremendously how we do it.

-Madeleine

Yearning To Be Together

A very merry Christmas to you, my
and may this season be a ti
of inward rejoicing for the lov
of mankind and for the power
that love.

May this be the season when w
can renew our faith in that
spark who which could e
between all men.

Keep the flame in your heart to
my sweet, you may think it
small, but you have no idea
how many lives it reaches.

May another Christmas find
us together — bound tightly with
power powerful force of love.

October 6, 1946 ~ Madeleine in Switzerland to Red in Gora Pulawska

(The village of Corcelles-sur-Neuchâtel is the ancestral home of Madeleine's mother.)

My third day in Switzerland. I've found a new family and a new country, and I like them very much. My grandfather's house is on a steep hillside, surrounded by garden and grapes, looking out over the village and the lovely lake of Neuchâtel. On the other side of the lake are low mountains, and beyond them, when it is fine, one can see the Alps.

Swiss houses seem to be simple, full of light and air and views, which is furnishing enough. I wish you could see one so you'd know if sometime it would be possible to incorporate some of their ideas. The kitchen here is red-tiled and gives on a garden that seems to come in at the windows. There is fresh milk and sweet butter and Swiss cheese—like a fairy tale after France.

The first word I think of to describe the Swiss is healthy: physically and morally. People look well. It's a deep pleasure to me just to see them, red-cheeked and cheerful, strong and hard-working. And morally, after the compromising and "arranging" in France, they seem sound as an

MADELEINE WITH HER UNCLE PAUL AND AUNT ANNA GERBER IN VINEYARD OUTSIDE CORCELLES-SUR-NEAUCHÂTEL. OCTOBER 1946
-PHOTOGRAPHER UNKNOWN

apple: responsible, forthright, scrupulously honest.

A little thing, but to get milk you leave a pitcher mornings on a shelf in the dairyman's barn and pick it up full on your way home. Dozens of pitchers, no names or numbers. Everyone trusts his neighbor.

The very air seems sweeter because of it!

Down the road a piece lives my uncle Paul in a little blue vineyardist's cottage. He's merry and hearty and a pillar of the village, spins a wonderful yarn, and is loved by the whole canton, I'd guess. They have a gemütlich little living room with a huge green tile stove you can sit on, a cat, and wooden stools to sit on when the armchairs aren't enough.

We had a tea there last Saturday (a cold gray day) that was like a supper. My ample aunt Anna has mushrooms drying in the kitchen, nuts in the attic, and preserves in the closet. My cousin Paulet is his father over again, and he's to be married in two weeks and live in a little house in the vineyards down the hill from his father's.

It sounds idyllic, I know, Red. It looks idyllic. After France it seems impossible. It's not perfect, I know. If I were here long I think I'd find it a little dull and unimaginative and intolerant. But as far as they've gone, the Swiss have been magnificent. As my uncle proudly says, "Here the people are master." They work, they work together, and they get along together. Today I saw three flags flying over Neuchâtel: the Swiss flag, the old Royalist flag, and the old Republican flag—the last from the time before Switzerland took in the canton of Neuchâtel. No one was bothered. (Think of that in Poland!) No one is upset by people speaking German and French side by side in trams and stores; they just print everything in two languages and let it go.

Oh Red, this isn't a travel blurb; it's to tell you what I'm seeing and how terribly I miss seeing it with you. I think I've never wanted so much for you to share an experience. Already I'm hoping to come back here before I return to America, and I nearly have to bite my tongue to keep from saying, "Next year there may be someone with me." Could you, would you? I'm proud of these people, and I'd like you to know them. I'd like you to know the easing of spirit that comes with a few days in a normal, happy country. I'd like to stuff you with good fresh food as I'm being stuffed. I'd like to walk along the stone-walled road at night and see the lights of the villages below. I'd like to have you with me under one of those great down puffs. Red, I'd like to know you and to share with you and to grow.

If I go too far too fast, tell me. With this damned long lapse between letter and answer, I feel sometimes as if I were writing into a void, as if I were thinking without knowledge of your reaction. But a deep-founded belief in your integrity and affection makes it not strange to say such things even before we have had much time to talk (write, rather) them over.

I've been cutting grapes with fourteen others in a steep vineyard overlooking the lake. It's cold and clear and hearty. At night I fall into bed and sleep like a stone. Now it's almost noon and time for me to go down the hill and help carry a hot dinner in buckets to the people in the field.

October 6, 1946 ~ Red in Warsaw to Madeleine in Toulouse

Lots of traveling again this week. Our talk with the Polish leaders in Kozienice was most satisfactory. Without our help, they said, the reconstruction would have to stop, and they gave us everything we asked for. In addition, they offered to put up a second wall to our barrack and pack straw in between the two walls to serve as insulating material.

Wednesday, Wojtek and I went to Kielce, and the chief there said the Poles were contemplating moving our team to Sandomierz and Opotow, another part of the Woje, in about two and a half months. When I said I would have to talk this over with our men and our chief in Warsaw, he said everything depends upon our willingness to move.

That last was quite a relief, because I was afraid he might be arbitrary.

It is on account of this interaction with the chief that I am in Warsaw. Friday night we had a team meeting, and the men were very much opposed to moving. It certainly does not follow Friends policy of living with the people and doing a job with them for us to move out now. What about the psychological effect on the people if their transport is taken away just as they are feeling encouraged with the rebuilding? Since we did not know whether this might be a political move on the part of some members within the Woje, or what commitments our contract with the ministry called for, it was decided that I should come to Warsaw and talk with Philip and Piascek, who is the Polish head of village reconstruction in Poland.

In addition, our men want to see another team come in. Philip thought it would be best to wait until after the elections to approach the ministry again about additional personnel. When Philip asked me what I thought, I said that when you live in the devastated areas as much as we do, international politics diminishes in importance in relation to what has to be done.

Personally, I am very anxious to see more transport come in immediately. We discussed the possibilities of a team arriving in the middle of winter and the hardships that would bring. Philip seemed convinced that more transport was the logical solution and that it would be best to split the present team and put the newcomers with those of us who have already had some experience in Poland.

On Thursday, I drove the jeep for the Kozienice team, and we were served a marvelous chicken dinner by the priest at the village where we were making the food distribution. Somehow it didn't seem right for us to be eating a chicken of theirs when we were having to bring food into that area. What does one do? It would have been an insult to them to have refused.

The next day, Wojtek and I went to Radom again and bought a barrel of gas and fifteen tons of coal.

The mayor of Radom was a Socialist before the war. He spent some time as a prisoner in Russia after the last war and was in the underground here against the Germans. Then he was a prisoner at Majdanek, the concentration camp outside of Lublin. He has lost a cheek bone and all but three teeth, had several ribs broken, and one arm deformed. He said he was fighting all the time. He lost his teeth when he bit an SS man!

He told stories that he said he would not believe had he not seen the incidents himself. England and America do not understand what the Poles have been through and what it is like here now, according to him. He said he and others were working on the lawn of an institution when some Germans came up in a truck and started picking up children and throwing them into a truck as if they were so many sacks of potatoes. It hurt him so badly, he had to turn his head and cry. He said that some of the men looking on were some of the toughest characters he knew and yet they cried. He cannot understand our treatment of the Germans today, considering the bestial things they have done to other people.

Last night Ralph, Arthur, two of Ralph's girlfriends, and I went dancing. The floor became too crowded at the Polonia, so we went to the Europa. I could hardly believe my ears; the music was really soft and smooth. The floor was much larger and not too crowded. We ordered a small salad and a beer each, danced two numbers, and were ready to settle there for the evening when the band started putting their instruments away. We were horrified! True to our suspicions, they were quitting, and we had danced only two numbers! The bill came to 1090 zl (more than four months spending money). That was pretty hard to take, but Ralph and I reminded each other that we learn the hard way and paid the bill. Had we spent two hours dancing, it would have been OK.

Ralph was going out to spend the night with the girls, and they invited me, but I decided that was too much for me. I was already getting too many invitations from one of the girls to visit her the next time I was in Warsaw; she also told me she would be in Pulawy to visit her friends soon. Do you mind if I tell people I am married? It would make such situations less likely to happen. I enjoy being with girls and dancing with them, but I don't want them to take it so personally. If they only knew that I was thinking of a girl in France more than of them, they might not feel so elated!

October 7, Monday ~ Last night, we saw *Faust*. The opera was superb. Although we could not understand the words, we could appreciate the music and acting. The scenery did not compare with *Madame Butterfly* but the acting was just as good.

This morning, I talked with Philip about the possibility of bringing in another team other than a transport team, but this will have to wait until after the elections, until the government can feel sure that we are nonpolitical. I told Philip that you and I would like to get within hailing distance of each other. He suggested that you write to Bill Huntington, at the Polish desk in Philadelphia, and state your reasons for coming to Poland. The decision to do that will have to be left to you.

Your mentioning the possibilities of when we can be married was rather startling, yet it seemed very natural. We have talked much about living together and growing together without having mentioned marriage, and that is the way it should be. We find our security with each other through the bond of a relationship that is established rather than through a license. Yet to meet the demands of the larger community, the license is necessary. As to when that should be obtained, I would say that I shall be ready as soon as the initial shock and excitement of seeing you again is over. Do you prefer to wait until we are back in the States? I am sure your mother would like to see you being married, yet there are some advantages to being married before we return. If some of the first steps to living together can be worked out before we return, we would not have to do that at the same time we are finding work to do and settling down. Also, with our limited finances, it would mean that we could have our honeymoon here where we might be able to afford it on our annual leave money.

Darling, both of us should feel free to say that we are engaged. Already the boys have become used to my fondly referring to you as my wife. Arthur has suggested that the team write a letter requesting your transfer to Poland because their leader is cracking! We have talked a great deal about a woman member of our unit, but each time we insist that she speak some Polish. We have not, however, found a full-time job for a woman as yet.

Madeleine, you said that you might become "skittish and uncertain." That may be; nevertheless, I have no fears. I have had no fears since leaving France. There is a bond between us that cannot be broken by a few uncertainties and doubts. There will be some, on the part of both of us, but the faith we have in each other and in the two of us together will overcome all.

October 15, 1946 ~ Madeleine in Corcelles to Red in Gora Pulawska

My last night in Switzerland, and I've just climbed up the moonlit street from my cousin's house where we had a magnificent dinner: a delicate lake fish with a sauce such as you read about and white Valais wine. All my relatives are making grand proposals for next summer: the high Alps, a cabin in the Jura mountains, St. Gothard Pass, and so on and on. We could stay two months doing it all. When I think of being in such beauty with you, I truly and soberly wonder how I shall get through the next twelve months, if twelve months it must be. It's awfully easy here to forget one is a relief worker. And I want so terribly to share it all with you—the people and the places.

WILLIAM EDGERTON TALKING WITH A MAN IN THE DOORWAY OF HIS BUNKER HOME
-PHOTOGRAPH BY RED

Two of your letters reached me here at Corcelles yesterday. I was overjoyed to have them, and there was much of you therein. I was overcast because they were only from you and a poor substitute for your presence. When there's more time, I'll go through them bit by bit and write my reflections. For now I want to tell you how good and vivid and loving they are. How stern, too, in the sense that they made me face up more sharply to the future and the possibility of a long, long wait. Time seems to come in six-month chunks. I don't know why I seem to feel that at the end of a chunk the miles will roll up and Red will appear!

Ever since your letters came, inside the pleasant time I've been having, a sort of battle has been going on. For the first time, I feel vividly that the next twelve months will be a hard, lonely pull and that it's up to me to make something rich out of the loneliness, as you do, or to squander and regret it. Perhaps because I've been more fortunate in my surroundings, I've drawn less deeply the past months on my own resources than you. Suddenly your letters, clear-sighted and comprehending, made me see, partly through your own difficulties, what a sacrifice our absence and distance is going to be. Not that I've not missed you already, but that being here, wanting so much to share Switzerland with you, perhaps seeing my cousin about to be married, has made the missing keener, more focused. I feel as if I were being tempered. It hurts, but it's a good hurt.

If I am being tempered, I'm afraid I'm molten right now; in fact, I'm weeping a little. It's OK darling, just let me be a woman for a moment. But Red, Red, so long...so interminably long. Partly perhaps because I lack and envy your assurance and calm; partly because it takes me a long time to know a person so deeply that whatever happens, I feel one with him. And our time together wasn't that long, my dear. I agree with you about doing and being apart sometimes, but first we need a long, long time together to learn each other.

You are not to be distressed or anxious about what I've written. If I hadn't great sureness of you, I'd not try so much to explain. None of this means that I love you less or trust the future less. It's perhaps like your saying that it hurts to love me. I hurt too now, but when I come over the hurt, I'll be closer to you than before.

October 15, 1946 ~ Red in Warsaw to Madeleine in Toulouse

I have much need for you today and tonight. I have not sufficiently overcome the effects of the team leaders' meeting to be really at ease, and now more than usual I wish you were here. If the proposals are accepted by the teams, I shall be coming to Warsaw within the next three weeks to take over Al Johnson's job with the idea that Peter Brock and I will become the heads of the Mission when Philip Zealey leaves. Darling, I don't know what to say. Tonight I feel rather small. I wonder what the transport team will say? Ordinarily this would be a time when congratulations are extended, but I would feel awfully foolish if anyone did so to me.

Before I left Paris, I was beginning to have a great deal of admiration for Philip Zealey. Since arriving here, I have looked with awe at the way he seems to know Poland and the Polish people. All of us have

known what a loss it would be to the Polish Mission when he left, just as
it was a blow when Bill Edgerton left. Now I shall be working with Philip
for three months before he leaves. That part I shall like very much, but I
am shaking in my boots at the thought of what it will be like when he is
no longer here.

It has been decided that the supply man should be in Gdynia,
so Johnson moves there, taking with him most of the supply headaches. That leaves me with the finances and working as Philip's second on administrative problems. Team supplies will most likely be for
me to do also.

Madeleine, what are you doing now? How was Switzerland? I
am anxious to hear from you and know that you had a wonderful vacation. You needed it after all the problems of a delegation.

Say, my Chicadillee, you certainly hit me between the eyes! I
gasped when you said it was your birthday, and then you came right back
and called me a dope for just what I was thinking! You are a wonderful girl
and I wish that I could kiss you. So consider yourself kissed and hugged
until you say it hurts, all for your birthday.

October 16, 1946 ~ Madeleine in Paris to Red in Warsaw

We had spring together in Paris; now I've come back in the
fall. You're all along the quays and at Notre Dame and the rue de Varennes.
Paris is still Paris, my Red, but you're sorely missed.

Strange, coming back here is like coming home. The names of
the streets, even the Metro stops, are full of charm and remembrance. It's
clear autumn weather, and the trees that were budding when we came are
yellowing now. Oh, I am so sentimental! So would you be, perhaps; to be
here alone is half sweet, half sad.

All of the offices are housed now at 17 Notre Dame des
Champs, and some fellows live there as well, I think. The cooking's
improved, the offices have been painted, and the group has more of a
family delegation feeling about it than before. ETU has a new garage
which I hope to see tomorrow and a Villa des Roses! Oh for the good old
days at rue de Civry!

I saw *The Taming of the Shrew* in French, done with spirit and
gaiety and color, and had a checkup at the American Hospital in Paris and
am completely OK.

I got back to find your long letter from Warsaw. There's not time now to say more than that it was wonderful, that I've asked to be considered for the new team they hope to form in Poland, that I like the idea of a honeymoon in Europe, that the idea of being engaged seems very strange to me, and that I love thee. Red, my dear, if all this doesn't go together to make much sense, bear with me. This is not the time or place to reflect on sentiment, it seems; during my holiday because life was more leisurely, I had time to miss you and think about our being together. Now that I'm back here, with the program threatening to fall about our ears— we've lost most of our IGC funds—it's difficult to look ahead.

October 18, 1946 ~ Red in Gora Pulawska to Madeleine in Toulouse

This past week, I visited a lady whose husband was taken to Russia about two years ago. Wojtek and I went to see her late one afternoon. It was a most remarkable visit. The young daughter is as pretty as she can be and well mannered; she misses her father and enjoyed our attention, and we had a marvelous time. The mother invited me to come back. I promised to make some inquiries for her in Warsaw, so I went to see her again Tuesday evening. Her brother was there, and we had a delightful time trying to convey ideas to each other in Polish. Unfortunately, neither of them could use a dictionary very easily, but we managed. It was my first evening speaking nothing but Polish. Now don't get the idea that I can understand or speak it! I can understand a little more Polish than I could French when I left France, but I cannot speak it as well as French.

Everything was OK until they began to make fun of the Jews. At first, I laughed with them, until I found out what they were saying. I am afraid I changed my attitude too quickly. I was sorry that I could not say more; at least I am sure that they know that I do not approve of making fun of Jews.

October 24, 1946 ~ Red in Gora Pulawska to Madeleine in Toulouse

Philip is here and met with us last night after a long session with the Kozienice team the night before. He leaves and will be taking this letter in a few minutes, so I'll be brief. The present changes in personnel are these: Al Johnson will go to Gdynia within ten days and I shall go to Warsaw within a week. Leslie Harris is to become the co-leader here with Van Cleve. There is some talk of Henry Dasenbrock going to Kozienice in place of Davis, who is on his way from England. Lou Taylor has arrived and gone to Olstyn. One of my first trips out of Warsaw should be to Olstyn. I am looking forward to that trip to meet the members of that team.

So far I have not heard from you since you left for Switzerland. In fact, I am not even sure that you went, but I do hope that you did and had a wonderful vacation.

There is much I would like to tell you about my feelings on accepting greater responsibilities, but there isn't time before Philip leaves. Naturally, there are doubts

VAN CLEVE GEIGER FROM OUR TRANSPORT TEAM AND POLISH CHILDREN. OUR TRUCKS WERE OFTEN USED BY VILLAGERS AS BUSES FOR LOCAL TRANSPORTATION.   -PHOTOGRAPH COURTESY OF AFSC

in the minds of those who know me well about the feasibility of my going to Warsaw. Everyone, however, including me, is fairly satisfied with the changes.

October 26, 1946 ~ Madeleine in Toulouse to Red in Gora Pulawska

The silver lining has appeared. For the first time in months, we're overwhelmed with good news! Hugh and I have found a house: it's a château, twelve kilometers out in the country, beautiful site, great trees all about, twelve large, bright rooms half-furnished (which is good because in a fully furnished French house you can't stir), central heating, and running hot and cold water. You were in France long enough, n'est-ce pas, to know what a remarkable combination that is!

Next, we think we can rent a piano for our center, which will enliven evenings for many refugees and French people. I'm going to teach carols to my English class who now give forth lustily with "Three Blind Mice" and "There is a Tavern in the Town." I love 'em! The class is the highlight of the week, and I only wish I had twice as much time to give. They have such enthusiasm, and all of them, even the dignified Spaniards and pedantic students, let down and give out with "Y-Y-Yippee" in "She'll be Comin' Round the Mountain."

And last, but very much first with me, your appointment as head of mission in Poland. I can understand your feelings, dear, but for my part, I feel confidence and deep pride and a quiet assurance that you'll do well. It's a hard assignment but all the more a challenge. I'm sure you have good people to work with you, and I'm glad of the months you'll have with Philip. More and more I'm coming to admire the English way of working together. American administration in France has been and continues to be pretty much from the top down. I hope you can change that tradition, Red. I should think that our learning to work with each other would be one of the greatest accomplishments and values of the European experience.

October 26, 1946 ~ Red in Gora Pulawska to Madeleine in Toulouse

Although this was put in the typewriter on Saturday, it is now Sunday afternoon. Instead of writing you last night, I played bridge for over three hours. It was one of the most interesting evenings of bridge we have had. John Robbins and I played Wojtek and Arthur Robinson.

Since it has been definitely decided that I go to Warsaw, I feel much better. Philip has mentioned a couple of times that he was anxious to work with me and has expressed confidence in me. This helps very much. This morning Ralph, Arthur, and I, with the help of some of the little boys around here, put all of our potatoes into the underground room that has just been completed. Yesterday Ralph bought some cabbages, and next week he hopes to get some carrots and beets. We have several cases of canned milk which we expect to put in there to keep them from freezing. You should see our house; it is large enough for me to stand upright, however the door is too small for me to go in and out with a load.

Al Malakoff is a valuable addition to the team. He spent thirty-nine months in prison as a conscientious objector and has now come to

Poland. His father came from what is now Russia, so he knows something of the life of Poland. Also, he visited Poland as a child. Too bad he does not speak the language; nevertheless, he has studied quite a bit and will be able to pick it up fairly rapidly. Al has a great deal of enthusiasm for doing odd jobs around the barrack and making suggestions. I do not mean obnoxious things; rather, he has more ability to see what is lacking. Al will be better able to see the relationships between members in the group and how we are operating as a team. Already I am becoming more sensitive to the way we are living. We are becoming callous to the condition of the people here, and yet if you do not acquire some objectivity, you become overwhelmed by the enormous problems. Still, I think we are losing some of the warmth we would like to show to these people. How do you do that and still do the job we came here to do?

Is there fall in southern France? Do the trees turn beautiful bright yellow and red? It is strange how I think of you each time I see a beautiful scene. The area around the camp has been wonderful, the trees losing their leaves and the ground getting a beautiful mat of yellow. Nearly every day there are two or three people around, raking them and packing them off on their backs. The leaves are used for fuel as well as for insulating the homes.

October 31, 1946 ~ Madeleine in Toulouse to Red in Warsaw

At this moment we find ourselves with no house and no prospect of one; all previous prospects fell through, and colossal hotel bills await us in the Victoria across the street from the office. Having moved, with no place to move to, we have stored most of our earthly possessions in a tiny room frequented by rats. In the Siege office, fourteen feet square, there are at the moment most of the appurtenances of our housekeeping: clothing, odd dishes, a bedraggled plant, several thermoses, a radio, odd automobile parts, a bread basket, two electric heaters, and leftovers from breakfast.

In and among these we try to work, but the telephone is getting tangled up with coat hangers, the typewriter is buried under records, and we keep losing correspondence in our clothes. Oh for a house!

Two days later. You can consider the above blurb a stream-of-consciousness effort. We are not so badly off, though things are in a bit of a mess. I feel like a heel for complaining when you write about people living in the ground all winter. On the other hand, when I reflect that our predicament is caused by muddle-headedness and lack of a realistic approach to the housing problem of Toulouse in this year of grace, I get mad all over again. We have bare, small, clean rooms in a hotel; occasionally there is hot water. But no place to meet together except the office, which means we eat, wash, write, read, cook, and work in the same place. This is OK for a little while, but certainly wearing on everyone's tempers (including our amiable German cook who is trying to get dinner with my washing dripping on her). If it were an emergency situation I shouldn't mind, but it's sheer dithering, if you ask me. (Ask Hugh also; he's eloquent on the subject.)

November 2, 1946 ~ Madeleine in Toulouse to Red in Warsaw

Today is the Day of the Dead and yesterday was All Saints—both important feast days here. The streets are full of flower vendors, and everyone is carrying chrysanthemums to the cemeteries. Yesterday after Mass, families paraded in the streets as we do at Easter time, all dressed in their best. It was pure pleasure to walk down the street, too, watching them. People look much better dressed than when we came to France; most of them have a warm coat or jacket, a pair of fairly good shoes, and an air of elegance about them. I know very well that for many people their Sunday outfit is the only decent one they own, and that it has been concocted with infinite pains out of secondhand clothes, castoffs, and hand-me-downs. The children especially look darling in little coats and hoods made from old fur coats and capes. The women manage to be very smart with very little; lots of them were wearing lovely sheer silk stockings, but you know that they probably can afford only one pair and have saved a long time for that pair. Whatever lies behind it, it means that people have some spirit and energy. Appearances are not everything, but they count for a lot, especially in a country that has been as low as France.

But now, seeing things looking a little better, I begin to wonder what it is that people need after they have enough food and clothing. I think that, with good management (which is something that France will probably never have), the French can get along from now on. But for all that, France is still a terribly needy country from the point of view of moral responsibility, cooperation, and self-respect. I wonder how it is that one helps a whole nation gain such attitudes.

France is very sick, and the physical recovery that is beginning to show only accentuates the moral illness. Every week a new scandal appears in the newspapers: first it is wine, then meat, then bread. There is a big drive to end the black market; there are arrests and threats of death for those who violate the rationing system. But all this fire and fury dies out after two or three weeks to be replaced by a new stir. Many intelligent and concerned people cease to read the newspapers or to vote; they consider that every party is so corrupt and self-seeking that one can trust nothing, and it's better to keep out of the whole dirty mess. There is fear of Communism and active propaganda for it—though it is a strangely nationalistic, materialistic, bourgeois brand of Communism, I must say. The latest stunt is a big raffle sponsored by the Party, giving away seven-tube radio sets, furniture, and smart clothes! As I've said before, doing relief work in such a setup is more difficult in a way than in a physically devastated country; the problems are more intangible and more like those we left behind us, unsolved, in our own country.

I think often and often of the future, Red. I'm not sure, either, where we should try to take hold, but certain it is that there is much to do. Seeing so much of the "de" attitude in France—débrouiller or take care of yourself however you can and the devil take the hindmost—I'm more convinced than ever that the real and only strength of a country is a citizenry that will stick out its neck in defense of the rights of everyone. I don't mean a future filled with "doing good"—the more I see of social service work as it is done, the more I think it is a pitiful apology for the lamentable state of our institutions and our understanding—but a stand like Henry Wallace's, for example. There goes a man, and maybe he'll make more of a stir in the end than all the careful, successful men who never got thrown out on their ears! (I look for you to get thrown out of something, somewhere, before you're through, my dear.) Not that I hold with being difficult as a matter of principle, but most people who know what they believe in and do it, get into some sort of disrepute sooner or later!

Speaking of the future brings me round to your letter from Warsaw on October 6 about getting married. Shall I confess that on first reading you sounded very businesslike and efficient about the arrangements we might make and the things to think about? Now, reading it over again, I feel much more warmly your concern and affection. Darling, this is not to hurt you...only sometimes I forget that words aren't your forte (though they are much more than you know perhaps), and being terribly sensitive to words, I miss sometimes those I'd like to hear you say. My dear, you shine through your letters like sun, and sometimes I have tears in my eyes at your sincerity and love. When we're together at last, I pray we may find each other all we hope and believe in.

Though it is far in the future, I think more and more that being married in Europe would be a jolly good idea. Shall I be efficient and precise? 1. We would, as you say, have a get-acquainted time before returning to the States and facing up to all the problems of a home and a job that will be waiting for us there. Getting adjusted to each other, and to a new set of living conditions all at once might be quite a handful. 2. We could have a honeymoon in Europe, practically paid for, I should think, by our leave allowances. 3. Although I know my mother would like to have me married at home, I think, after having seen the elaborate, hectic, and utterly fatiguing preparations that most of my friends have undergone, that I'd much rather do it simply and out of range of showers, bridesmaids, and white satin gowns. 4. I'd like to be with you as soon as possible. 5. Your comments on all points, and any others, will be gratefully received and carefully considered!

Let me have a quiet chuckle over your request to say you're married! Tiens! You mean you can't fob off the women in any other way? Of course, say so if it helps; I know just the sort of situation you mean. Red, you know already, I expect, that both of us are attractive to the opposite sex. I've wondered if it would be a problem, for us and for other people, after we're married. I've thought much about what is usually called love; it's a composite of many things, and theoretically speaking, the basis of it is common interests, understanding and affection, and a kind of mystical need for unity and community with other souls.

This next is a piece of feminine inconsistency that will probably drive you bats, but I want to tell you anyway. It's this, about your saying that we should both be free to say we're engaged. Red, though I think with pleasure and impatience of the time when we shall be together, though it is as natural to think of being with you as it is to feel the sun or to fall asleep, I have not said, in so many words, to anyone that we're engaged. There's a curious hiatus in my feeling, perhaps because we were together so short a time. I don't feel engaged.

November 8. A hectic week has passed when I couldn't seem to be alone long enough to finish your letter. I am alone now for a little in the hotel room, writing you propped up in bed after a bath!

Perhaps what I'm trying to say is that I don't believe I am engaged. Having been once or twice before ready to marry, it's hard for me to realize that this time I've arrived at that point. I've decided against it so many times that it's hard to follow through on the results of saying yes. (By the way, did I ever say "Yes"? I don't think you ever asked me!) Not being together, we're missing—putting off, rather—the thrill and discovery and enchantment of the period of engagement. Red, the first time I was ever in love, I truly thought I knew what the phrase means: "a new heaven and a new earth." I had a clarity of vision, of hearing, of understanding, that made me think I was beholding a fresh creation. I look for that to come again with you, but it has not yet. If I knew you and myself better, it might come even when we're apart. You are nearer to that perhaps than I.

It's asking a very great deal of you to try to understand all this and still not trouble over it. For I don't want you to do that. There is, in me, I think, a large capacity for loving that's never been fully used. Some of it has perhaps been misspent, some has been dormant. But if you can help me to tap it and use it wisely, I think I may yet be something.

Another thing I'd like to tell you. One of the delegates in the south has proposed to me. He's been a good friend and a good companion, but for a number of reasons, not the least being you, I've said no, long ago and again now. He's going back home soon, and though I shall miss him, I'm glad he's leaving. It's difficult to be always with someone who is very fond of you even when you're quite sure of yourself. I think I'd rather be lonely and have you to think of. Perhaps I should not risk troubling you with this. I know what the outcome will be; I've not changed my mind. But I'd like you just to know, that's all.

November 2, 1946 ~ Red in Warsaw to Madeleine in Toulouse

From a single room in a hotel in Warsaw, my home. This is my first opportunity to be by myself in a long time, and it is good.

This is a big job for me and the living conditions are strange. Never before have I lived in a city; never before have I lived by myself. Only last night I met one other American who lives on the fourth floor of this hotel. Philip lives in another hotel. Sometimes the thought of my being here in such a strange city frightens me; when I think of Philip's leaving, I shake. I wonder how it will be when UNRRA moves out and we seldom see an Englishman or another American. Yet I know that I must put my faith in something greater than myself, greater even than the people with whom I work.

Never before have I had the opportunity of living with myself. So often there were others around, and I could exert myself so that my energies were in the main devoted to their problems. No, it is not my intention to brood over my own problems now, but to see if I can discipline myself. Is it possible to set aside time for studying Polish, for reading, and meditation? Can I train my mind to concentrate on one thing for a period of time rather than wandering off and then thinking of something that needs to be done and doing that instead of remaining with myself? Do you know how hard it is for a gregarious person to have to live alone? No, I am not complaining; I am rejoicing for the opportunity before you and I are together for keeps.

I am beginning to get excited about the prospects for new work in Poland. Philip has already been in Krakow and met with some students about food we are sending to Poland for university students. Now there is a request for an investigation of children's homes. It may be that we shall help with institutional care in Krakow. It's all up in the air; we just have to sit back and see how things develop.

Of course, one of the reasons why I am excited is that this would mean new personnel coming to Poland, either to fill the relief team if they take over the social work or actually to do the social work. If only you spoke Polish!

The more I am with Philip, the more I like him. Both of us like to linger over meals, and we also like to discuss problems from all angles. The relationship between Philip and me is much sounder than I have had with many people previously. What I mean is that often I hold such high regard for a person that I am next to idolizing him until we get to know each other very well. Philip and I work on a man-to-man basis, willing to give and take as necessary. He is quite anxious for me to take some of his load, and there is enough for three people.

Since coming to Poland, I have felt more strongly than ever the need for a religious experience as the motivation for service. For a long time, I felt that intellectual honesty, combined with a conscience, was all that was needed. It is more than that, unless the conscience incorporates something much deeper than intellect. Oh Madeleine, it is one of the many things I would like to talk over with you. I express myself so poorly. The situation here is tough. I need strength; so much strength is needed that I fail to feel it within myself. Yet I know that I am growing in understanding. Words fail me.

Please do not be disturbed. It is still Red searching for a way of life that is satisfying. Each time I climb higher, the better I can see the valley below, but the horizon broadens, and once again I find myself searching for something more. It is a time when I am glad that I have you, but oh, how I wish we could work on this together and grow together. Maybe we are doing this, more than we realize.

You know, I bet that when we meet again, it will take us several days before we can relax and really have some good talks. Oh, we shall talk about the trip, a few people, and interesting events, but it will take time to talk and feel free to ramble on and on with a few serious thoughts coming into play and stimulating more serious conversation.

November 3, 1946 ~ Madeleine in Toulouse to Red in Warsaw

I'm in bed with a cold which was presented me by the delegation on my return from Switzerland. Working 'til midnight encouraged it, so I'm going to nurse it this weekend. Nothing serious!

I'm sending a small Christmas package (how many shopping days?) just in case we don't get any closer by December. You will follow the usual rules about not opening until the 25th! But I'm hoping your new duties will call you urgently to Paris about that time or even to our château in Toulouse.

I have requested transfer to Poland if opportunity offers, otherwise to Germany, Austria, or Hungary. I have also agreed to stay on six months beyond my original year. There is a reasonable chance, I imagine, of some transfer coming through, but it will take time. I expect to be here for several more months.

Pity you can't come for Thanksgiving! Charlie Thum and I have planned a colossal menu, and the Americans are inviting the English to come see what Thanksgiving really is! At the same time, we'll warm our château, and the place is so huge and the floors so smooth that we'll probably have a dance as well. Now we have to send out the transport team to run over a turkey. Do come!

November 3, 1946 ~ Red in Warsaw to friends back home

I'm writing from room 101 at the Hotel Terminus, which I expect will be my home for many weeks. Three days ago I came to Warsaw to help Philip Zealey with the central administration of the Anglo-American Quaker Relief Mission, of which the transport team is a part.

First a bit about my room; this is the third best hotel in the city. As Bill Edgerton said when he lived here, "It rates third only because there are only three hotels left." My room is on the first floor (second floor to you) and next to the stairway, which makes it rather noisy, but I am seldom bothered by noise when I want to sleep. The window opens onto a court, and that is most interesting because of the people going and coming through it. The bed is a long way from being that innerspring bed that I used for several months in Florida; in fact, the mattress is made in three pieces, and you can easily feel the ridge between

WAR DAMAGE TO WARSAW. THE CITY WAS NINETY PERCENT DESTROYED. IN ALL OF POLAND, TWENTY-FIVE PERCENT OF THE POPULATION WERE MISSING OR DEAD. OF THE CHILDREN LEFT, TWENTY-FIVE PERCENT WERE ORPHANS. 700,000 FARMS WERE WITHOUT A COW; 65 PERCENT OF THE HORSES AND 80 PERCENT OF THE HOGS WERE GONE. THERE WERE FEW HORSES AND NO MACHINERY TO PLOW THE FIELDS. 1946

-PHOTOGRAPH BY RED

the sections. I prefer the English camp bed that I was using at Gora Pulawska. Fortunately, there are running water and electric lights. There is also a radiator in here; here's hoping they can get heat into it this winter.

Some of you may have been disappointed that I have made no comments on the political situation in Poland. That has been deliberate. It's not that I have lost interest or have not been trying to understand the intertwining of political thought here, but rather that I am connected to an organization that does its work purely on a nonpolitical basis and is able to do work here only because that is the policy we follow. We are free to write as individuals, but we must realize that we are in reality representing the Quakers; already by bitter experience we have learned how far an innocently told story can travel. So if you will be patient, I hope that I may have some evenings of discussions with you on my return to the States.

Friday was one of the largest holidays Poland has celebrated since I arrived; in fact, most businesses took three days off. It was All Saints' Day, and everyone made a visit to the cemetery or to a memorial in the city where a loved one died or was buried. One does not have to walk far here to find a cross or a plate enshrined where a Pole was mortally wounded.

Thursday night I spent in Philip's room, and as we were dressing the next morning, we saw one truck after another loaded with coffins come by. Since we had heard nothing of a recent riot, we wondered what they could be. Later we learned that one hundred bodies had been uncovered in the ruins of Warsaw recently and were being taken for burial that day. Last December, they estimated that 100,000 bodies were still buried underneath the ruins of Warsaw. Have you read General Bor's account of the Warsaw Insurrection? It is certainly a vivid account of the life during those sixty-three hellish days; his pictures of it are no more horrible than the stories we have heard here. It is hard for us to realize the part the women played in the underground in Poland. In fact, women have fought alongside the men before in the history of Poland, so it was only natural that they should be active here when the fighting was being done in their own streets and homes.

Today was the first real snow this winter for Warsaw. It is beautiful and yet tragic, as many have no means of heating their small rooms, and it is a pitiful few who have more than a room for their family in Warsaw today. There has been very little heat in this room today, but I have a hot plate on which I make coffee, and that has been enough to make it comfortable.

Those of you who know anything about transport and its problems will have some sympathy for our condition this past week, when eight of nineteen vehicles which we have in Poland were out of order, and the Warsaw jeep was not capable of leaving the city. So far we have received no parts from Paris since the seven trucks left there last

July; neither have parts for the English and Canadian Fords arrived from England.

In France we were able to get the army to help out in emergencies, but there are just no parts to be had here. We have broken several springs, and these have been replaced by ones made in blacksmith shops; you can imagine how long they will last in a five-ton truck. There must not be a spare jeep part in all of Europe, and yet we must keep these trucks rolling if our program continues. Tires are another question; the truck from Paris came by boat and brought five extra tires with it. Two weeks ago another truck left Gora Pulawska for a 185-mile round trip run and in the two days that it took, we had eighteen flat tires, including two blowouts and one tire that was ruined because the driver did not know that he had a flat.

Yes, you guessed it, transport supply is one of the jobs allocated to me; it may take many weeks or several months to get supplies, but I intend to have some parts if we have to buy extra trucks to obtain them. It is impossible to carry on the work we do without vehicles.

November 10, 1946 ~ Red in Warsaw to Madeleine in Toulouse

Tonight I feel very close and near to you, and yet there is no hurting inside because you are not with me and I am not in France. Your last letter written in Switzerland was the best yet. No, I do not mind your tears, neither do I mind your dreaming. There are two reasons. First, remember The Prophet when he said, "The deeper that sorrow carves into your being, the more joy you can contain"? So it is with your tears. I know that there is much happiness within you to compensate for those lonely moments. Remember that today is the present, and the present is what is real. Enjoy it and cherish it because that is something you can never regain. Second, your dreams: yes, dear one, dream, because your soul is part of you and it needs nourishment just as your body does. Dream, and may I be included in your dreams!

Steve and Irwin arrived with about three packages from you. Now I will have less time to read, but you can be assured that someone will be happy to have the books. Above all, I cherish most the note you enclosed in Lin Yutang's book. Already I have read the first chapter and hope to read some from it each week. "For Red, in anticipation of all we

shall learn about it together." We have learned much already; life is fuller
and has more meaning each day.

Oh, how I wish you knew what four months in Poland has
done for me. Maybe you can tell by the letters. I know from yours that
you have grown in strength and understanding. Your scope is broader and
your vision is greater.

November 15, 1946 ~ Madeleine in Toulouse to Red in Poland

This must be the relief work they talked about: candlelight in
an unheated hotel room and no house in prospect. It's funny at times,
infuriating at others. The city of Toulouse is saving electricity and capri-
ciously cuts the current by day or by night. After trying to write a monthly
report by an oil lamp I share with Hugh, I decided I'd rather ruin my eyes
on Red!

Darling, what's happened to the postal system? No letter for
nigh on three weeks. The longer I wait, the more sure I feel about you,
deep down, but each day clouds over a little when there's no long brown
envelope from Poland.

I'm bursting with excitement and want to tell you so much.
Hugh came back from Paris yesterday saying that by a great stroke of luck
there were three openings for Americans in FRS teams in the British zone
of Germany. I may go in six weeks! Red, I said yes at once. It means no
Poland, but that was a faint hope. I know some German, I've always wanted
to go east, I'll have some direct field experience, and I'll work with a
British team, which from my experience represents tops in democracy
and team work. I'm terribly pleased. Can you be happy for me as well?

My first enthusiasm is sobered by the fact that Germany in
winter may be a difficult place to be. Even with only autumn weather,
cold becomes a vital enemy, a real presence. And we are well fed and
clothed and in good health. For others, what can it be? Often and often I
remember Bill Edgerton's words about the thinly dressed Polish children
and his own warm boots. Life and the good things of life seem very simple
here: hot soup, a fire, a candle, warm stockings, a glass of cognac to cheer
you up, a tight tin to keep out mice. Whatever privations (that's too strong
a word) we have are merely annoyances; they can illustrate other people's
difficulties, but we can't really say we share them. I can be irritated at the

perpetual clutter of our office, where clothes, books, food, and auto parts are heaped together for lack of space, but what of refugees who've lived for years in one small room?

Oh Red, I want to talk, to match your experiences with mine, to find out with you what it means. If my going to Germany means that we don't see each other before our service is over, we shall just have to steel ourselves to it. I feel more up to facing that than I did a month ago. But how I hope for a meeting!

November 22, 1946 ~ Red in Warsaw to Madeleine in Toulouse

If you only knew how many letters I have composed to you while I have walked around the streets of Warsaw, you would be overwhelmed. It is most frustrating not to have the time to express myself as I would like at a time when I feel a more personal contact between us would be so helpful.

When you see Steve Cary, he may tell you how tired I look. Please do not be disturbed. I have had more difficulty in adjusting to this work than any job I have ever tackled. That is as it should be; never before has a change been so great. It is now well after eleven; we have just finished our last long confab with the visiting firemen, Cary and Abrams. Tonight I received a telegram saying that Lou Taylor would be here in the morning looking for some spare parts, which means that he will arrive here about 6:30 a.m. Oh what ungodly hours! Every night this week has been filled, and so are the next two. Already my hair is so long that I shall soon need curlers to put in it at night. Each day I promise myself a haircut, but too many things arise, and it is put off until the next day.

Your telling me of someone proposing to you made me not jealous of him but envious of you. There is always the risk that a relationship like that could cause a breach in ours, yet I am willing to take that risk. Yes, both of us will continue having close friends of the opposite sex. That "charm" will not disappear because there is a marriage license. The main thing is for each of us to recognize it and appreciate it; never will I be able to meet all of your needs for communion with other souls. In fact, I would be disappointed in you if your capacity were that small.

Your comments on the demoralization of the French intrigue me; I have been trying to grasp how far the Nazi occupation went in destroying the morale and morals of the various countries. Their techniques in Poland were interesting: very little food, but much vodka at low prices.

There go the lights again!

November 28, 1946 ~ Madeleine in Toulouse to Red in Warsaw

Happy Thanksgiving, and do you like chestnut, sausage, or bread dressing in your turkey? The whole Refugee Program, nineteen of us, had ours on Sunday, with all the trimmings. I personally cut the heads off the two turkeys (they were already dead), cleaned and stuffed them. Then we formed a procession to take them to the baker, along with two mince pies that Connie whisked together. In view of the coal shortage, we cooked the birds with forty cigarettes.

That is to say, we paid the baker the cigarettes in return for his roasting the birds in his ovens, which were already hot. It was quite a sight, our riding in an open jeep through the streets, cradling the turkeys, and then returning for them several hours later. They were beautifully, though unconventionally, done. There was even cranberry sauce, from Charlie Thum's personal package.

We had few flowers to decorate the table, but Dick Sherrington, who is an artist, ransacked our stores for bright packages of American foods, and from them constructed a colorful centerpiece. And we made a Christmas pudding which everyone stirred and dropped something into and wished over. You may guess what I wished, but it's against the rules to tell, and I want very much for it to come true.

Oh Red, if we could have Christmas together! Thank you for the hope of the spring, though; I shall wait for the new life that's spring and the new life that's you with equal eagerness.

A small scold: how are you going to have anything to open on Christmas Eve if you've opened all your packages already? Or didn't you get the letter telling you to wait until after Steve had arrived with your gifts? The package had silly things in it, just to make something to open, and why did you think they were tied with red and green ribbons? Never mind, if you're pleased with them now, I don't care. But I do wish for a real Christmas with a tree and candles and our friends with us and carols and cake. We shall probably go to Perpignan, all of us, and spend Christmas together. If you could come down to Paris, I could certainly go up, or whatever the direction is. I don't mean to sound like a spoiled kid. You know well that if we are not together, I shall have a good Christmas, think warmly of you, and think of the next one. If we were together—I can't say it—I think I should be beside myself with happiness.

November 28, 1946 ~ Red in Warsaw to Madeleine in Toulouse

Hurrah! There are the lights again! They went off shortly after I came in to work this afternoon, and since then my eyes have begun to burn under the strain. I shall have to take it easier in poor light.

Of course I am happy that you are going to Germany. The main thing for me, darling, is that you are happy. The chances of your going to Poland become slimmer all the time.

May I ask you to read again Bill Edgerton's report on Poland (I've enclosed it here). He suggested that relief workers going into Germany live in an occupied country first. Yes, I know that you have been in France, but what happened there is nothing compared to what happened here. First, there were so many people in France cooperating with the Germans that the French themselves were often the ones to do the dirty work. Second, the Germans always regarded the French as having a higher culture than the Poles. And last, the Germans did not get to southern France until the latter stages of the war.

Maybe I should compile some stories for you, yet I wonder whether it is worth the trouble. They

REMAINS OF A CHURCH IN WARSAW. 1946
-PHOTOGRAPH BY RED

are too hard to believe. Men tell me stories and say that they can hardly expect me to believe them. Stories of Germans dancing in the streets and taking pot shots at civilians; throwing children onto trucks like so many sacks of potatoes; tying women in front of their tanks; tying women to ladders and pushing the ladders and women across a street to make a barricade. I do not say these things because I want to have bitterness and hatred spread more widely than it is already, but because Germans have a great deal of self-pity. Unfortunately they have no idea of what has gone on in their name. If they have heard of it, they will not believe. Maybe some of the stories are exaggerated, but there must be some foundation to have so many respectable people tell you such similar stories.

I know that each of us is to be blamed for what has happened to humanity. We are to be blamed for what is happening in Germany now. But the bitterness and hatred will remain here until Germans are willing to acknowledge their guilt and take positive steps to make things right with the people they oppressed.

To me, it will be interesting to exchange experiences with you even if it will be by correspondence. Together we should be able to help each other to broaden our views and scope in regard to the mixed emotions in Europe. Maybe you will be working with Poles in Germany; many are still there. If so, the experiences will be even more interesting.

Now the government is encouraging people here to write to those who have refused to come back. Mail can pass freely from here to Poles in the camps in Germany. This effort is being sponsored by UNRRA; conditions here are not as bad as they are made out to be to people in the camps. If accurate statements can be sent back to them by people who have already been repatriated, maybe more people will volunteer to return.

Madeleine, you speak of your life there, comparing it with how the refugees live. Now compare the occupying armies and their life to that of the German people. Did you know that the English relief teams work as part of the army—at least they did. I am not trying to frighten you away from Germany but rather trying to point up something that you might have to face. I find it difficult to do, that is, to be in a position of living so much better than the people we are trying to help. Philip says that in the British zone "everything is laid on." If you go in under the auspices of the British army, you will have the opportunity of obtaining those same privileges.

Here is Bill's report:

April 24, 1946 ~ William Edgerton in Warsaw to AFSC

(William Edgerton was the AFSC representative in Poland)

I told Philip Zealey (FRS) the other day that I wished all Friends workers destined for work with the German population could first have a period of work in Poland, and he said almost that very thing had been considered by FRS but rejected because of the practical difficulties involved. The proposal had been that no FRS member should work in Germany without having first worked in a country formerly occupied by Germany. As Germany's principal national victim, Poland would be the most suitable country for such experience, because it would bring Friends up against the very grim realities that the German people themselves must face honestly if there is ever to be any kind of reconciliation between them and the rest of Europe.

Most of the Germans are not facing all that. My impression is that the great majority of them are sinking deeper and deeper into a slough of self-pity, almost totally oblivious of Germany's legacy of destruction and suffering inflicted upon the rest of Europe, and each of them is frantically intent on convincing himself and everybody else that he personally had nothing to do with the whole thing.

I have extremely grave misgivings about any relief program for Germans carried out by Quakers fresh from the States, or even by Quakers fresh from Britain, to whom the war came much closer to home than it did to us.

I know what will happen. American Friends will probably first land in France, where they will be impressed more by the present moral, economic, and political confusion of French society and by the Frenchmen's hatred for the Germans than by any evidence they can see of what the Germans actually did in France. Then they will proceed to Germany, where they will be appalled by the sight of most of the German cities in ruins.

And they will find as they expected to find, being men of good will, that most Germans are friendly, pleasant, and of course quite human. Having seen destruction and suffering in Germany beyond anything they were prepared for, and not having seen with their own eyes the almost incomparably greater suffering and destruction in Poland, they will be filled with pity for all the Germans. Their pity will be reinforced by the conduct and attitudes of some of the occupation troops. This one-sided pity will correspond exactly to the one-sided pity the Germans already have for themselves, and therein lies the grave danger that Friends will do more harm than good.

The Germans have created against themselves a hatred in Europe that I believe is completely beyond any hope of ever dying down by itself. It will be passed on from generation to generation as long as there are Germans to be hated and other Europeans to do the hating. The only possible hope of reconciliation that I can see is through a movement of national repentance starting within Germany itself. If we Friends try to help bring about this reconciliation by applying Quaker sweetness and light to the countries that do the hating, there will be more need of reconciliation when we have finished than before we started. And if in our sympathy with the Germans, we in any way block the difficult road that would lead them to repentance and to facing their moral responsibility, we shall fail at the very point where the Germans need help most and where we, of all groups, might do our most effective work.

I have been interested to see the effect that just a suggestion of German repentance could have on the Poles. I have become acquainted with a Polish woman who was in Oswiecim Concentration Camp (Auschwitz) for a year and a half. Her husband, an intellectual, was sent there, too, and the only time she was allowed to see him during the whole period was on the day of his death, when the Germans took her out to watch him being killed. I think she is probably the most violent hater of Germans that I have met. And yet one day, after she had told me some more things the Germans had done here, I said to her: "Suppose a few Germans should feel repentant about what Germany has done and should ask to come to Poland and help voluntarily in the rebuilding of what their nation had destroyed. What do you think the attitude of the Poles would be?" That idea jolted her. For a few moments it seemed to clear the air of her hatred, and she became calm and thoughtful. The effect of it was remarkable.

November 30, 1946 ~ Madeleine in Toulouse to Red in Warsaw.

Beth Clarkson arrived in Toulouse this morning, invited down by Hugh and Juanita Jenkins to speak at our community centers in the south. I restrained myself from personal questions for as long as I could—a few minutes—and then asked how you were. It was very good, darling, to talk with someone who had so lately seen you and to have her say that you really are well. She told me, too, how sure she was you'd do a fine job in Warsaw, and in her unexaggerated English way she added, "You have good taste, if I may say so," which warmed the cockles of my heart. This evening, while I was stirring chocolate pudding for our dinner, she recalled that you had wondered how we'd ever arrange a kitchen for the two of us, a wonder which had not disturbed my somewhat impractical mind but which quite charmed me.

It made you seem so close, but the closeness made me miss you more. For so long Warsaw has seemed as far away as the moon, and I simply accepted the distance. Seeing someone from there makes it seem nearer and that makes the separation sharper.

A few days ago five letters came from you, and as always I felt overwhelmed by my sudden riches. I thrilled over your words on living alone. It will be hard, my love, terribly hard sometimes. But I'm glad you're glad for the chance. It's something that's been in my thoughts for years, but I've never really got down to doing it, living alone, purposefully and strongly.

I wonder if you know the constant sort of quandary I find myself in: that of wishing to see people happy and doing small things to give them pleasure, and at the same time almost hating them for eating up my time and spirit with little unimportances and hating myself for giving in so easily? I don't dislike people, as you know, Red, but I have a deep feeling that one does not do her best for other people or for herself by letting herself be frittered away in small services. I don't mean small in the sense of importance or prestige, but in the sense of essential-ness.

MADELEINE WITH A SPANISH CHILD IN TOULOUSE.
1946   -PHOTOGRAPHER UNKNOWN

More and more I'm coming to think that the most tremendous thing one person can do for another is to be herself or himself, with courage, conviction, and honesty. And yet that being oneself is the hardest job anyone can undertake and one that I most usually shirk by doing some-thing instead of "remaining with myself," as you say.

You will probably know by now that Poland is out for me, at least for six months or more. But I don't see why we shouldn't count heavily on a spring vacation together. I shall have another two weeks due me then, and you'll have four. Switzerland should be surpassingly beauti-ful in the spring! Here I am beginning to appreciate what winter means, and has always meant, for millions of people: a stilling of activity, a constant battle against cold and darkness and dullness, an almost animal hibernation, and a looking toward the rebirth of nature. The hope of being together makes the promise of spring seem doubly wonderful: the fresh new world, which has always been an almost delirious delight to me, and the new life of our affections when we can know each other more closely and perfectly.

Supplies have been turned over to me. It is a diminishing job, since most of our training courses are now set up; it consists mostly of heckling London and Philadelphia for what they promised us months ago. In addition I am responsible for the allocation of secretarial help, which I foresee will be a grade-A headache but certainly useful personal experience. I have rashly taken on another English class, German lessons in French, and the writing of Christmas cards to friends. In my spare time I chase rats and mice out of the office and store room.

Another bit I've wanted to share with you: the organization of our monthly meeting, which has brought democracy, sweetness, and light to the southern delegations. I mean that quite literally. The program had been a hierarchy run from Paris before Hugh came down here, with all the internal dissension and resentments which that sort of organization brings. Now, once a month, the head of each delegation, and another member selected by the delegation, meet with Hugh and me. We usually alternate delegations as the place for the meeting, and often everybody gets together the day before, as we did for our Thanksgiving dinner.

The meeting is always held on a Monday to give us a chance to meet for the weekend if we wish. All matters of policy within and between the delegations are discussed, ideas and suggestions are exchanged, and if there is business to be brought up before the Home Committees, recommendations are made. Minutes are made of all decisions, written and approved during the meetings, and these minutes are for us the Law and the Prophets. If we find that we have drawn up a minute that later doesn't fit the situation, we amend it, but we don't just allow the matter to drop.

It may sound like a fussy procedure; I thought so at first. But it has proved extremely valuable. There are too many possibilities for misunderstanding and misinterpretation, even with the best of intentions, to let important agreements be made verbally.

Sometimes in the evening I dream: of a fireside, some comfortable chairs, books, and time for the two of us to talk as long and reflectively as we wish. I hope my life will never be cluttered with elaborate desires; I think not, after this experience. I've never realized so keenly how much of people's strength and stability comes from their family, civic, and social ties. I've never realized either how simple the appurtenances of those ties can be. A home doesn't need the apparently fantastic furnishing I see, unbelieving, in the American magazines we get here. It does need calm and privacy and cleanliness (i.e., no rats) and friends and much love.

December 16, 1946 ~ Madeleine in Toulouse to Red in Warsaw

I had a date with you last night, an evening I had jealously set aside to visit with you, in front of a log fire. I was almost cross when two guests came for dinner, though it was fun having them in our new house. Will you come for tea next Sunday? It's little, queerly arranged, and dark; all the same, paint and scrubbing and bright curtains have transformed it already, and at least we are chez nous. I hope I never have to clean out a muckier place. Sometimes when I was grubbing away, I wished I were doing it to make a place for us. Some day we will, Red.

My bedroom is tiny but has a fireplace, which is my idea of complete luxury. Most of the rooms have fireplaces, actually, but they're more picturesque than practical, I'm finding. My dear, if we're cold here, with no snow yet, what must it be in Warsaw? Never, in all the northern winters I've known, have I felt so chilled. It's cold in bed, cold out of it, cold in the office, and cold in the street. Cafés and cinemas are warm and some people's houses. But I've never realized that cold could be so pervasive and so important. Washing is an heroic operation; the first job is always to see how much wood there is. (I learned to split some yesterday under Hugh's tutelage.) All one's work is slowed down and one's thoughts occupied by the temperature. Perhaps after a while one gets used to it! Madeleine Chevalier, Connie, and I are seriously considering a three-person bed, since we haven't the benefit of husbands to keep us warm!

This is not supposed to be a gripe, more an astonishment. I begin to realize dimly what Europe suffered during the war and suffers still from lack of fuel. It's as bad as lack of food, and if you haven't enough heat, you need more to eat. I've never been healthier, and I have all the clothes I can stuff myself into—stadium boots from my family, for example, which are remarked on in the street whenever I go out in them. I feel uncomfortable about being seen in them here.

This is a brilliantly bright day. I went out this morning to get films for the children's Christmas party and bought a great armload of the glossiest holly, and a graceful sprig of mistletoe, which grows in abundance around here. Our house looks most welcoming, with holly in vases and the mimosa which a dear German refugee woman gave us as a welcome to the house. Juanita is a genius at making a place look homelike; all of us have brought out our books and pictures and bric-a-brac. In spite of the cold and no maid, it's far better than the hotel.

Three boxes of Christmas presents have already arrived from America, everything from tinsel to a filmy nightgown, fudge, and bedsocks.

Wish you were going to open some of the gay packages with me. You know I'll be thinking especially of you on the 25th. Our next Christmas we should be together!

December 22, 1946 ~ Red in Warsaw to Madeleine in Toulouse

What is the latest on your going to Germany? I have heard nothing since the first mention you made about accepting the invitation, and that you might be going in six weeks.

Last night I was talking to Ted and Ken about Germany. Ted's fiancée is working there. Evidently some of them are pretty unhappy about the conditions under which they are working. Each member becomes part of the British Army machinery. Everything is done through the army, even to schedules of leaves and vacations. FRS members have the opportunity to have all their household duties taken care of by Germans. They can live in nice homes or apartments; transport is by the British Army. In other words, the relief worker has to struggle not to live a life of luxury. This means, of course, that they are unable to make themselves part of the German community. There have been some strong feelings expressed in London about the situation in Germany. Philip said that liquor flows like water, and there has been some difficulty among the FRS workers on that score. I would not care to be quoted on any of this, as I have received it through people who themselves are not familiar with the situation except through other people. Nevertheless, I did want to let you know what I have been told. You might make some investigations for yourself or at least become familiar with what to expect in Germany.

I do hope that you will be able to work there; it would balance our experiences to some extent. Here all I get is a very anti-German sentiment, and quite naturally so. In fact, I would like to work in Germany awhile after leaving here. Another year might leave an impression on me about Germans that would be hard to overcome except through personal contact with them. No, I am not becoming anti-German, but it is often hard to understand how humans were able to inflict such punishment on a people as was inflicted on the Poles. It must be a place where a person renders all to the state. I have recently purchased a book called German Crimes in Poland. It is illustrated with pictures, drawings, and plans of the camps. I am hoping that I can finish it before Henry leaves for Paris, since I would like you to see it. Oh yes, it is emotional and biased, but it gives data that is graphic without comment. Imagine a country with a population of 35 million reduced to

BUNKER IN THE VILLAGE OF LUCIMA. AFTER THE WAR FAMILIES RETURNED TO LIVE IN THESE BUNKERS UNTIL BUILDING MATERIALS COULD BE HAULED TO THEM.
-PHOTOGRAPH BY DICKIE AND TONY CHAPELLE

24 million in six years! Less than 69 percent of the original population left. One man said that an average of sixty Germans were killed in Warsaw every day during that six years. This figure seems pretty high but indicates how the Poles resisted and how often reprisals were executed.

December 22, 1946 ~ Red in Warsaw to friends at home

A belated season's greetings to you! We understand that a Polish Christmas is something worth experiencing, and I have been honored with an invitation to spend Christmas in a Polish home in Gdynia. Wojtek, the young man who serves as interpreter for the transport team, will meet me in Warsaw tomorrow, and we shall take the night train to Gdynia. Today I was surprised to see in a Catholic country most of the stores open on Sunday afternoon; it was like most any night prior to Christmas in most any American city: many people milling about, bright lights on in the windows, and what colorful windows! The Poles know how to make a thing attractive with only a little paper and a small amount of color.

There was little evidence of buying. Although the shops are only one-room affairs built on the ground floor, they are not crowded. Newspapers have said that the toys are too expensive for the children and that most of them will have to just look at them in the windows and know that toys do exist. Yet what toys! I have seen one electric train ...a very small one. Most of the toys are made from paper, cloth, and wood. I would say that the prices run from seven to ten times what they would in America; hence, the toys are very poor quality in order to have them low in price. Even so, I saw dolls marked at 500 zl which would sell for 25 cents to 40 cents at home. Cheap 10-cent and 15-cent toys sell for 70 to 125 zl each.

Yesterday I read where the government claims that no child in Poland would be forgotten this Christmas; just what they plan to do for them, I am not certain. If they could even get a small gum drop to every child, I would be both surprised and happy. UNRRA personnel had a party and raised money for some children's homes. One home received most of the money with the hopes that at least this one could afford to have a Christmas party for the children; the UNRRA staff was informed that they bought two pigs and a load of potatoes for the children. A few minutes ago I gave the professor who lives across the hall two children's books (in English, but with many pictures), a box of crayons, a couple of pencils, two cans of milk, and two pieces of candy for his two little children. I was extremely surprised at his genuine pleasure and excitement in being able to have something for his children. It is a pretty rough life for them, four living in one hotel room with no private bath.

You may get tired of my writing about the hardships of the Poles; yet we cannot afford to forget them if we want peace, because we shall never have peace as long as masses of people are struggling for security. You can read of these things once in awhile and then you become preoccupied with your own duties, of which each of you have many. Yet these people have been living under strenuous conditions since the fall of 1939! One-third of their people are dead, and their country is destroyed.

We are laying aside food for our teams for the time when we shall not be able to obtain food according to our contracts with the government. Already the FRS teams' diet consists mostly of potatoes and bread. Even now they are taking account of the calorie consumption per team to see if they are getting sufficient food. It is a hard life for them, as they work in the cold under trying conditions, and yet the physical hardships seem small in comparison with the mental agony of knowing that so many of the people we see each day will go to bed after eating just a bowl of hot potato soup and a piece of black bread, while we can enjoy a meal lavish with potatoes, a little meat, a vegetable, and tea with sugar and milk.

The transport team has found it most difficult to operate this winter; for a short time, the roads were so muddy that they would send two trucks together in order to pull each other out. Finally, they quit operating altogether. Now they are sorry they did not stop sooner, as the roads are frozen and passable now, but they have ruined brake drums and who knows what else by the continued operation on the muddy roads. We hope that they are able to find other work during the spring thaw.

Despite transport troubles, the Czerwonka team has continued to distribute food to about 9,000 children and pregnant women plus several clothes distributions. One team member is a nurse and has clinics in several villages. It seems to be a common thing for the girls on the team to walk home—anywhere from three to fifteen kilometers (two to ten miles)—when a truck fails to go further.

The Kozienice team is continuing with its food and clothing distributions and now has a nurse to do similar work as the nurse in Czerwonka. They, too, have had transport trouble but have been better able to cope with it than either of the other teams. As you may imagine, all of these teams are working under extremely primitive conditions. I marvel at the spirit with which the girls especially are able to do it. Yet there is a deep concern for the people; otherwise, none of us would be able to take it.

Now we are hoping that we can help with some children's homes in Krakow; however, our budget is limited and the needs of this country are great. We do not care to spread ourselves too thin, so we are trying to figure a way to continue what we have started on at least the same scale if not larger and include the children's homes as well.

Philip Zealey leaves on December 31; that is going to be a great blow to the mission, and everyone who knows him hates to see him leave, including his many Polish friends.

Recently several reports on university students have come to my attention; we are giving them twenty tons of food per month in cooperation with the World Student Relief Fund. Not much, but it is a big help when you hear what they have. One university reports that they have tea with no sugar for breakfast with a sandwich made from black bread; soup for lunch; and tea with sugar and another sandwich for supper. I was horrified! Some of our members have visited these canteens; other reports say there is not enough to serve three times a day. Still there is a keen interest to learn; for six years students had to attend underground schools, so they know how to manage. Imagine trying to study on this food. Johnson reports from the Gdynia and Gdansk area that one building housing students is beautiful except that all the plumbing was stripped and there is none to replace it. This means that all water must be brought in buckets for a distance of two to three blocks and all refuse carried away.

The teachers are faring about as badly; it is common to see professors in canvas or wooden shoes, yet they are eager to teach.

December 29, 1946 ~ Red in Warsaw to Madeleine in Toulouse

Since the plane did not bring first-class mail two weeks ago, and there was no letter from you the previous week, I came back from Gdynia yesterday with such a positive feeling that there would be a letter. Then Peter said, "Why yes, there is a large pile of mail for you," and I knew there must be at least two letters from you. It was not until long after lunch that I had an opportunity to get to the office, but once there I eagerly thumbed through the mail to pick out those with French stamps. There were none. Oh, how my heart sank. Before, when there was no letter from you, I would be disappointed, surely, but I could find something to do and feel comfortable, knowing that whether letters came or not, the affection was still there. It's not that I momentarily lost confidence or faith in us, but rather that I have been so anxious to hear from you, to know where you are, what you are doing. Your letters are such a joy! I often wish it were possible to correspond daily, though I wonder when there would be time.

I opened your little Christmas card beside the Christmas tree on that celebrated day. And I did have "warm thoughts of the merry Christmases together to come." On the evening before, when we all thought of our families who could not be with us, I thought of you and of the Christmas trees we may have and of the stockings we shall fill with fruit and nuts.

Just then in walks Reed Smith with no place to spend the night except in my crowded room, and I had just started out to write to you. Not only that, but he burned out a bearing on the jeep coming into Warsaw. Now I have him and a jeep on my hands.

January 4, 1947 ~ Madeleine in Toulouse to Red in Warsaw

Last night, after dinner, around an open fire, six of us were lounging, listening to a beautiful Mass on the radio, and looking over new copies of *Life* and *Time*. I came across this article on Marian Anderson and in the quiet and flickering light and the music, it seemed suddenly to bring together many thoughts and many people. I'd like you to see it, too. I thought of you and a young pacifist couple I know who have gone to work in Georgia and of Si Courtney in Perpignan who is hoping to settle in the South and of Herb who is thinking of going there (he was born in Alabama). I wondered if there might not be some sort of new Concord in the South, a renaissance of high thinking and plain living, and whether we might sometime be a part of it.

I read that Gene Talmadge had just died before being sworn in as governor, and although hate and ignorance do not die with one man, perhaps there is one tongue less to poison us towards each other. I remembered again the possibilities that sometimes exist in downtrodden and despised peoples. I once wrote something almost like that about the Germans, but I had not thought of Negroes in that way. I remember, too, the great earnestness and devotion in colored people in Philadelphia towards religious cults that seem to us fantastic but are perhaps closer to a primitive Christianity than we are. And I sat in the firelight and wondered....

I missed you very deeply, my dear, with a kind of accepted hurt. Sometimes it hurts much, but not always; mostly it's a calm and sustaining knowing that you're there and that you're going on.

Hugh is leaving the Refugee Program to be secretary of all the field work at Friends House in London. Bill Stanton (do you know him— ex-Starvation Unit?) is coming down Tuesday to take his place, along with Margaret Wright from Le Havre who is going to replace Connie Madgen who is to replace me. Got it? We're going to meet Bill and Margaret in old clothes and a horse-drawn cab, just so they won't get any high-and-mighty ideas about this delegation! We've got to get home now, build fires, and scrounge furniture for the two new arrivals.

Oh Red, if only you could drop in for a meal. Our funny house is cold and damp, but when a fire flickers over the walls and the table is laid and holly glistens in the light and we get a symphony on the radio, it's a pleasant home.

I hope the letters are getting through to Warsaw better than they're coming here at the moment.

January 5, 1947 ~ Red in Warsaw to Madeleine in Toulouse

This is the time for a confession. We did not get the American mail until Thursday morning, so I was overly anxious to have a letter from you. There had not been one on the two previous planes. In fact, I thought maybe there would be two, greedy as I am. Anyway, there was loads of mail, and Peter and I were busy sorting, preparing to open and discuss the official mail, when I saw a letter from you. Although

we do not usually read personal mail at that time, I took time to open yours and to glance at it. The first thing that caught my eye was the date ...December 16th, which meant you had not written for sixteen days! I was horrified.

Since I have been ever anxious to know

ETU TRUCK CAUGHT IN THE SNOW. THE WINTER OF 1946-47 IN EUROPE WAS THE COLDEST IN MANY YEARS.
    -PHOTOGRAPH COURTESY OF AFSC ARCHIVES

whether you go to Germany or not, I looked hastily through the letter and could find no word telling me what was happening to you. Frankly, I was hurt. That was a busy day and not until late at night did I get a chance to read your letter. It was quite short to be the first in sixteen days, yet you could not have put more warmth and affection in a letter if you had taken ten pages. Though I still do not know what your plans are, I do know that the love and affection are deepening. Your letter was more satisfying than I ever hoped at the beginning of that day. Forgive me, darling, for judging too hastily.

The temperature has dropped to 13 degrees below zero. Van Cleve Geiger had trouble Friday night on the way from Warsaw to Kozienice because the gasoline line kept freezing. The grease in the gear boxes freezes, and it becomes impossible to change gears.

Monday night Peter, Philip, Hanka, Hanka's cousin Kinia (our secretary), and I had dinner together. We ate at a small restaurant where there is dancing. We had a marvelous time. Philip gave each of us a small Polish diary; then we passed a paper around on which each of us wrote something in memory of his leaving. I wrote in English, one girl wrote in French, and the other three wrote in Polish.

Philip left Tuesday and what a sad day! It was not until then that I really felt as though I were losing a personal friend. We worked together well, but each of us has been so intent on our job that I did not realize how much I liked him.

January 6, 1947 ~ Red in Warsaw to Madeleine in Toulouse

How I wish I were bringing this package to you! It's a book on German crimes in Poland, and I would like you to see it. It tells stories I have heard many times here, differing in details, but essentially the same.

I had planned to take two days of holidays and be by myself, but too many visitors have kept me from it. I am not overworked as I was, and I don't feel tired; rather, I have been wanting to do some thinking. There are times when I become concerned about our Mission and our real purpose in being here. Here we are, twenty-eight people with a few tons of food and clothing plus nineteen trucks. What does it all mean? We are living in a country where tension is great, where people do not trust one another, where there is hatred and fear. We are trying to help them. We say that we are more interested in the personal contacts we make since that is the real way of getting across the Quaker meaning of our work. Yet we spend most of our time with the mechanics of our program.

The transport team spends most of its time in an isolated island. They have failed to impress the people with the real reasons why they are there. Many still think that they are UNRRA; some think they are spies for the Anglo-Americans. They have more contact with people coming to the barrack asking for rifles than they do with the people to whom they are hauling building materials. The welfare teams find their men in the garages too much of the time. It takes two man-days each week just to fill jerry cans with gasoline for the trucks at Kozienice! Everything one does seems to take many times as long as it would anywhere else. In Warsaw, we do nothing more than one does working in any office in an American city that calls for many outside contacts—nearly all business.

These criticisms are no more than have been leveled against other Quaker missions, both present and past. Personally, I think my trouble has been that my approach has been too much on the intellectual side. This time is similar to the time in CPS when I realized that my reasons for being there were not strong enough to take me through. Here I am finding myself more in need of spiritual strength. More than ever I need to listen to the "quiet inner voice."

January 9, 1947 ~ Madeleine in Toulouse to Red in Warsaw

It's a cold drizzly morning with the rain spattering on my skylight, but just as I got settled at my desk, in came someone with your gay square package. Thank you ever so much. The red ribbon I'll keep to wear in my hair; I got a Christmas sweater exactly the same color. The tin I'll keep, too, and someday in our home, we'll use it for a tea canister and laugh and remember how far it has come: from America to Poland to France and back to America again.

We had a riotous time last night, welcoming Bill Stanton, Margaret Wright, and Hollis Wyman down from Paris and Hugh and Juanita and Madeleine Chevalier from Switzerland. The funny little house was fair bursting at the seams with people, but it's good to have the rooms full, and we do enjoy each other. Oh Red, I so wish you could be with us for times like these. You have them, too, of course, and there will be others when we're together. I remember when three of us shared an apartment in Philadelphia; we often wondered if ever we'd have such fun again as we did then with all our friends, and here it is halfway round the world in a city I'd never given a thought to that I find the same friendship and thoughtfulness and fun. It will happen with us, too, whether it's Warsaw or New York, Poland or Switzerland or Sweden.

There were white tulips on the flower stalls this morning, an incongruous spring. And I thought of our spring, and where we shall pass it. Oh darling, if we could begin now to plan, it would seem so much nearer. But I don't yet know when I go to England, much less when I go to Germany. My next leave is due in April or May, but I doubt that I'd get it before June. I didn't know that leaves were arranged through the British Army; the best I can think of now is that I try to arrange something as soon as I get to my new post, and see how it works out with you.

Your Christmas message reached me in Perpignan the last day of the year, and a beautiful one it was. Thank thee for it. I've read it often and often—that first day sitting on a rock in a lonely, lovely gorge and other times just before going to sleep. And if you're sometimes discouraged these days, as you sound occasionally, let me send back to you some of your own words for the lightening of your heart: "a time of inward rejoicing for the love of mankind and for the power of that love. May another Christmas find us together, bound tightly with that powerful force of love."

And letters—oh Red, I do hope by now that the bottleneck's been broken. Part of the hiatus was my not writing for a couple of weeks, as I told you, but part is surely the mail service. I didn't hear for over two weeks either, and well I know that sinking feeling when there's no post, the waiting and the wishing. I try to remember back to the other times when I've been impatient and wistful, and how letters usually come in batches, but that's not much help when what one wants is a letter today. Whatever the weather, the post, or my own shortcomings, remember that you're much thought of and longed after and loved. How many times, waiting for a streetcar or riding in a train or sitting with a book, does your picture come out.

Yes, love, I do a bit of wondering about what we shall be doing for a job and how we'll work together or apart—more wondering than concrete thinking, I'm afraid. I could wish for a clear-cut sense of mission, but that I haven't got. There are numberless places to tackle the problems of the world, and I don't feel strongly gifted for one more than another. In one sense, it doesn't matter greatly what we do; it does matter tremendously how we do. As for our working together or alone, that depends partly on circumstance and partly on our choice. I think it will need a lot of talking and thinking together to know what we should aim at. I confess that on this point I have some misgivings; I've seen, unhappily, two marriages of gifted, devoted pacifists break on that question. In both cases, there was a lack of understanding and companionship that was accentuated by separation of work. But those two cases have made me doubtful all the same of what's the best policy.

It's hard to explain, Red. I believe in independence and a certain amount of aloneness like you'd believe in the Gospels. I wouldn't want to marry someone who was too dependent on me or who let me be too dependent on him. And yet, there's such a multiplicity of delight and strength in sharing that I should like to find with you.

I remember that Herb once wrote: "There is more real love-making between a man and a woman in a day spent working together than in a night sleeping together." And I think that's true, because love comprises such an infinity of expressions and attitudes. I don't suppose I've often known a deeper content than when working with Harold in Philadelphia or Hugh here, sitting across the desk, exchanging ideas, or each doing his own job, with a comment or a word here and there. Or when, each of us with his nose buried in a report or an account book, Hugh and I sing strong old hymns in parts, half unaware that we're doing so, the murmured notes making an obbligato to the job. It's such that I'd like to share with you, Red: the weariness and the successes, the funny and the tragic. How we'll do that, I don't see now; surely we'll find the way if we desire it ardently enough.

Two days later ~ In desperation at never having a quiet time to think and write in, I've gotten up at six this morning and am batting out to you until breakfast time.

Red, this is going to be awfully personal; I hope it doesn't follow that it's trivial. But Bikini bombs or Polish disaster, it seems to me it's all rooted in people, in their ignorance and fear and blindness. The more I see the "hangover" that the old Secours Quaker left us here to muddle through, the more I'm convinced that it's only by becoming more understanding and honest that we'll have anything to give to the terribly complex problems of the world. And although sometimes it seems silly, in the face of the tremendous things happening today, to spend so much time and thought over our personal relations, I think really it's OK.

The way we feel and think will color all we do, and I want what we do now, and perhaps later together, to be strong and sure and honest. And so, although it's not according to any Hoyle I ever heard of, I'd like to share with you some of the things Herb wrote, after I wrote him about you, in trying to help me straighten out my own thinking.

Something that you might use, Red. "One love does not contradict another. Rather, it explains the other and gives it dimensions. Do you think that having loved a man, that love could ever leave you, unless you poisoned it with pride?"

Do you mind if I quote Herb? Red, I wonder if I'm asking too much of you? I don't know just how I'd feel if you did this. In the past, the rivals I've had have been inalterable circumstances or custom or ideas, not other women. I admire tremendously Herb's integrity and intellect, and I hope I always shall. He has made me rich in some ways, and I want strongly to share the riches with you, but I wonder how you feel about it? You wanted to know all about me, and I guess this goes along with it.

Red, for all that's mis-said or left out or bungled, use your love for understanding.

January 18, 1947 ~ Madeleine in Toulouse to Red in Warsaw

I hope that by now my Christmas and New Year letters have come to you and that wretched fortnight lapse in December is not leaving you empty-handed and empty-hearted any longer. Oh darling, if I had imagined how difficult it would be for you, I'd have written just for the sake of something on a piece of paper.

Tiens, Red, you've been in this relief game long enough to know that I wouldn't buzz straight off to England! I'm sorry if I neglected to mention the Great Move, but I've heard scarcely a word since I was accepted for Germany! Whenever we talk with Paris I say, "Heard anything?" and they say, "No," and I go back to my job in the Refuge Program. Hugh's replacement has arrived and so has mine, which makes my office resemble Grand Central at rush hour. This noon when your letter arrived, I did so joy over it that I could have written you like the wind in my rush to meet the spirit that you sent in that letter, but with five or six people shouting, scrabbling in the files and wanting gas coupons all at once, I plain couldn't. For the moment there's plenty of work for all of us, and if I should get called to London this next week, Bill Stanton would have fits. However, I hope for February. You shall know as soon as I do.

This last week it's been almost spring: soft air, long light evenings, and the morning sky sweet with pink clouds. The half-hour's walk to the office along the canal is a joy now; the still-bare trees reflect in the green water (that looks almost clean, for a wonder), and the barges, loosed from the Christmas ice, are edging through the locks again.

Now that I'm about to leave Toulouse, I'm beginning to appreciate it. The filth and ugliness shock me less, and I like the pink and orange buildings reflected in the water, the bright patches of moss on the falling tile roofs, the funny little cafés with a waterfront air and the inimitable French names that we pass along the canal—Bar Fluvial, Chéri Mouton, and best of all—Café de la Langouste Qui Chante (the lobster who sings).

Night before last, Hugh, Juanita, and I had a memorable meal. Not that eating is all of life here, but it does seem the traditional Midi way of showing friendship is to spread a good feed. The head accountant in our office, M. Pérez, has worked with Secours Quaker for seven years, during the hard days of the occupation, sometimes without pay. He always invites departing delegates to dinner at his brother's home, since he is a bachelor. So the three of us, escorted by this genteel, dignified Spaniard, went to a refugee's one-room home and were served a bountiful meal in the poorest of surroundings with utmost graciousness.

The room was about fifteen feet square with a bed and crib (they have an adorable, fragile eighteen-month daughter) in one corner and a small gas stove and a curtained cupboard in another. The table is rough wood, made by the husband; the chairs were borrowed from the neighbors, and still there weren't enough to go around. The table was covered with clean bits of cloth, neatly laid together. And under a hanging electric bulb we were served a huge plate of salad with mayonnaise; then a mold of rice with spicy tomato sauce in the center; then fried eggs; then roast chicken and lettuce salad; red wine; chocolate pudding; little biscuits; and coffee.

You were in France long enough to realize what it means to offer a dinner like that. And the conversation—I haven't had a bat like that in months: Spain, relations with Russia, the demoralization of France, America's role discussed in Spanish (which I can understand now but can't speak), with me in French. Not a word about food prices, which is, sad to say, the most-talked-of thing in France today. No bitterness, in spite of the fact that the brothers had been in camps, seized for forced labor, and are still living under extremely difficult conditions for people of culture and refinement. We came away humbled. All of a sudden, I thought I knew why we were here: to help people like this, to share with them, to encourage them if we can. And the dignity and generosity of their hospitality outranked that of many a statelier home that we've been in.

Your book and letter came down from Paris on Friday. Thank you for them. You've started a seminar here with the *German Crimes*. Everyone's had a go at reading it, and after a few pages, they drop the book and start talking about it. I'm glad of it, because as I've written you before, the whole problem is very unclear in my own mind (and in almost everyone else's, too). And too, I've felt often that we gabble an unnecessary lot about trivial matters and work out of office hours, and sometimes I get deathly sick of it.

Red, I do share with you that feeling of unrest and seeking about our work. There is a good deal of feeling among the people working in France that work should go on here, but I honestly can't see how it can be on a relief basis as that is understood in a country like Poland. And yet, the need here is crying. But it's primarily a moral need, and how do we minister to that? And who are we to do it anyhow?

Sometimes I envy the people who are doing hard work, like Ex Williams and her clothing distribution. At least there, I think, one could see the need and answer it in a direct, satisfying way. But I know that there, too, there are frustrations, inadequacies, and above all, the same deep spiritual lack that all of us feel, wherever we are. And trying as our situations are, Red, where we deal at second or third hand with human needs, I think it's primarily important that we try to work out some sort of answer. More and more I feel, perhaps too strongly, that Lady Bountiful handing out food and clothing looks pretty silly beside atomic bombs.

What these people need basically, what we all need, is for some leather-lunged prophet and seer to preach among us of the faith that moves mountains and atoms, of a love that can knit the world together, of a vision that can mark out a future that is worthy of the spirit of man.

Sorry if this sounds soap-boxish. Here, as in most situations, I talk mostly from my own experience and my own need. And these last weeks, I've had recurring times of lostness, when I wake up each morning wondering: What am I for? What is God? And, What does it mean to live? Those times come now and again, and they are empty, trying hours. I suppose that in a sense they are something to be thankful for, since as long as I'm pricked by a sense of isolation and non-understanding, I may put forth more effort than I do now. Why, oh why, is it so much easier to concentrate on a monthly report than on the eternal verities? The spirit is willing but the flesh is weak, I guess.

PS: I've hung on to this a couple of days, and now I have some news for you. Phone call from Paris this morning; I go up on Wednesday and should be in London Thursday January 30. Write me from now on at Friends House. I guess it'll be my turn to wait for mail now. I'll look up Philip Zealey for firsthand news about you. Wish you were going to be at the station when I get in. Do be someday, n'est-ce pas?

I only know that the spirit of man, whenever it is
honest and courageous, is a tremendous thing

-Madeleine

CHAPTER FIVE

Precious Moments

April 9, 1947

Dear Red,

Ha — so we get everything done for us here, and our petrol tanks filled by the chauffeur so we don't know how much we have, so we run out ⅓ of the way home! Serves us right, but it lands us up parked on a sunny street in a small town, the curiosity of all the kids, while James goes off to get a jerry-can full.

It's been a typical day: going into a new town, talking with the Mayor and Refugee Representatives, going around visiting homes and schools. It's hard work, in a way. People are often suspicious or resentful of us at first, though always docile;

... & that they expect, quite

January 1947 ~ Madeleine in Toulouse to the AFSC

I shall be leaving the south of France and the Refugee Program soon to go to England on my way to the British zone of Germany. But before I go, I'd like to try to share with you something of that I have seen here and some of the unmet needs in France that might someday become part of the concern of the Peace Section.

This has been what is known as a second-stage relief job. Life here is still hard and uncertain, but there is no mass starvation or wandering homeless people. In some ways, this kind of work seems harder than that of first-stage relief, where the problems of devastation and distress are tangible. There is still real and tragic need in France. The fact that much of it is probably chronic and grows out of long-standing institutions and attitudes does not make it any the less urgent.

The greater part of our work here in the Midi is with Spanish refugees, a gallant group of people in exile for what sometimes seems a lost cause. But the problems now confronting these refugees are very much like those confronting the French, except that they are aggravated by differences of language and tradition and discrimination because of nationality.

Although many of the problems of France seem so close to our own that it is exceedingly difficult to know how to remove their mote until we have got rid our beam, there are some things which I believe we do better than the French and which we might usefully share with them.

It is the young people of France who need help, encouragement, and direction. France is an old country, run largely by old people on old ideas. All sorts of cumbersome restrictions and regulations surround the ambitious young person who wants to strike out for himself, whether in business, education, or social work. The result is a frightening apathy. The one hope of the more ambitious young people is to leave France: for America, still the traditional land of promise; for the colonies; for South America—anywhere to have a fair and fresh start.

Those who do strike out find little encouragement or financial support from their elders. For example, I met a young teacher who, with the help of two or three colleagues, has started a school for delinquent boys and girls. It is run on the most humane and constructive principles, and the results have been truly amazing. But they are running the school on a shoestring and a precarious one at that. Neither private nor public help seems to be forthcoming. A sense of social responsibility seems not to be highly developed among the French; voluntary social work of the sort we have at home is hardly understood and little practiced. Government support is the accepted and essential thing.

I doubt that I have ever talked with a student who didn't believe that wars could be prevented if people of different countries could get to know each other. By the same token, one finds a goodly number of ardent Esperantists who are convinced that a universal language will bring in universal peace.

Among the more thoughtful French, the bitterness and rancor left by the war and the German occupation are beginning to fade in the face of the necessity to find some way of getting along with Germany and the obvious interdependence of the European economy. In all the cities and towns hereabout, there are two days a week without electricity.

STUDENTS' SUPPLEMENTARY FEEDING AT TOULOUSE. 1947
-PHOTOGRAPH COURTESY OF AFSC ARCHIVES

There is no electricity because it doesn't come from the Ruhr. It doesn't come from the Ruhr because of lack of coal. There isn't coal because there isn't enough food to feed the miners, and so on.

For many, this is their only positive tenet as regards peace. Otherwise they take a gloomy view of the future and fully expect a war between the east and the west in which France, finding herself between the two, will be overrun and destroyed.

French students are flocking to American universities. Many more would go if they had the opportunity and the money. Because of their sense of frustration in the present, French students tend to turn to intellectual pursuits and interests for satisfaction. In the student club we have here in Toulouse, I have heard passionate arguments over some point of literary style but barely five words on the organization of the United Nations or the current election. There are, of course, the science students who are passionately interested in American technology and research. It's a queer feeling, having your country judged chiefly by its purely technical and material achievements.

When I have had a chance to tell these students about our foreign service seminars, they glow with enthusiasm. If only such a thing could happen in France! Just the prospect of meeting American students would draw many. There is plenty of reconstruction still to be done, and I can think of nothing that would be better for students than a rousing work camp experience. Manual labor still carries a stigma here, a stigma that present day France, with all her devastation and disorganization, can ill afford.

A religious approach to the problems of the world is usually suspect, at least at first hearing. The Catholic Church still remains sufficiently political and reactionary to make the free thinker a positive and opposing factor. Especially in the Midi, near Spain and Italy, the Church retains an almost magical character that is anathema to anyone calling himself a liberal or an intellectual. In such a situation, I believe Quakerism could have much to offer in bridging the gap between the position of the anticlerical atheist and the narrow, orthodox believer.

I have found in this part of France no pacifist groups, only isolated individuals who have usually come to their pacifist convictions by way of a religious humanism. There is probably a much larger group of people who would be sympathetic to the pacifist approach if it were expounded, and above all, lived among them. As in every other country, I suppose, there is a group of people seeking a better way, but they often do not know in which direction to seek.

February 1, 1947 ~ Madeleine in Paris to Red in Warsaw

My last note to you from France. The roses do not bloom now by the Gare d'Austerlitz. Notre Dame is etched in snow; I saw it last night by a pale moon. My dear, let's try to come back to this city again, this Paris where we saw the spring together.

Oh Red, at the last moment I'm reluctant to leave. All the quirks and annoyances of French life are suddenly endearing. And in Toulouse everyone was so kind and so regretful that I felt as if I were abandoning them. For some reason or another, we had a party three nights running at our house (a party being any occasion when all the gang plus lots of visitors plus lots of food are all together).

The dressmaking class of our retraining course whipped up a charming pink blouse; the staff gave me an album of Toulouse pictures, a traveling clock, and a leather diary. Most touching of all, Chick Moran, Bill Stanton, and four French friends took me to the station, waited around for three hours, and gave me a warm send-off at 3 a.m. of a very chilly day!

February 2, 1947 ~ Madeleine en route to London to Red in Warsaw

The rest of the compartment (I'm on the Flèche d'Or) has gone to dinner, so I can type on the little table without bothering anyone. It's a queer feeling, leaving France. I feel a little rocky inside; this isn't going to be an evaluation but just a lot of impressions. It seems all of a sudden as if I were understanding France better than in all the months gone by.

There are four very nice English people in the compartment with me, going back home. Somehow their solidity and their un-understanding comments on French life make me rise up in defense. I, who have cussed out French bureaucracy and sanitation with the best of 'em, find myself defending her.

Things are certainly better here than they were that sunny day last March when we careened through the streets of Paris for the first time in Joe Howell's truck. It's a joy to me to come back and see how much better people are dressed, how much more food there is in the stores. But it's still hard for me, knowing the inefficiency and internal strife and lack of mutual confidence, to see how it has happened. I wish I had the knowledge and subtlety to understand what it is that makes a country go.

Here is Paris, beautiful and modern, old and traditional, full of past glories and present frustrations. And there is the Midi that I've known, dreaming in the southern sun and carrying on commerce in a casual Latin manner. And the isolated little villages that can't have changed much since the Middle Ages—the peasants with their superstitions in their eternal black and their wooden shoes. What holds it together? What makes it tick? And most puzzling and important of all: will it go on ticking? Sometimes I've been quite sure it wouldn't—sure it was too demoralized, too worn out, too lacking in adaptability to go on. And other times I think, "No, a people's will to live is too strong to die so easily. A long and glorious tradition dies hard." France still has something that every other country would be poor without: Paris, which as an

Italian friend of mine told me, is a little the city of tout le monde.

Last night looking at the gray outline of Notre Dame in the snow, beside the black river, I was almost frightened by its mass. Think of the faith and energy that went into that building, and the others like it. People can accomplish almost anything if they believe in it. When they have a faith, however mistaken, however cruel, everything they have goes into it: energy, greed, selfishness, altruism, competition, love, beauty, and they can move mountains. Whether they move them wisely is another question altogether.

Reg Rountree and Hugh happened by in my first night in Paris; we went out to a café together. Reg said with passing pride, "I've a home of me own," with such wistfulness and pleasure that my heart turned over. He's tall and lank and somehow reminded me of you; it made my eyes sting with tears, I don't know quite why.

February 3, 1947 ~ Madeleine in London to Red in Warsaw

So, I'm in London, which is cold, wet, and dark. I walked about yesterday seeing the sights, which were rather dismal. But so was Paris that first Sunday—remember? And afterwards I lost my heart to it (and in it, my dear). The Channel crossing was smooth and bright; just before dark we came in sight of the white cliffs of Dover, which are gray and sheer and futuristic against the sky and sea. It was a moving moment, Red; England still seems very small to me, and I marvel at the thought and poetry and power that have risen out of that island. I wonder whether it will produce more, or whether its great days are over. For the moment, I feel dépaysée, rather lost here—in spite of a warm welcome—and wondering what Germany will be like. That's all right; on a fine morning (if there is such a thing here) I shall wake up with a great thrill at knowing I'm in London!

What's pleased me most today is an announcement that Philip Zealey is talking to us tonight. I'll try to find out about you, Red. It always makes you nearer, to meet someone who's been in Poland. But oh for the days when we won't have to do our understanding at second and third hand!

PS: It may be Solingen for me, Red; not certain yet. We hope to get off in two or three weeks.

February 3, 1947 ~ Red in Warsaw to Madeleine in London

Tonight I am trying to figure the best way to send you a telegram. Oh, gosh, it has been hard to sleep lately; everything seems to be topsy-turvy, and my thoughts are more on where and'how we shall meet than on the reason I am being called to Paris.

Now, I wonder if we shall not be together before you receive this. However, just in case something happens, I shall tell you what has taken place so far. This past week we received a letter suggesting my going to Paris to talk with Bill Ensor about Polish mission accounts; Cary suggested my going and said he would leave it up to Peter to decide. We had a team representative meeting this past weekend, and they not only approved my going to Paris but strongly urged my going on to London to help coordinate supplies. Tomorrow we send a telegram to Paris approving the trip and asking them to notify you of the arrangements.

Peter thinks I should take two weeks in addition to the official week. This will depend, of course, a great deal upon where you are and what you are doing. If you will still be in Toulouse, I would like nothing better than spending some time with you there. I am in need of a rest, so if I could sleep a great deal and just do nothing; it would not have to interfere too much with your work—or would it? Anyway these are things to be thinking about, and unless I hear from you before, we shall wait until we are together to make any plans. I am not even sure that you will not be in London by the time I arrive in Paris. It would be grand if we could go to London together after spending a few days in Paris. What about it?

If it were only possible to tell you how happy I am!

February 6, 1947 ~ Madeleine in London to Red in Warsaw

I'd meant to write you a slow sort of letter tonight, sitting in the kitchen which is the only warm, cheerful place in all Gordon House. Going up into the hall to bring tea to the rest of the gang, I found an envelope airmail from Toulouse with a much-garbled copy of your telegram! Oh darling, my heart, it almost stopped! Do I gather rightly that you may be in Paris toward the end of the month, with leave time as well? Let me wail a little wail—why couldn't it have happened before! If we have luck with our validations and travel arrangements, we may be on our way to Germany by that time!

On the other hand, I think it's going to take longer than most of the group knows. I shall talk to the personnel secretary of FRS tomorrow and see if she can give me the inside dope. I rather think, though, that it's just a matter of waiting for the official wheels to turn, and that is anybody's guess. If we were still here, I'd be so busy that I couldn't get away. It would probably mean paying for the trip out of holiday allowance. Oh hell, none of that would make any difference if only we could get together. Or how about you coming to London? I expect by the time this reaches you, I'll have a letter from you with more details.

Oh Red! I'm only just beginning to realize what it would mean to see you soon. Waiting until next summer hasn't seemed so hard, but if we just miss a chance now, it will be tough.

London's been pretty grim; I'm afraid I can't write with much enthusiasm. Most snow in years, a bad coal shortage, and fog, gray skies, and damp every day. I landed a week ago tonight, and sun is merely hearsay.

The high spot of the week was a visit to Parliament, conducted by Lord Darwin, a Friend who was made a Labor peer with the approval of his Meeting! I got quite a charge out of that; here's the noble House of Lords, traditionally reactionary and conservative, spiked with new Liberals.

You can ride on the double-decker buses for miles without seeing much war damage; then you come on whole blocks blasted down to the cellars, hidden behind billboards. It is a sobering sight—the spire of a lovely church against the evening sky and nothing else left of the church.

Red, I do hurt for you when you speak of the depression of the endless rows of bombed, jagged shells. Even a few blocks are down-heartening. But most dreary of all, to me, is the kind of living that most people return to, or aspire to, at the end of this war.

Hah—at last I'm learning to drive—on the wrong side of the road! Transport at Toulouse was always in such bad shape that we almost never got to practice, so the English Friends have sent me to a motor school. I've a patient, non-flusterable instructor, and so far, in spite of foul weather, I've run over no old ladies or dogs. Having got my reflexes tuned to left-handed driving, I now go over to Germany and switch to right; however, it's all to the good. Who knows, someday I may graduate to a truck, and we can go into business together!

February 7,1947 ~ Red in Poland to Madeleine in London

Tonight I am disturbed; your letter has just arrived saying that you are due in London on the 30th and in Germany by February 5th. By this time you must already be in Germany.

I am afraid that it will be difficult for me to visit you in Germany. Since I know that it will be difficult for you to leave Germany once you are there, maybe you can make application for me to visit you. I do not even know where you are!

If this trip is made all the way to London and back without seeing you, oh how dreadful! I do not like to think of the possibility.

February 10, 1947 ~ Madeleine in London to Red in Warsaw

The end of this week is Valentine's Day, and we, my love, have a special Cupid. He's very tall, fair-haired and lank, and he squints amiably through thick glasses. No rosy cherub and no wounding bow and arrows, but all the same, we are being watched over.

It's David Jenkins, who called me this morning to say that Steve Cary had told him that you might be in Paris and that we'd like to get together, etc. etc. He was very sweet and English about it and outlined three possibilities: if our validations don't come through before February 20, I go to Paris if only for a day or two; if they don't come through until the end of the month, you might then be in London; or if all else fails, you might go back to Poland by way of Berlin, and we could meet there! An awful lot of ifs, but after all, darling, not every couple can choose among three world capitals in which to meet! I can't help feeling anxious, but for the moment there seems nothing much to do but sit tight and hope. Dave assured me he and Steve would keep an eye on developments and do all they could to make things work out.

I wonder if I should say this—it's only the whim of a moment, and when one writes things down they seem more important that they are. I half feel unwilling to see you. All of a sudden the lost opportunities of the year, the things I might have done and didn't do—the meditation and discipline I might have practiced, the understanding I might have gained, the situations I might have helped, the people I might have known better—overwhelm me with failure and frustration. And I have so wanted to come to you a bigger person. I feel now, as I have so often in the past, overwhelmed by the opportunities and privileges in my path and saddened by the little I've done with them. I wonder if you know what I mean? It's partly an unhappiness born of the endlessly dreary days. There's been no sun since the day I came; sometimes mist succeeds fog, or fog turns into rain, or rain into snow, but the sky never clears. One's spiritual skies ought to be less dependent on the temporal ones, but I'm afraid mine aren't.

Today, coming back from our German class, Bob Byrd showed me a flower shop he had discovered, where people are invited in just to look and sniff around.

It was lovely past saying: great clusters of lilacs, and all spring flowers, hyacinth and daffodil and tulip, branches of flowering cherry and forsythia. It was wistful seeing; almost it's hard to believe that such loveliness will burst out again amid these gray streets under gray skies.

February 15, 1947 ~ Madeleine in London to Red in Warsaw

Today I sent this telegram: "Leave impossible remaining in London until Feb. 25. Can you arrange earlier arrival?" Any similarity between our correspondence at the moment and what is usually known as love letters is purely coincidental; anything more like official business I never did see!

Two letters from you arrived yesterday, and I cherished them for the day. We had a Valentine party last night—but of that later.

As you will now know from my letters, there is no chance of my having leave. Actually, in spite of your letters, and in spite of my great wish to be with you, darling, I have not asked for leave. I have no time coming to me, the teams in Germany are waiting for replacements, and as it is, I shall be almost the last of the American group to go. Don't for a moment think I don't want to—no, you'd know how much I do—but it simply doesn't fit in with my job now, and I can't let myself think too much about it. You must need a rest very badly by now, and that's perhaps one reason why you feel so desperately the need that we get together. Don't think I don't feel it, too; actually, this is about my lowest and driest period since coming abroad, and I look forward to seeing you—if only for a day or two—as I look forward to spring sun and rain.

Because FRS feels it is very important that I drive well and that I have some practice on lorries, I am staying on after the others to pass a driving test scheduled for the 24th. All FRS, as I've told you, and AFSC in Paris, know that we hope to meet, and I believe they'll do anything they can to make it possible.

I wonder if you could come directly to London from Paris and discuss business later, on your way back. My days here are not over-full, and while London at the moment is the lousiest possible place to spend a leave (cold, foggy, no heat, no electricity), it would seem warmer and sunnier if we were just together. There are some pleasant spots in the city and countryside that we could enjoy. I don't think this alone would be the rest and recreation you need, and since you can't lounge in Toulouse, how about trying a real leave somewhere else? I'm truly anxious about that, my dear; I've had two short breaks already, and both times I felt I needed them and was much better balanced and able to do a better job after them.

Look Red, this suggestion I make in much seriousness—so at least give it a think, dear. How about your going to my relatives in Switzerland? You would find the friendliest of welcomes. I've told them of you, and even though you come alone this time, I can promise you that you'll be taken in as part of the family. It's just their way. Two or three of my cousins speak good English; with the rest of the family, between French and German you can get along. You could have all the rest you want, good food, and most reviving of all, you'd be in a healthy, happy atmosphere. Before this trip ends, there are going to be a lot of threads to untangle, but do above all try to arrange a real rest, away from relief teams of any description and in lovely surroundings. Nothing I can imagine would be more beautiful than our doing it together, but for the moment that can't be. So do it for yourself this time, Red, and in June or thereabouts we'll do it together.

I hope it works. I need very much to see you; my enthusiasm and inspiration seem to be used up, and there's a great empty place inside waiting for you to fill it.

1993 ~ Madeleine from Monan's Rill

Red finally arrived in London, and we had five days together, a time of no great activity but great meaning for both of us. I was fighting a severe cold; Red insisted on bringing me breakfast in bed each morning, much to the disapproval of the housemother. "You're starting off on the wrong foot," she warned.

We went walking on Hampstead Heath one evening and fell upon a pub whose lights shone invitingly across the snow. The regulars inside were warmly welcoming. Red played a game of darts with them.

One night we stayed up until the wee hours in a small room that had an electric fire which we kept going against the prevailing cold. This was strictly forbidden because of rationing; I believe the housemother knew what we were doing, but she recognized our need for a few hours alone and said nothing. We talked urgently; Red was ready to marry then and there; I was not yet quite sure. It was a precious, stolen time.

One morning Red woke up with severe pain; no doctor was immediately available. Frantic, I dashed out into the snowy street and rang the bell at a nearby nursing home where mothers gave birth. A Sister came back to Gordon House with me and was able to relieve Red. It was after that episode that I was able to convince him to go to my relatives in Switzerland for a real rest.

February 27, 1947 ~ Madeleine in London to Red in Paris

Do you feel all of a piece, darling? Because part of you is certainly here. I almost catch a flash of your red head around the corner of a door, and this afternoon when I woke from a nap, it took me several moments to sort out the fact that you wouldn't be coming in to sit on the edge of my bunk and kiss me awake. Shall I be seeing you in Germany or no?

Now it's settled that I leave on Tuesday.

Remember my telling you on that ride to Marseille that your braking reminded me of an organist? Well this morning I went out in the three-ton Bedford, and truly enough, I almost had visions of your long black shoes moving about on the pedals with such sureness. Not that my stubby boots moved with any sureness. But I did all right, chum! My instructor said so, and I felt so. I could double-clutch without screeches after an hour, and by the end of two hours I was trundling the thing through fairly heavy traffic around Hampstead, where we walked yesterday.

Red, it's fun! I haven't had such a bang-up good time in ages. I wouldn't be surprised if that isn't partly what's the matter with me—no physical work and absorbing concentration for too long, no garden, no wood to cut, nothing except myself to ponder on, which is a darned dull occupation sometimes.

I was tired out at the end of two hours; I can't lean back in the seat, and every time I changed down I'd grind my teeth, and you have to kind of bash the gears around, especially when they're cold, but golly, I loved it. You feel so high up, and you've got such a lot under you, and you're not afraid of any goon who might come dashing into the road. I like it fine. I gathered from a remark the instructor let fall at the end of the drive that the other men thought he was nuts to take a novice out in a lorry on such bad roads, but he's a game guy, and I guess he wasn't sorry in the end.

March 3, 1947 ~ Madeleine in London to Red in Warsaw

Red, I did it! I confess to having some apprehension when I went to the doctor this morning for a contraceptive, but I might have saved the trouble. She was stubby and brusque and fitted me as if she were fitting a pair of shoes. Ordinarily one has to go back at least once, after practicing, but I got it right the first time, so she packed me off with her blessing. You may have to help me with it at first. It's more in your line anyway, being a sort of engineering affair. I am very small, which may give us some trouble at first. Do you think we should ask one of our friends at home to send us a helpful book on techniques and so on, or do you think that together we know enough to work things out? (Apropos, I shall never in my life forget the spectacle of my old roommates Beppy and Janice practicing instructions on positions while I read the directions out of a book!)

It's very curious, this matter of sex. I never thought that I could be so dispassionate about the preparations, having a perfect mountain of unsound attitudes and worries to overcome. Still less did I ever think I could find it in some respects amusing, and yet when it comes to the final act, I expect a very great deal in the way of loveliness and delicacy. As with so much else, my dear, it will take a lot of patience and understanding.

March 4, 1947 ~ Madeleine, traveling to Germany, to Red in Poland

It's now eight in the evening, and we're tearing across France toward Belgium. I've been remembering my first—our first—journey across France, and how we fitted ourselves into the carriage and spread our coats over each other.

There are four girls in this compartment tonight, nice people, most of them civilian Military Government. And we've just had an excellent meal—best since I've been in England—finishing up in good French fashion with cheese, black coffee, and Cointreau. So I feel much happier, especially in my tummy, than I did a few hours ago. The Channel was choppy, with a cold driving snow. The first hour I had a wonderful time, standing on top deck and watching the gulls and the waves; then I smoked a cigarette and spent the rest of the time fighting down nausea. Remind me not to smoke on our next rough crossing.

When I was enjoying the trip—and when I was wishing it would end—I half expected to see you standing over me if only I turned around. Oh Red, it's going to be hard not to let these next months be just an interlude. Even if there is not as much to do in Germany in the way of material relief as I had expected, there must be something I can share with people there, and surely there is much I can take away to share with people at home.

March 4, 1947 ~ Madeleine's journal

There are little kids begging along the side of the train, thin and ragged, as kids are all over Europe. We sit on plush seats smoking cigarettes, and occasionally someone tosses a sweet out the window. I HATE IT! Going through a station on a military train is like running a gauntlet. The tired faces, the hungry faces, the faces of people crouched over the couplings or on the roof, they follow us along.

March 5, 1947 ~ Madeleine in Vlotho to Red in Poland

This is it. We've arrived. All we saw of Belgium was the lights of Brussels last night and dark canals crisscrossing the flat land. The Ruhr early this morning was only blackened ruins standing in the snow, fading out into the gray fog. Here and there a lighted window shone out of some apparently uninhabitable building. All the things you ever said or wrote about Poland come back to me. It's a sad country to come into, and some of the sadness penetrates my mood.

The billet here knocked me for a loop—a huge room with heavy German furniture, spotlessly clean, a proper bath, and central heating! This last is almost too much for me now; I had a nap this afternoon and slept as if I were drugged. The food at the mess is good and more plentiful than in England. I have a most unbird-like appetite now that there's something to eat—I'll take you on at a pie-eating contest any day!

Red, you should see me—this isn't the girl you fell in love with—gray stockings, shirt and black tie, English beret, and all. I hardly know myself; maybe you wouldn't either. The cold wind has given me an English complexion, and by the time I learn to polish my shoes up to British standards, I'll be a proper English lass.

March 6, 1947 ~ Madeleine in Vlotho to Red in Warsaw

Tomorrow I go with the Vlotho people to Bielefeld for the conference. Wondering if I shall see you there, but my guess is not, so I'll write you a letter while I'm waiting for the dinner hour.

At the moment I'm enjoying a feline existence, luxuriating in warmth and plenty of food, but that will pall shortly. I'm anxious to get to Solingen and dig myself in. Apparently the work there is going to expand to include the expellees who are swarming into neighboring towns. The great snag is that all that kind of work needs lots of supplies, which we just don't have. The townspeople don't take kindly to these Volksdeutsch refugees (people who were repatriated to Germany from the lands returned to Poland) who are thrust upon them. The authorities don't usually allow them to work, and they are either interned in big camps or billeted on unwilling families with a welfare allowance. God help us—if we can't do better than shove people around like cattle, ignoring their creative capabilities and their human needs, what can we expect but upheavals!

1997 ~ Red from Monan's Rill

After the war, Poland was given the areas that had been called East Prussia. In addition, the western border of Poland was moved further west to compensate for the Polish territorial losses that had been given to

Russia in the east. Most of the Germans living in areas that was Germany before the war were forced to move inside the new borders of Germany, but postwar Germany was not prepared to take care of its own residents and was certainly not prepared for the flood of German refugees coming from the east. Oftentimes these refugees were housed very poorly in barrack-type buildings with only hanging blankets to provide privacy from their neighbors. These were the refugees for whom Madeleine sought housing in Germany, where shelter was already scarce.

March 8, 1947 ~ Madeleine's journal

In Bethel (Germany) this evening I stayed with the Wagner family: Frau and Dr. Wagner. They have a small, comfortable house, shared with the family of a sister who is a Flüchtling (refugee). One room was heated. I was given a small, clean room with a white down comforter.

They spoke of Russian atrocities and said: "The Germans never did anything like that." They didn't believe tales of German crimes in Poland. They claimed that the Poles were not using the homes and farms from which they had been evicted. In any case, they said, "That was war, this is peace." There is no apparent understanding of what Germany did in Europe, how other countries are now suffering as a result, or of how other nations feel toward the Germans.

The women tended to harp on small things: no tea, no milk except for children under six. "Things were better under the Nazis." They said they were very little disturbed by the Hitler regime. No books were taken out of private libraries, they claimed. I felt the tension of taking sides against pleasant people who were my hosts. Dr. Wagner showed a much more understanding mind than the women. He was three years on the Russian front and believed the Russians were good men, but he fears Bolshevism.

March 8, 1947 ~ Red in Corcelles to Madeleine in Solingen

This is the next best to spending a vacation with you. Your folks are spoiling me. Already I have slept fourteen hours and now should be in bed again. But I slept this afternoon instead of writing to you. Then your cousins Claudine, Hélène, and Marthe came unexpectedly. Tomorrow I visit them in Neuchâtel. Oh Madeleine, I'm running over with joy, and yet I feel as though I'm sharing it with you without having to write about it. Everything points to you: a piano, your bed, Uncle Paul—just everything. They love you, my dear.

Oh, where can I start? Mimi has taken charge of my affairs. Now she is knitting me a pair of mittens; her mother has already knitted me a pair of foot warmers, which I shall wear tonight. Uncle Paul is delightful. Aunt Madeleine is in bed, but I understand she spends most of her time there.

Tonight we had dinner at M. Charles' house. Yesterday I saw Krista, his granddaughter. They teased me that you want three babies. Darling, if only we could have a Roland! Everyone just assumed that we expect to get married; in fact, I was asked frankly if we expected to marry in June. The first time this was asked, I must have blushed; however, I said our plans were not definite. Now everyone wishes us to be married in the church at Corcelles where most of the family has been married. They even brought out the wedding suit, but all that fits me is the tall black hat! There is a wedding dress for you. Thank goodness, Claudine was here to translate, and I could explain that it is difficult for foreigners to get married quickly, and we will have only two weeks.

Oh yes, I am staying at Uncle Paul's, but in June I shall stay at M. Charles'; possibly you will stay again with the old maid aunts unless we are married.

Madeleine, can it be that we shall have as much life and love and devotion as Uncle Paul when we are his age? Tonight he pulled his wife into his lap and kissed her tenderly; then I saw you with an aged body but young in spirit and matured in love.

March 9, 1947 ~ Red in Corcelles to Madeleine in Solingen

Darling, we have just finished dinner and coffee with, of course, the traditional wines and whiskies. They tell me that you can consume your share, plus some. Now I come and match Uncle Paul glass for glass—it IS good wine. He has given me a liter of whisky to take with me. What does one do about all of this hospitality?

Last night I went to bed shortly after 11 p.m. and did not get up until 9:30 a.m. Had a hot bath and breakfast, then went with Uncle

Paul to see the rabbits and his wines. He showed me wine that he is saving for Roland's wedding.

I am anxiously waiting to know about Germany, about your living conditions, your companions, and any Germans you get to know. As for me, I did not know it would be so easy to forget about Poland—oh, not entirely, as people want to hear about it, but no longer am I anxious about the budget or personnel or many other problems. I am being extremely selfish and enjoying all of the hospitality that is being laid on.

I am beginning to come alive again. I wish you were here to witness it. You will meet a new man the day I am not tired and anxious but relaxed and well fed with plenty of sleep.

March 11, 1947 ~ Madeleine in Bethel to Red in Warsaw

It's a quiet evening, with purple light coming through the woods around the house. But first I want to tell you about a bright snowy morning the first day of the conference when I came in to breakfast and sat down beside Claude Shotts (the AFSC representative in Berlin). Says he, "Where's Red Stephenson?" Says I, "I don't know, thought you could tell me." A fine thing! So up speaks Bill Huntington from across the table and puts us both right.

Oh Red, I was glad to know that you'd gone to Switzerland. I'd love you to have been here, and some of the discussions you'd have found stimulating, and some rather CPS-like and redundant, but it was all shoptalk, and a real vacation had much better be away from all that. Whenever I went out walking in the crisp snow, I'd think how it would be much the same in Corcelles, and I hope you had a mound of down to sleep under and a warm kitchen to sit in and good Swiss cooking. Bethel has been as pleasing an introduction to Germany as one could have. It's a town of about 8,000; half the population are epileptics or mentally ill, cared for by the nurses, doctors, and deaconesses who make up the rest of the town. It was begun by a Protestant pastor in the last century, and carried on by his sons and grandsons. The religious aspect seems a bit overbearing: black-coated, white-bonneted sisters and nurses; Bible texts painted inside and outside on the houses and hospitals; a long, solemn Sunday service for everyone. Listening to the hour's sermon, looking at the poor, half-made faces of some of the children, I could have wished something brighter and sunnier for them.

Almost miraculously, the town suffered little either from the Nazis or from bombing. Early in the war, a stray bomb hit a hospital for children, killing sixteen of them. The incident was seized on by Goebbels as an example of Allied atrocity and trumpeted all over Germany. Bethel, City of Mercy (how strange that sounded in the mouth of Goebbels, said the pastor), had been wantonly attacked. No more bombs fell, but when the greater menace of euthanasia threatened, the work of Bethel had become so well known that the Nazis never dared touch the patients.

Back to the conference. The theological school in which we met has a large room with windows on two sides, looking out to the woods. The clean, scrubbed tables were centered with pots of prim cineraria. Portraits of Martin Luther and the founder of the institution hung on the walls. There was searching, but inconclusive discussion about the role of relief workers. Service in Germany, or any other country in Europe, came to seem to us untenable on a short-term basis. Perhaps there would be something to be hoped for from our returning later, with our families, to live and work for five or ten years. We saw our possible functions as being go-betweens, promoting reconciliation, offering friendly encouragement.

March 11, 1947 ~ Red in Corcelles to Madeleine in Solingen

This is like a paradise amidst an ocean of suffering. In fact, it is easy to forget about the suffering of other people. Sometimes I wonder what it all means. Can the Swiss be complacent in the midst of Europe today? Or have they found something that is indestructible? Uncle Paul has something that many of us do not acquire in a lifetime. Is it because the Swiss are so close to the soil? Maybe Louis Bromfield and others were right when they said that a civilization becomes decadent when the soil and forests are exploited. That certainly has been the case in Europe and, now, America.

Regardless of where we go or what we do, there should be one prerequisite: a place where we can get our hands into the soil. Also, there should be a place for a few rabbits, chickens, and a hive of bees. One does not have to have a large place for these, or for a couple of nut trees. In Salem, Oregon, the streets are lined with English walnut trees. Beautiful and useful. The main trouble is that in order to get real benefit from these things, one must become settled. Oh well, we shall work it out somehow.

Madeleine, everywhere I turn here there is something to remind me of you. In fact, while we were eating yesterday, a car door slammed outside and for a moment I had a queer feeling that it would be you. All the time I have the feeling that I've just left you, and we shall meet again in a few hours. How can I miss you, when you are still with me?

Everyone is so concerned that I sleep, eat, and not exert myself, but I'm breaking into the kitchen by peeling potatoes and wiping dishes.

Tuesday après-midi.

I've just returned from a two-and-a-half-hour visit with Aunt Madeleine and Aunt Tida. Oh, my dear, how can I tell you about it. I'm so happy, even the rain does not dampen my spirits. Madeleine, I sat and ate from the same place you ate in your room. I looked at the picture of you and your brother Walt on the piano; for a moment we could see the Alps across the lake. They love you dearly, and I did not tire of talking and hearing about you. Although I must admit, twice I became absorbed in looking at your picture and missed what they were saying. Then they brought out pictures of you as a baby, a little girl, then with glasses, and last as you became a lady. My eyes burn still from the passion I felt as I tried to imagine you through those years.

There was a time when I had fears or apprehensions about raising children in this troubled world, but now I know that what we need is faith and a new generation with faith. It is not that we should mold the child or direct the child, but we should rather give to him opportunities to obtain those things which we consider basic: a good diet, a loving home, freedom, and faith in himself and in that which is greater than us all.

March 12, 1947 ~ Madeleine in Dortmund to friends at home

A cold, gray, dripping day. We drove through the ruins of this, one of the most destroyed cities in Germany. Ruins and pictures of ruins may be getting to be an old story at home, but they are still terribly real here; pitted roads winding through piles of rubble; carved columns sticking up through landslides of brick and mortar; a gold-figured clock on a square tower, all that is left of a church; clean-curtained windows in the two or three rooms that are still habitable in a block of apartments; vistas off the main street into still more streets, all of them only shells or façades or piles of ruin; two beautiful statues on either side of an arched door leading into a roofless, gutted twelfth-century cathedral; the dome of a church lying crazily against its foundation; stairways going up into nothingness; and everywhere the sodden mass of brick, twisted girders, toppled pediments, crumbling stone, that is Dortmund—and Cologne and Berlin and Warsaw and dozens of other cities in France and Poland and Russia and Germany. Already weeds and grass are beginning to grow on the rubble.

I was traveling with an architect, and it seemed to particularly pain him to see the structural parts of buildings, so carefully calculated for their use and beauty, strewn about like the dismembered limbs of a body.

Destruction on a dark day is depressing enough, but added to that is the overwhelming realization, no matter what ruined city you are in, that it is only one of many—and that it might easily be Paris or London or New York or Chicago. It is not just the ruins of a city you are seeing, but the ruins of a civilization. Over and over again the words of Stephen Spender echoed in my head: "It [the destruction] is the shape created by our century as the Gothic cathedral is the shape created by the Middle Ages ....It is a climax of deliberate effort, an achievement of our civilization, the most striking result of cooperation between nations in the twentieth century." (From *European Witness*, which I commend to you as the most sensitive and moral analysis of Germany today that I have yet seen.)

In this dead city, life goes on with a kind of blind drive. Women pick their way among the mudholes with their ration of bread and vegetables; children play on the rubble heaps; workmen hang on the cream-colored trams that run irregularly through those streets that have been partially cleared. Here and there, in a building that seems a total ruin, a room has been fixed up, a piece of glass found, and a store opens. If it is a food store, you recognize it by the block-long lines waiting to buy rations. We saw several shops with smart, bright dresses in the windows; their gaiety and incongruity seemed almost indecent in the surroundings.

The actual rations in Dortmund are about 1,300 calories a day. You have only to look at the passing faces to read what that means: yellow, lined faces of the old (and people grow old soon here); pinched, gray faces of working men (despite the fact that they have extra rations or they could not work); pasty, dull faces of children. The painful procession goes by slowly, slowly; no one has the energy to move quickly. If you drive, you must make twice the usual allowance for the reaction time of pedestrians. It gets to be very hard to look the stream of passersby in the eye; every face shows misery, hopelessness, dull resentment.

March 13, 1947 ~ Red in Corcelles to Madeleine in Solingen

The week is nearly at its end; I feel like Cinderella at midnight, yet I can dream of returning here this summer with you. Last night I dreamed of you again; it's a poor substitute, but soon we shall be together. Yet the time (until then) must not be spent concentrating on our trip to Switzerland in June so much that we forget to live today. That may be one reason why we did not feel rushed during those few short days in London. We have begun to live each day for itself. Of course, there are outstanding days, days of great joy and days of great sorrow, but as Bernard Shaw says, "You do not retain the flavor of good wine by always holding some in your mouth."

Madeleine, relief work by its very nature is frustrating. Why? Because relief work in itself has demoralizing aspects, one cannot overcome them but rather do enough good to change the balance.

-Red

Our Relationship Is Tested

superior noticed I hadn't drunk
my café au lait (it's that and
mud-colored stuff) and was
inquiète. Now who the Mother
Superior is I haven't the fog-
giest, but she must have an all-
seeing eye.

There's a huge park here, and
wonderful view of the countryside.
An interval of several hundred..... did I say I wanted
to be alone? The Mother Super-
came to talk to me, then a nun
from Ecuador - a jolly woman
who studied in a convent in
Michigan and loves New York
City! They were so sorry to
come I'd been alone since
last night! Next time I

March 14, 1947 ~ Madeleine in Solingen to Red in Poland

Well, I've been here two-and-a-half days, and though I've been in and out of bed that time (a streaming cold from the Channel crossing and driving around the country in drafty cars), I've come to know the team. They are all pleasant, if somewhat unusual people, and I don't yet see the conflicts I was warned of. Aside from a certain lack of American spontaneity and general rambunctiousness (which I inadvertently supply), I find them very amiable and easy to get on with.

The house is magnificent—the manner of living to which I should like to become accustomed! Green-tiled bathroom as big as a bedroom, enormous sitting room, ditto dining room, grand piano, organ, modern kitchen, etc., etc. It's the house of a big industrialist who joined the Party to keep his job. It's fun to luxuriate, to have a steaming hot bath, to have all you want to eat, well cooked (the army rations are tremendous after England), but the contrast between that and the misery in refugee camps and large cities is hard to take. As you know, there's little one can do about it, short of rejecting the whole setup under the Military Government.

The whole question of food and accommodation was brought up at the conference and thrashed out, rather unrealistically, it seemed to me. One high-principled young woman suggested we live on German rations and packages from home, which is balmy to my way of thinking and was to most of the others. The consensus was that it was better to take our privileges and share them as much as possible with Germans, who need the lift of an evening in a real home and a good meal now and again. Since coming here, however, and seeing the abundance of space, heat, and food, I wonder if we share as much as we might. The contrast with our way of life in France and England is so great.

But why is it, Red, that so often it is dour, severe, unattractive people who propose austerities? And that other people, like me, revolt against the personality more than against the idea? I think all of us could give up much more than we do, but I'm damned if I want to do it out of a stern sense of duty or self-sacrifice! When the person comes along who preaches joyful austerity, I'll probably trail along, but not after anyone who is severely good!

I think the basis of much unrest among the teams here is the fact that the relief job is so much bigger than can be handled, and along with this is needed a spiritual reconstruction which we all see is necessary but which is beyond the compass of Friends Relief Service. The second point troubled me already in France, but since the conference in Bethel, I've had some new thoughts on the subject.

Red, dear (here I'd give you a short kiss if we were talking together), it's obvious that the job in Europe won't get done this year or next or on an emergency basis. It's also clear that we probably can't make

FOOD AID (BRITISH) FRIENDS RELIEF SERVICE DISTRIBUTED SUPPLIES IN GERMANY. THIS IS THE SON OF A "STATELESS GERMAN." 1947
-PHOTOGRAPH BY DICKIE AND TONY CHAPELLE

a large contribution by staying on indefinitely in the present circumstances. I at least feel that, by the end of my term, I shall have pretty well used up my spiritual resources, and I'm getting anxious to be back home and do some thinking and replenishing and just living.

What struck me was this: how about going back to the States, starting a family, getting into some useful kind of work, which might also be a preparation or possible contribution to European work, and planning to return here in perhaps five or ten years, to settle in some country, live among people on a normal basis as a family, and really dig into the problems of international understanding and interpretation? How long one would stay—two years or five or ten—would depend on situations and needs and abilities. One might come as an individual, earning his living, or possibly as a representative of AFSC. I wonder—what do you think?

I am going to start a club for the Relief of Relief Workers in Germany Engaged to Men in Poland: RRWGEMP! In Dortmund I found Hetty Tinkler, about to tear off to meet George McMillage; here I find that Grete Ravn is engaged to Ted Harris; then there's a certain little American who thinks often and fondly of Red Stephenson and loves to slide his name—or at any rate, Poland—into the table talk.

1993 ~ Madeleine from Monan's Rill

One of the ways our team shared with the Germans was to exchange the big, crusty loaves of white bread, which we received with our NAAFI rations, for German bread made largely of cornmeal. There was little flour on the German rations; cornmeal was supplied instead. But German bakers were not accustomed to using cornmeal, and there was little to add to it to lighten the bread. So we put aside our white bread for people on our welfare caseload who had stomach trouble and took their cornbread in exchange. Made into sandwiches for lunches when we were out with the trucks all day, it was coarse and dry. But we could handle it better than many others.

Most of us received packages from family and friends at home, and most of these gifts went into the team's storeroom to be distributed by the team social workers along with relief supplies. Packages from America were often lavish by English standards and were greatly prized, but I never opened a package from England without a special sense of gratitude and humility. These small gifts, perhaps a tin of sardines, a small can of evaporated milk, and a bar of chocolate, came from people whose rations were:

Butter: 1/4 lb. a week
Eggs: 1 a month
Cheese: 2 oz. a week
Sugar: 8 oz. a week
Bacon: 2 oz. a week
Tea: 4 oz. a week
Candy: 4 oz. a week
Lard: 2 oz. a week
Syrup: 2 lb. can a month
Bread: unrationed until 1944, then 1 lb. a week
Fish, potatoes, and vegetables were not rationed, but one had to get them when they were available.

The Save Europe Now parcels came from people of goodwill to their former enemies and represented real sacrifice.

Clothing bales came from both the U.S. and England. Again, the American bales were usually of better quality, but the English contributions came from people whose clothing was rationed from 1939 to 1948—again, gifts representing real sacrifice and concern.

Mid-March 1947 ~ Red in Warsaw to friends at home

I have been in seven countries and six capitals in the past four weeks. First stop was in Berlin, and my disgust for the way the Americans are living there was as great as it was last July. Lois, secretary to the local AFSC representative, said that all the German youth that she knows are very much depressed. She is most concerned and is trying to figure ways to improve the morale of those she knows. Also, they were most concerned about a large group of old people who have no one to get food and fuel for them during this cold weather. There was no central building to which they could be brought; so it meant a large force of personnel to care for them. Of course, this is not being provided; so the old people are just dying in their beds.

The next morning we were off again above the clouds, a rather dull ride to London during which time the RAF (Royal Air Force - British) boys fed us sandwiches, for which they apologized and kept showing us where we were by means of a map.

How is London? Gray, dreary, and dismal. Everyone was apologizing and saying that it was too bad that I had to visit London at this time, as it was dirtier and uglier than it had been all through the war. The food was poor, and there was very little, yet I had the impression that they did not do the best with what they had. No imagination in cooking, but after all I am spoiled by the restaurants of Warsaw. The streetlights were not on, and electricity was off for part of each day. The gas pressure was low. Yet I am glad that I was there, because it is easier to understand how the British face a crisis like that, plenty of griping and yet taking it all philosophically. You had the feeling that everyone was being treated the same; there were no favored classes. Their food situation is worse than it was throughout the war. In spite of all this, they were interested in exporting food to Europe!

Took the Golden Arrow, which is supposed to be the best train from London to Paris. We crossed the Channel from Dover to Calais. Ah, sweet Paris. After eight months, it was grand to take a stroll around Notre Dame Cathedral again and along the Seine. It brought back some very pleasant memories of last spring.

I stayed in Paris for a week and then took the train for Neuchâtel, Switzerland, where some of Madeleine's relatives live.

I took this trip because I was extremely tired after eight months in Poland and needed a rest. Madeleine wrote to her uncle and must have given them a good story, as they treated me like an invalid. They live simply, growing vineyards, yet I felt more security in their home than I have felt in seven years or more.

Uncle Paul is a hard working man, and his wife works along beside him in the fields. It was too wet and rainy to do much while I was there, so I was given a back room where it was quiet.

All I did was eat, sleep, and drink wine. Chocolate, apples, and oranges were always beside my bed. They made heavier woolen mittens for me, as they thought what I had were too light for Poland; also, they made nice foot warmers for me to bring back. I could sleep as late as I liked, and breakfast would always be ready after I washed. It was paradise, but I would hate to live that way for long.

Since they spoke no English—though their daughter was there with her small son for a few days and she spoke a bit—it meant that my French improved, but conversation was still tough. However, it did give me an opportunity to do some thinking.

Here is a man who probably inherited his land from his father and fathers before him. When his children receive the land from him, it will be as productive as it was 100 years ago. This man is not taking from the soil, but giving to it. He knows that you cannot get something for nothing.

So ended four weeks of traveling. Madeleine has now gone to Germany (Solingen, in the Ruhr). Both of us are having experiences that will help shape the rest of our lives; yet we are anxious to see more of each other. That must wait until this summer when we hope to be in Switzerland together. (Did someone say that relief work is a great sacrifice?)

March 17, 1947 ~ Madeleine in Solingen to Red in Poland

It's spring again today, snowdrops are out, and children are skating and scootering down the hill beside our house. You wonder where, in their thin bodies and pipe-stem legs, they find the energy to do it, but they do. Two boys are hilariously kicking a homemade ball around the street; one of them is wearing shoes big enough for a man, and to keep them on his feet, he has to hop rather than run; the other has broken-down women's white summer sandals with runover high heels. It makes for an awkward game, but they're having a wonderful time.

As we were going to bed (there are four beds in our large bedroom), one of my roommates said: "Listen, hear that noise?" I did—a deep whirring sound. Presently came the crash of a felled tree. Another of the red hawthorns that line our street has gone for fuel. It's illegal, of course, so people do it by night, but once the trees are down, anyone may come by day to hack away at the stumps and carry off baskets of chips. Bebelallee, that in spring used to be bordered with pink blooms, has scarcely one tree in four left.

You get a queer, island-like feeling here; it won't surprise me if we don't get our back-and-forth correspondence established for quite a while. The vagaries of army post offices are too many for me!

Our house is beautiful. It is too damn beautiful. About three times the size of an ordinary American house—huge rooms, plate-glass windows, through which we watch the inhabitants pushing pitiful carts or hacking away at stumps for fuel. Steam heat, almost too much. Wonderful food, compared with England, but a bit heavy, and there is always cabbage. The potatoes are always dried or powdered, but otherwise excellent. A battery of servants—five or six, I think.

A team of twelve, when I came. With that many people and no housekeeping duties, we should be able to turn the Kreis (district or county) right side up. I know I've only been here a week and shouldn't squawk yet, but it's only you and I feel like saying it: I cannot see what the hell we are doing! A little supplies work, a little youth work, a little refugee work. The most strenuous thing I've done since coming here was to pass round sandwiches and talk to refugees at an evening "do" we had.

I am doing what is known as "settling in," which consists in poking about trying to see what other people are doing, begging for odd jobs, and being tired out at the end of the day from sitting on my derrière. Another team member and I were asked by HQ at Vlotho to go to another Kreis north of here to do a survey on refugee conditions, which are apparently very bad. For lack of transport we didn't leave on Monday, but I hope to heaven we leave tomorrow. The team was rather against the idea because they felt so short-handed! But two men and an English truck went off this morning just to make a friendly call on a man in Bonn—an all day job!

Toulouse all over again. Just sit there, darling, and let me blow my top and presently I'll feel OK. It's all bound up with the transition of relief work, and the fact that we're not well equipped either technically or emotionally for the long-term job and that the problem of Germany is so damn big that neither we nor anyone else can see it all in a piece. People say over and over again that just our being here helps, but unless you think you're a vestpocket god, that isn't much justification for living off the fat of the land.

Next item: The team morale is something to write home about. Three days after I got here they had a team meeting that—for spite, bitterness, and accumulated misunderstandings—tops anything I have ever heard. The team is split into two cliques: the Old Guard and the Poor Relations or new arrivals. Curiously enough, I think I have the liking of people on both sides, though it happened quite by accident. I just wanted to get to know everyone and did before I discovered the great cleavage.

A further snag is that the team leader is engaged to one of the girls on the team, and since they're both Old Guard, this causes an added feeling of separation between the two groups.

So for the nth time, it's our own muddle, which we must straighten out before we can hope to help other people's, and a sorry condition it is. The fact that several people are leaving and three replacements are coming in April should give us a chance for a fresh start.

I have hopes, but I must say at the moment Germany is not panning out as I had expected it to. I came here thinking there was a pile of work to be done, and eager to get on with it; and it's the same story again—we don't seem to know what our job is and have to go looking for it before we can do it. All of which doesn't give me much of a chance on a six-month basis.

I can try to get all I can out of the experience, in language and understanding. As far as I, as a person, am concerned, I think it will be richly worthwhile. But as for helping the German people or extending peace—I dunno. It's easy to ask too much of a job, particularly of jobs like these which are so untried and uncharted, and so difficult to visualize now without the acute conditions of emergency which we first imagined would exist here. I remember Hugh saying once, "The time to do relief work WAS."

Well and a day. You may give me a swift kick if next letter I yell about being too busy! Right now I can hardly wait for August to come. I shall continue to swot at the Polish—not that I'll be able to ask for a direction by the time I get there—and hope that we can be together in Warsaw for a while.

Do you know, Red, something that pleases me very much: whenever something happy happens—if I wake up and see a spring sky, or if people are having fun together, or if Kjell plays his lute and sings

Swedish songs through the halls in the morning before we get up (he's one of the swell members of this team, someone you'll hear more about)—my thoughts fly to you and I feel all smiley.

Next day: I do go off today to do a JOB. I WORK! Soltau (the Kreis north of here) has asked for a relief team, and they're sending in four of us for an emergency job and survey to see what needs to be done and what we can do in three weeks. Maybe it'll be repeated and I'll stay for six. There seems to be a general feeling that it would be nice if I stayed here and spread sweetness and light around, but I confess I'd rather spend myself tramping around camps and feeling I'm DOING something.

March 20, 1947 ~ Madeleine in Soltau to Red in Poland

Drove from Vlotho to Soltau with James Patrick over shocking roads, through minor floods, and across precarious bridges. Most of the bridges in the Rhineland and north are out, and many roads are flooded. Incredible destruction at Hanover. I'm beginning to wonder if Poland has anything worse to offer in terms of mud! For kilometers we bumped over roads that were no more than logging paths, traveling in the company of three- and five-ton trucks, sometimes with trailers. The roads were not much to begin with, but after that traffic, they'll only be good for gravel pits. We were misdirected over a moor and ploughed through some of the loneliest country I have ever seen: stretches of rolling grassland broken here and there with clumps of fir, with only a flock of black sheep and a shepherd to be seen for miles.

On the way, we picked up people. One man said he had been deported twice from the East. There was a boy who had been in Belsen; they were told the camp was for Jews to be guarded before going to England and America. The camp was surrounded by woods where dogs ran loose. Then we came to Belsen. Low concrete buildings with barred windows twisted with barbed wire. We saw pits in the forest, graves scattered about. There is a Jewish monument and a wooden cross. Great twenty-foot ditches backed by a sinister concrete wall. Arches in the hillside were probably crematoriums. An utter desolation: gray sky, black mud, somber forests. A cursed earth, if such is possible.

Today, the four of us in the survey team were just outside the town of Soltau visiting a youth center. In a grove of fir trees with moss-greened trunks was an old red brick church, and beside it a squat, square wooden tower that housed a tremendous bell. At one o'clock the bell boomed out, and the members of a little wedding party began to arrive at the church.

There was only one car, and the driver did a shuttle service between the town and the church until they were all there. Finally the bride arrived, stepping across the mud on pairs of bricks that had been laid down for her. Although the rest of the party was simply dressed, she had a white gown and veil and the bridegroom a black suit. Two little girls in pink scattered green leaves before them. We peeped in the open door as they stood before the minister in the freezing church. And because it was coming on spring, and because the little scene before us was so simple and lovely, I found myself thinking

CURIOUS GERMAN CHILDREN WITH A TRUCK OF FOOD SUPPLIES
-PHOTOGRAPHER UNKNOWN

of our wedding, my dear. It won't be just like that one, but—oh Red, it's hard to say what I feel. It begins to seem to me that the ceremony of marriage, though in a conventional sense unimportant, is symbolically of very great moment, and I pray that ours may be sincere and beautiful because we are so to each other.

Later we visited the pastor of the church. His little boy clicked his heels when we were introduced. The pastor had fought in the war. "We had to," he said. "But did everyone fight?" we asked. "We HAD to."

This job in Soltau isn't as neatly cut out as I had hoped when I came; evidently we are to mooch around, spot-checking refugee conditions, bring suggestions and recommendations to the attention of the German and Military Government officials, and distribute a minute amount of supplies. Maybe it's me, always yelling for a concrete problem to tackle, but I don't think so. Everybody I have talked with in German relief work feels the same vagueness about our work, and I'm beginning to feel that perhaps everybody in Germany is vague and unsettled in his mind about what he's doing and how he's to do it. There's the incredible duplication of two sets of officials: German and Military Government; there are the almost endless political divisions; then the divisions between parties; between church groups; between residents and refugees.

And in it all we are strangers; we are not wanted here and to a large extent we do not want to be here (I am speaking of the whole foreign colony). All the efforts of NAAFI to provide refreshment and recreation have a strained, unreal air, and sometimes I feel sorrier for the English, or any occupying power—with all their privileges and easy living—than for the Germans, who at least belong here in a fundamental sense. I think I have seldom been more deeply lonely than in Germany, and that in spite of being among good comrades. But we are Ausländer—people out of the country, foreigners—sometimes that is good, sometimes bad, but always the distinction remains.

March 19, 1947 ~ Red in Warsaw to Madeleine in Solingen

If only you knew how good it is to be back; it was a thrill to see Warsaw again. Everything is in ruins, yet it has a certain character about it as well as a spirit that is good to witness again. Honestly, it was as though I was returning home. I have been so happy that it seems childish. Everywhere I go, it is as though springs are under my feet, a song in my voice, and a smile on my lips. Warsaw is not the only cause of my happiness, but the prospect of seeing you. Anyway, just knowing you makes me happy, and the thought of our marrying this June gives me thrills. Yet I still insist that if we do not, I shall be happy, because we shall marry sooner or later.

We arrived in Prague late Sunday afternoon; everything was crowded on account of an exposition that was being held there. No hotel rooms were available; so they asked if I would be willing to accept a private home. Of course, I consented, yet when I arrived there they spoke only German and Czech. However, the lady called to a girl in another room and asked her to speak English to me. What a lovely girl walked out. My first thought was that Red's luck was still holding good. It was not only beauty, but her charm and dignity that made up a most appealing personality. We chatted a bit, and she made arrangements with the lady for my room and breakfast the next morning. I was also attempting to find out what happens in Prague on a Sunday night. Her boss came in, and she said they were going to meet some Belgian buyers for dinner and asked if I would care to join them. Not knowing just what was coming, I was adventurous enough to accept. We had dinner, and she was the only lady. What a hostess she made!

Darling, this may sound strange to you, but I enjoyed looking at Maja as I would have enjoyed a beautiful painting, and this beat a painting because the feeling could be exchanged. We later went to three different night clubs. It was a grand evening. Some people would say that my actions were outrageous for a person expecting to be married to another woman, yet I broke no trust between us, and besides, I was enjoying Prague as I would not have enjoyed it otherwise. We had dinner together at the House of Representatives restaurant the next day and saw much of the fair together. Then one of the Belgian men, her boss, and I saw her off to her home. She kissed us all good-bye, and I was actually sorry to see her leave as I had five more hours in Prague.

Why do I tell you all of this in such detail? Because, darling, I witnessed and experienced something that was wonderful. Knowing that we had only night and day together, I felt freer to let my emotions go. No, my sweet, I did not sleep with her. Neither do I have a guilty conscience.

Maybe I, myself, don't know what it is that I'm trying to say, unless it be that I have the capacity to enjoy beauty in other people and, through that, to be happier with you, just as you witnessed the beautiful scenes of Switzerland and for it loved me more. I enjoyed an evening with another girl and loved you more deeply for the experience.

March 22, 1947 ~ Madeleine in Belsen to Herb Hauck back home

Harold Chance flew over from England last night. You, my friend, have won a famous victory. Remember your questions about "What would a pacifist do if . . . ?" Harold's been in Sweden, in Holland, and Belgium. Friends there, good pacifists all – many of them imprisoned and sentenced to be shot for refusal of military service – entered almost totally into the Resistance Movements. They started out by trying to win over the occupation troops; gradually the things they saw and knew drove them to try to help Nazi victims. They hid Jews, passed on ammunition, stole, and lied like the best of their compatriots. According to Harold, they still believe in pacifism as the only solution, but they couldn't make it work, and what they were able to do, they'd do again. It's magnificent and tragic together.

Personal sacrifice in the face of organized brutality, in the face of mass slaughter, seems almost completely ineffective. These people judged it better to try to live out the persecution than to fight it in a hopeless way. I don't know. I only know that the spirit of man, whenever it is honest and courageous, is a tremendous thing. I honor these people, the more so that they did what they thought they had to do with torn hearts. I'm beginning to learn, a little, how people can do half-good things in great sadness, knowing it is imperfect and incomplete, but knowing too that it's the best thing they can do at the moment. God, but it's a hard thing.

March 22, 1947 ~ Red in Warsaw to Madeleine in Solingen

Once again this is one of those long periods without word from you; although it is a bit of a strain, I am trying to be patient. Only today we received Paris mail that was posted March 8. Oh, how can we ever plan anything when it takes so long?

As yet I do not know how you are finding Germany. Peter asked me today what I thought about your going there, and I said that quite frankly I did not think that you would like the way you would have to live in comparison to the Germans. I told him you would be too sensitive to the differences and the restrictions. However, there is a job to be done.

I am glad that you can be in Germany. More and more, you will be asking yourself what you can do; that is one of the most asked questions in relief work. Tonight we received a letter from Arthur Little telling about a Polish man from the embassy in Washington telling him that he knew about the work of the Quakers in Poland and was well pleased. One never knows how far-reaching a kind word or a smile will be. Yet neither Germans nor Poles can live on words and smiles alone. Who is to say that living without those things is life?

Last night Anna Krossowska visited in my room for more than three hours. She told me of a Jewish boy who was stoned and beaten so badly by some Gentiles during the occupation that he needed medical attention. The hospital treated him but refused to keep him, as it was too dangerous. A friend of hers took him in and cared for him; however, he died. This caused more complications because no doctor would sign the death certificate—too dangerous. So she and her friend decided to put the body into a sack and take it on the tram to the edge of the city. As luck would have it, this happened to be one of the trams that the Germans checked. They knew that they were doomed, when the Germans opened the bag. You can imagine a soldier's amazement when he peered into a burlap bag and saw the body of a Jewish boy. The soldiers ordered the people to dig a hole and bury the boy and then to the complete astonishment of everyone, they freed all those connected with the body!

Anna is a grand person, and she has been a great help to us here. Sometime after my visit to Kozienice, I am to meet her husband; she will be the interpreter.

If only you could be here, then experiences like this afternoon would not be so tempting. I was offered an invitation for drinks and supper with the promise that more pleasant things might come later; it was from a lady I have known and expect to meet again. Honestly, I felt like a fly in a spider's web. Nevertheless, before leaving we had a complete understanding, and I do not think it will be embarrassing for her to meet me in public. In my opinion it hurts a woman's ego more than it does a man's to be refused. As I have told you before, I cannot promise that a refusal would always be my answer, but today there was little temptation. I know that though it might be satisfying physically, it would be repugnant emotionally.

I like the company of women, and I trust that I shall continue liking her, but I must be more careful and let the impossibility of a relationship be known. The fault is not hers alone, because I have responded to the wink of an eye and the pressure of a hand in spite of the fact that there was not emotion behind them but rather a feeling of adventure. What is the adjustment that one has to make when those things are expressed to one person only?

Oh, Madeleine, we have so much to learn together. This idea of living with someone is going to be strange, but wonderful. If I arrived in London with any fears, they have been minimized to the point of nonexistence. Is this blind love?

Today has been spring! One of those days that you love so well. Many people are promenading to see the ice floe, the museum, and the art gallery. Oh my sweet, tonight is beautiful. The window has been open all day and evening. I walked back beneath the stars so wonderful and refreshing, and I wondered if you saw them tonight. 'Tis strange, but I always connect you with those things everlasting. Tonight, I gazed upon the stars, thought of you and was at peace. There was a quiet stillness within and I was happy.

March 25, 1947 ~ Madeleine in Soltau to Red in Poland

It's the beginning of a day that's been fitfully spring-like. Around our house and up the road are woods—pine and white birch—touched with sunset clouds. But it's another day with no letter from thee, Red, and I'm beginning to be sore lonely. Darling, do you know I've no news of you since you left Paris for Switzerland? I can't think what it is; mail from you in Paris was waiting for me in Solingen, but nothing since.

Oh Red, I do so miss you. Days without post are a keen disappointment. Yesterday I had to go for a walk in the pines to remember that our thoughts are together even though we are not, that the same sky is blue over us and everyone, and that love knows no time or place. I wondered as I walked whether we might some time walk together in the Polish forests. They are magnificent, these pine forests—the only wealth of this part of Germany, which otherwise is moor and marsh. They're being recklessly logged now, and the timber being sent to England.

The little temporary team here is tops: Frank Farnell, a Yorkshireman with a sense of humor and an easy way of talking; Peg Atkinson, a nice American girl; James Patrick (from Solingen, too), a liberal Anglican parson, and me. We spend our evenings roaring with laughter! You're part of the joke, chum. When I told them about you, and that you're as tall as I am short, they burst into gales and haven't stopped since. Frank delights in telling everybody that "Madeleine's Mann ist zu hoch" (too tall).

Work is getting on. We're well into the technique of mooching around: meeting officials, both German and English; scrounging supplies; listening to problems and trying to help; spot-checking refugee housing; and so on. We wine and dine, and are done the same unto by officers of the Military Government. The net result of such an evening is, or ought to be, a bunch of mattresses or a new welfare office. If I do say so, as I shouldn't, I'm considered good at liaison!

March 28, 1947 ~ Madeleine's journal

I wish the men in Moscow who are talking about boundaries had been with us today as we went about the Gemeinde of Dorfmark visiting the camps and private billets where 1,500 refugees are housed. Driving through the neat villages and the countryside with the ample half-timber, half-brick houses, you could not guess that the number of refugees here is greater than the number of natives. The farm homes, set far back from the road, closed in on three sides by fir and birch forests, look spacious and prosperous. But when you go up to the carved door of such a Hof, you notice a neat list tacked up, with the names of the thirty-one people who live in the house; the first seven are the owner and his family, the rest refugees from the east, from New Poland.

We visited some of them. Frau Peters and her mother, who were ironing in the sunny room where three of the family sleep and where they must also cook, eat, sew, and live. A smaller room is used only for sleeping, the three beds as close together as in a dormitory. We noticed the snowy feather beds. They are the pride of every housewife here, but rare indeed among refugees, who too often have had to leave their homes in a matter of minutes.

When Stettin, where the Peters lived, was occupied, soldiers ripped the beds open with bayonets, and the feathers scattered for meters around, but the women patiently gathered them up, washed them, and remade the beds. In spite of the crowding, the room is amazingly neat and attractive. Flowers bloom on the window sills, and bunches of pussywillow bring in spring. It is not until the Peters begin to talk of their homeland that you realize the constant hurt that lies behind this homelike exterior. Stettin, they say, "is a city as German as London is English." They can understand Poland's taking back land that has long been disputed territory, but their country has been "German for a thousand years." They feel they are being punished for the concentration camps, but they say ordinary Germans didn't know about them. They only knew that sometimes people disappeared, they knew not where; there was no free press, and one did not dare listen to the foreign radio. "By the time we saw which way the wagon was going, it was too late." Not very profound thinking, but pitifully human.

Upstairs lives Frau Rohrs, an alert old lady, with her daughter and two grandsons. The son-in-law is still in a Russian prison camp. Frau Rohrs has been twice a refugee, once in 1919 and again in 1945 when she had to leave with her two ill grandsons on a four-week transport. "When can we go back to Brandenberg?" she wanted to know. When we told her of the latest boundaries proposed by the U.S. at the Moscow conference, her face lit up with a momentary hope. "Tell them when you go back there that the refugees want only one thing: to go back home." And I thought of the Spaniards in southern France, waiting to go back home to the other side of the Pyrenees, and of the thousands of Poles still in camps in Germany after five or six years, and of prisoners of war, all wanting only to go home.

Not all the refugees can be billeted in private homes; some are still in camps like the Schweinkaserne, where 108 people are living in buildings where pigs were once fattened for the slaughterhouse. Five families have been there since 1939, and by this time they have made their quarters quite comfortable. Only the long, low building and small, high-up windows betray the lowly origin of the camp.

A collection of wooden barracks in the woods, once a youth work camp, now houses large families. There we met Herr and Frau Tantov and their seven children, the youngest only five weeks old, who live in two rooms. It was washday, and the living/dining room/kitchen was dim with steam. Whatever the odds, these people manage to keep themselves and their children clean. But there is very little more Frau Tantov can do to keep her children covered, in spite of all her darning and patching. Two little boys were wearing baggy trousers made from a bit of soggy army cloth their father had picked up in the woods. The little girls' dresses and pinafores were patchwork that wouldn't hold together any longer; the socks drying on the line had been darned and re-darned in a dozen different wools.

But even more than clothing, people beg us for shoes, especially children's shoes. Most of the little boys who have anything at all to go outdoors in are hopping about in men's old shoes, four or five sizes too big. When schools have been open this winter (and most were closed for weeks and months because of "coal holidays"), many children are not able to go because of "shoe holidays." It is not at all uncommon for one child to go to school in the morning, come home at noon, and give his shoes to another child in the family so that he can go in the afternoon. Now that the snow is gone, children can go out in wooden soles, tied on with bits of leather or string, or in straw sandals. Every imaginable makeshift is used, but makeshifts come to an end at last. Already, in a cold spring when we are still wearing woolen socks and heavy shoes, I have seen children barefoot on the country roads.

March 29, 1947 ~ Red in Warsaw to Madeleine in Solingen

What a hectic week this is proving to be. Tomorrow we expect to have fifteen members of the mission in Warsaw!

I was to take the mission's books to Koz and work on them this week and visit with the team there. However, before I boarded the train, we were informed that floods near Warsaw had turned for the worse, and the ministry was asking some of the voluntary agencies to send representatives over the area in a plane. I couldn't go and still catch the train; so Lou Taylor went. The next morning, I received a wire saying that they wanted some transport; so I went immediately to Gora, where we received another telegram saying that they heard there were floods around Pulawy and if that was so, not to send trucks to Warsaw if they could be used there. Since the bridge is out, Wojtek and I had to cross the river by boat, but after two hours, could find out no sign of problems. The next morning four trucks left Gora for Warsaw. Today a fifth one arrived, but so far none have been used.

Two bridges in Warsaw and one at Modlin have gone; every bridge in the Kielce district has been destroyed. Now there is an ice jam on the Vistula north of Warsaw which acts like a dam; the ice floe has collected until there is a block one mile wide and nearly four miles long.

It is difficult to get accurate figures, but over 250 square kilometers are under water in this one place and more than 15,000 people are affected in one Wojiat; of these more than 6,000 are stranded. It is practically impossible to get to them as boats cannot get through the ice. Now they are dropping food from the air.

The water is subsiding, but there is a chance that the Bug River will cause the Vistula water to slow up in which case the Vistula will rise again. Now there are increased floods in Poznan and Gdansk.

Everyone is helping and doing what they can; they have gone through the hotels asking the guests to contribute to relief. We have given one hundred Care packages and two tons of sugar. We would like to do more, but our supplies are near the bottom, so are everyone's now as we have had no ships in since the big freeze several weeks ago. Nevertheless, much food, clothing, and bedding is being given and some agencies have promised to take several hundreds of the children who are homeless.

As you can imagine, it is difficult to find out where our transport can be used. Now that it's here, the Polish officials do not think that it's needed. Some of the fellows are rather disgusted, and it's easy to understand when some of them stayed up late at night and then were up at five o'clock in order to get their trucks up here. However, my attitude is that we have made an offer, the trucks are at the disposal of the officials. If they have need of them, we are glad to help and they know it. If they have no need for our transport, I see no reason for our meddling. We are not here to run the show.

The Polish people are very grateful for our interest and what little we have helped. Although we are considered one of the smaller agencies here, the ministry specifically asked that we send representatives on the plane. As one man at the ministry told me, "We knew that we could depend on the Quakers to do whatever they could."

Your two letters were waiting for me when I arrived yesterday. Your first impressions of Germany are not surprising. Madeleine, relief work by its very nature is frustrating. Even when you have a lot of supplies at your command and all the work you can do, it is still frustrating. Why? Because relief work in itself has demoralizing aspects, and one cannot overcome them but rather only do enough good to change the balance. Already, I have heard much about the way the workers live in Germany. It is not good, but as long as you contact the German people freely, you have an opportunity to be hospitable to them.

Many of them are hungry for outside stimulus, for news of other people, for the warmth of a friend. You have few supplies, 'tis true; therefore, you have more time for the personal contact. Although, I must agree with you that one wishes to have a job which makes his stay profitable; otherwise, we are saying that we have such a pleasing personality that just being ourselves pays our keep.

It is easy to see why they would wish you to stay on the team in order to be the weld between the two factions. Certainly, you have the personality and ability to hold the confidence of both groups. Your idea of leaving relief work in the fall fell upon very favorable ground. Yes, we should think of starting a family soon (and that is not easy to do while running around Europe) and then returning to Europe for a longer period. That is something I once dreamed about doing in India or South America –going in and living with the people until part of them had grown into me. This should take a long discussion and much thinking.

March 30, 1947 ~ Red in Warsaw to Madeleine in Solingen

This is one of those nights when it would be good to be able to tell you six things all at once. If only we could talk and talk and talk! The conference ended today and the mission is saved! We have managed to figure out a solution to the supply problem that will safely carry us through July, and we are keeping our fingers crossed that America can find us some aid by then. Also, the prospects of a work camp are more encouraging than ever before. Enough so that Peter, Van Cleve, and I are expecting to take a proposal to the ministry this week.

There were several things which we thought might be touchy, but all of them were cleared, although there is too much jealousy between the various members about insisting on more supplies and personnel for their pet projects. Peter has worked extremely hard—one night until three o'clock—attempting to formulate a plan whereby we could save our supply projects. The mechanics went along nicely, but once again we did not discuss the basic reasons why we carry on the work here.

Maybe I am too sensitive, but often I question why we spend so much time and energy on the mechanics of relief. Is it possible for us to accomplish more by some other means? Are we not taking the easier way? First, what do we wish to do? Satisfy our own conscience by overworking ourselves? How do we relate this experience to what we expect to do when we leave here? Is it not possible to stop now and then to share our ideas and thinking and from that profit in the future?

The teams are expected to bring in nominations for my replacement at the next meeting. I become scared when I think of the qualifications for the job. An American driver is willing to handle finance and transport. He doesn't have high qualifications, but few American team members who care to come here have those. They have other qualifications, but not driving, transport, and finance. It may mean that we shall ask AFSC to furnish someone, in which case it may take several months. The next meeting should take place at the end of May, at which time we should know whether we can find a replacement here.

April 3, 1947 ~ Madeleine in Solingen to Red in Warsaw

The spring's springier and the sun brighter. As Frank said, "If a card will do that, what'll a letter be like?" It was one from Corcelles telling about fondue and quietness, and all of a sudden it brought you very close. Where all the rest of the Swiss mail is, I can't imagine; when all my back mail arrives, it should be Alpine in height—I hope.

Tomorrow three of us set out for a Young Friends' conference in Goslar, which has been described to me as a medieval town where you expect to see knights in armor riding up and down. As always, there's so much here I'd like to share with you and talk over with you. The work continues to be fun, and I feel full of beans—good food and lots of going about in the fresh air. What we see and hear in the course of our investigation is discouraging and sometimes despairing; I've been in so many bar-

SPREEKANALSTRASSE NEAR ALEXANDERPLATZ LOOKING TOWARD
FORMER BANK BUILDINGS IN BERLIN, GERMANY. 1947
                    -PHOTOGRAPHER UNKNOWN

racks and seen so many ragged kids and heard so many pleas for children's shoes and been asked so many times, "When can we go back home?" that if I were prone to nightmares, I think I would dream about it. So very much of what you have written me about Poland is reproduced here; until my German gives out I keep repeating the fact that conditions here are shared by millions of people all over Europe, but the immediacy of the present is overwhelming.

The psychological plight of refugees underlines very sharply the basic faultiness of the materialist philosophy on which the western world has been living. Over and over again people tell you of the home or the farm or the business they had in the East, before they were driven out by the Russians or the Poles, and paradise seems to be lots of goods. It's completely understandable in a country where the butcher shops have nothing but plants in the windows, and you need a spool of thread to buy a bag of potatoes; the discouraging part is that resumption of production and consumption remains the highest good that any of the democratic countries can dream of.

April 4, 1947 ~ Madeleine's journal

Through hilly country we drove into Goslar, the sun brightening a rainy sky. A promise of spring in the still bare fruit trees and ploughed fields. A lark singing.

Goslar is indeed a fairy tale: an old free city of towers, slate roofs, wood carving, mottoes and verses on homes and public buildings, and flowers in the windows.

Young Germans, totally disillusioned at the end of the war, for a time refused to believe in anything or anyone. Now the time seems ripe for new ideas. They are desperate for information about the rest of the world, having been virtually cut off during the war years except for managed propaganda. Two young people at the conference said to us: "We think worse of the Germans than you do."

Young people are more realistic than their elders about the chances of returning to their former homes in the East. There is universal fear of Russia: "Just another form of dictatorship."

April 7, 1947 ~ Madeleine in Solingen to Red in Warsaw

Your Corcelles letters and your second letter after your return to Warsaw have just come. It was a joy to know of your stay chez Oncle Paul, and I lived my days there over again with you. What fun to know that when next we walk up the hill and ring the bell, they'll know both of us! So they're trying to marry Red off—I warn you, the Gerbers will make an honest man of you yet!

Much as I hate it, this isn't going to be a pleasing letter. If you've waited long and this is the first of the many I've posted to reach you, wait a bit before reading it and remember while you read that we do love one another.

Red, I've not really answered your first letter back in Warsaw because it took me a bit of a time to appreciate the story of Maja—mostly, I think, because that letter had been so terribly awaited for, and then when it came it hadn't much of us in it—or so it seemed to a rather too-sensitive me. But truly, my dear, after rereading and thinking, I did thank thee for telling me about it. I think I do know the possibility of sharing with one person and loving another more for it—sometimes it seems to me that all one has ever known and felt goes into the wonder of loving.

But then, Red, came your Warsaw letter of March 22, and I really was upset over the supper-spider web affair. I'm writing the same evening, which maybe isn't wise, but if you were here I'd be telling you of it right away, and it is something we both need to work out. Damn it,

Red—it sits strangely in the same letter to read of a tête-à-tête "with the promise that more pleasant things might come later" and connecting me "with those things everlasting" and being at peace. I know loneliness drives people together; often and often I've known that myself, but we both know deep water when we see it, too.

Oh hell, I hate writing this, and yet it's not fair not to say it. We're both rather unusually attractive people, with considerable experience and freedom. What are we going to do about it now? I have no desire to be—in fact, I couldn't be—self-righteous. My interpretation of sexual relations has been, in a certain sense, freer than most of my friends. But (largely through temperament, perhaps) it has been limited to people for whom I felt respect and integrity and affection; casual relations have seemed to me, perhaps unfairly, shabby.

We agreed long ago that neither of us believed in rigid restrictions. I think that still, but obviously there is some adjustment needed, and I doubt that either of us has found it yet. I believe deeply-founded—spiritually-founded, if you will—relationships of any sort between you and other people and between me and other people can only enrich our life together. I have very grave doubts that casual or "adventurous" relationships can. It could be easy for adventures to become a matter of competition—one person engaging in them just to prove that he could, too, or because the other had. The one with fewer opportunities, because of the job or the home, might easily resent the freedom of the other. Maybe I'm imagining problems where none exist. But I've seen too much of half-marriages to want to start out with misunderstandings.

Red—will you see that if I'm crabbed or unfair here, it's because I hurt? And I hurt because I am small and you are small—and can we help each other? Darling, if you were here I should probably climb into your lap and weep a little, but I'd have to go on thrashing it out.

I think I shouldn't be so easily disturbed if my fears, like yours, had been minimized to the point of nonexistence. But Red, there's part of me that you still haven't reached or reassured. Partly that's my own fault; I bring to loving you the scars and failings of spirit that living has brought, along with the richnesses and joys. We agreed early and easily that marriage as a ceremony wasn't very important; I wonder if we knew—or can know even now—how terribly portentous it can be as a fact—the fact of two people living closely, changing each other, creating and shaping new life. Those first evenings in Marseille, when we came to know so much of each other, it seemed easier to me to imagine being always with you than it does sometimes now, much as I long for it.

Forgive me, my dear, if this is unfair, but sometimes I feel that you—being happy and fulfilled in love—don't look back very often to see how I come on through my more devious path to love. There's no *fault* involved, Red; it's just that if we are truly one, you will suffer from my lacks or unhappinesses as much as I, and I from yours. We shall double our burdens as well as our joys when we decide to go together.

I hope this doesn't reach you at a poor time; I hope you've leisure to read between the lines and pour understanding into any hurts I've made. Just writing has made me feel closer to you; I pray it hasn't made you feel distant from me. I expect this is only one of some hard problems we're going to have to work out together. If we can work it out, we shall have added something strong to the beautiful and lovely already holding us to each other.

April 9, 1947 ~ Madeleine in Solingen to Red in Warsaw

Ha—so we get everything done for us here, including having our petrol tanks filled by the chauffeur, so we don't know how much we have and run out one-third of the way home! Serves us right, but it lands me up parked on a sunny street in a small town, the curiosity of all the kids, while James goes off to fill a jerry-can.

It's been a typical day: going into a new town, talking with the mayor and refugee representatives, going around visiting homes and schools. It's hard work, in a way. People are often suspicious or resentful of us at first, though always docile; if not that, they expect, quite naturally, that we bring supplies, or why would we want to find out the need? By the end of the afternoon, though, the two officials who took us around were as amiable as over-the-back-fence neighbors, and we met one or two families that I should like to know better.

So much of what we do is just listening: welfare workers ask us for shoes, and we have thirty pairs for a county. They ask for clothes, and we have one bale. And much worse than that, the stories people tell. Oh Red, sometimes I'm torn in two. One woman today told of her brother, shot by the Russians as a hostage. "Beasts," she said. But I had to remember the French and the Poles were shot that way, too. And "Why did the Russians destroy our beautiful cities in East Prussia if they wanted to occupy them later?" I could hardly hold back from saying: "Why did the

Germans destroy Warsaw?" And yet—to people ravaged by suffering you cannot at once say such cold things, not without the time to talk and understand more deeply. Later we met a woman who had been taken from her three children to do forced labor in Siberia. She fell ill there and was sent back, one of the few in the transport who survived. Her story was so simply told and betokened such suffering that none of us could say anything; we only stood silent a few moments before saying good-bye. It struck me in a stark sense that here was a Quaker Meeting.

I remember Clarence Pickett's saying that Friends suffer with both sides. That seems to me more and more true—and we suffer at the same time from our lack of understanding and our shrinking from this great burden of suffering to which we are exposed.

April 10, 1947 ~ Madeleine in Solingen to Red in Warsaw

You're getting a businesslike letter for a change, but inside I feel all bubbly and excited. I agree with thee about arranging life and then sort of fitting things in as fancy comes; in practice, since you plan more easily than I, you may get to do more of it and I'll enjoy the results and tease you for being efficient. OK?

Look, there are a million things to iron out. Amazing what miss-ups can occur when we can't get answers from each other in a month.

About our being married. As I've written you in an earlier letter, which I hope you have by now, it's being hard for me to settle on June. I dunno what it is, darling; sometimes I guess I need a little more wooing! That's so old-fashioned that I blush, but I don't know how else to say it. The idea of finally committing my future to one person (insofar as that is possible) has never been a very real one before. I came nearest to thinking about it with Herb, and then I remember a feeling of near-panic like that I feel now occasionally. I tell you with all the honesty I can muster, Red, that I do not think it is lack of love, but rather a too-sensitive and too-apprehensive spirit that needs to be quieted and strengthened. And when you can be with me for a longer time and help me to that, I shall be able to come to you one day and say, "Red, I'm ready to be married." I'm afraid this may be hard for thee, and I'm sorry for it; I can only tell thee that I am trying to put as much integrity and understanding and affection into this trying time as into a fully joyous and confident one that is surely coming.

For many reasons—convenience and the fact that now we both have family and friends there—I should like to be married in Switzerland. But it seems to me all other concerns except our personal reactions are secondary in this matter. Perhaps I'm putting too much stress on it; thee has half of this to decide, so speak thy mind! Germany seems more and more difficult, in addition to the fact that psychologically it is not the spot one would choose for a wedding. Maybe I'm overestimating that, too, but I have a hunch that once out of Germany, I'll feel as if I could soar with wings. It was like that when I went to Switzerland from France; from here it must be a thousand times more true!

What I'm thinking is this: let's get all the necessary papers to enable us to get married, and then we can go ahead wherever we are, whenever we feel the time is right.

What's your favorite color, and will you help me pick a wedding dress this summer? Mother's sending me some money for one.

Leave. I've asked for June, but what time? Or doesn't it greatly matter? About what we do—one of the reasons I wanted so much to go back to Switzerland was to re-

MEN CLEARING RUBBLE IN BERLIN. THE CHURCH STEEPLES IN THE BACKGROUND WERE ALL THAT WAS LEFT OF THE FAMOUS KAISER-WILHELM-GEGAECHTNIS KIRCHE. 1946
-PHOTOGRAPHER UNKNOWN

ally get into the Alps. I'd half planned to stay in Corcelles just a few days and then go to some hotel or pension high in the mountains and climb and look and wonder my fill. You've only seen a corner of Switzerland, darling; there are the mountain meadows, the glaciers, the German Swiss villages that look like gingerbread, and the Alpine horns.

About the job. It is time we began thinking about it and letting the Service Committee know we are. It needs talking over, but we can make a start here. I'm afraid my ideas, like yours, are hazy. That's not good, but maybe we'll clarify one another. At the moment, my concern for international affairs overshadows everything else. Like you, I felt

Truman's speech was full of doom. It sharpens the situation, which is probably good, but the direction it points is ominous. We Americans tell the English with some bitterness that they needn't worry about their country bowing out of Empire; we're taking up where they leave off. Bitterness, however, is too easy and mends matters not at all. Whatever we can do to bind the world together, I feel we must, wherever it may take us—within the limits of our abilities, of course.

I must tell you that the South has taken a second place in my thinking and feeling since being in Europe. Perhaps once back in the States, I'll feel differently. You remember, Red, that I've never been close to the southern problem as you have, and for me it is one of many injustices.

I am all in favor of offering to travel for AFSC if they want us. Sometimes I think all the relief teams ought to go home and relieve the misunderstanding and un-informedness of America! It's getting to be an obsession with me. People have GOT to wake up. Ideally, I'd appreciate a few quiet months when we get back, but practically it may not work. I rather expect that, if AFSC could use us, it would be right away on our return.

As to our working together, I don't feel that should be a deciding factor. It would be both pleasant and difficult. So would working apart. It seems to me that the thing to do is find out what openings there are, and then how we can fit into them. Of course, I want a chance to do something, but if a smashing job turns up for you, I can certainly fit in something near it.

One reason I'm not campaigning for a definite and full-time job is that I expect we'll want to begin having a family fairly soon after we settle down, and much as I don't wish to be Hausfrau, I think some of that's inevitable for a few years anyway. Do you know how to change a diaper?

Someone casually mentioned that it was usual to inform the Service Committee of one's matrimonial intentions. So I'm telling Jack Hollister of the German Desk. OK?

Although I didn't think it would be otherwise, my mother and father have given us their blessing, even to not raising any objections about our being married in Europe, which I thought might be the one sore point. I expect Mother's already written you; if you don't hear from my Dad, don't feel hurt—he doesn't write easily and his spelling is worse even than yours!

April 11, 1947 ~ Madeleine in Solingen to Red in Warsaw

Here's a starlit night I'd like to share with thee. First a ride through a gold and blue sunset to an Anglo-German meeting where there were people amusing and friendly and odd.

Today I experienced the tearing of heart I feel so often here: two intelligent, vivacious girls who spoke good English and who told us of the international students' club they had belonged to in Berlin before the war. Then they said they had been interned by the British because they had worked with the SS as secretaries. And I cry out inside, "How could you?" There isn't time over tea to talk through something like that, but I feel always on such occasions there's a knife in me.

Most pleasing of all was a gray-haired woman with a face full of humor and experience who had lived a long time in France and could talk about Marseille and Paris. And, oh Red, that meant talking about thee! Strange, how eager I am to find someone these days who speaks French and how it falls on my ears like music. Partly because France, from here, seems a country of freedom and energy, and partly because it means us.

Driving back through the night, Peg and I sang French songs, and I remembered so distinctly the evening at Les Oubliettes, and your head over me, and your calling me a witch! That WAS a witching night, Red. I wonder if we'll find it again? I wanted so intensely to have you here, but all without hurt; and I sang, "Il y a longtemps que je t'aime," as sweetly as if your arm had been around me.

I'm sorry, as I should have known I'd be, for that letter about Maja. It was written too hastily, and to someone whom I don't find in Switzerland at all. It's still something to talk over, but not just as I did, perhaps.

April 13, 1947 ~ Madeleine in Solingen to Red in Warsaw

It's a long lazy Sunday afternoon; in the country, beside a pool too icy to swim in, on a farm that looks and smells like all the farms I remember from my childhood. Four pink and white lambs, a day-old calf, a puppy, and great lilac bushes beside the door. Let's have our rooms white-washed, with red curtains and rafters like these here.

Oh Red, so we're both coming heartless back to America—you with yours in Poland and me with mine here! I know what you feel about wanting me to see the places and people there in Poland, and I want to—but darling, I feel the same about this! Much more strongly than in France somehow, perhaps because the work here is much more with people. And I'd like you to meet them all, and to go through this Bergische Land (hill country) with me.

Every trip with supplies, every case visit, is a marvel: fields of a green I've never before seen; lilacs and apple blossom; black and white half-timbered cottages; hills and valleys and rivers. And bouncing through it all with the exciting feeling of a powerful lorry under you. Some of the roads are shocking, and some of the trucks are stubborn, and at the end of a morning I feel tired but good.

I know several German families well enough to drop in on them for a chat, which takes some doing in this formal country. I have more opportunities to go out with German friends than I can accept, and the house is so full of visitors that sometimes we have to run away to escape—like today. And every visit, every meeting, is an occasion of excitement because it means more information, more understanding, of this huge, amorphous problem of Germany. And if I were to try to tell you half of what I think and feel and see, it would take hours every day!

More than I ever did, I wish now we were working together. The work and fun and affection and problems I share with the team here, I'd like you to be in on. Every morning it's a fresh wonder at being here, and every day I hate the thought of leaving it. My personal satisfaction probably shows I'm not as close to the German problems as I should be. Yesterday, bouncing with good health and good spirits, I met a friend who told me the rations for next week would be one kilo of bread and very little fat—nothing more! I am honestly surprised that there are not demonstrations or attacks on us. It is inconceivable that the food situation could be worse, and yet on the whole, the Germans accept British authority as docilely as they accepted Nazi authority. It's a never-ending puzzle.

April 15, 1947 ~ Red in Warsaw to Madeleine in Solingen

A letter written in long hand on March 25 arrived this afternoon. A beautiful letter, darling, but disturbing news about the mail—or lack of it. Each day I become more anxious to start feelers for a job; yet it should be a cooperative affair. How can we correlate our affairs at such a distance with no mail service?

The more I think of going back home and settling down the more it becomes repugnant to me. Yet I know that I wish to stay put in one place long enough to get some roots started: some flowers growing, a few rabbits, a child or two (or more), and to become attached to a place. I want time enough to know you and find out who you are and what we are. How can that be done without becoming a part of the whole trend of America at the present time? It seems as though the idealism on which America was founded has been replaced by lip-service.

America is following closely the steps taken by the Romans; they were forced to protect their borders from the barbarians, so they sent out expeditions. Each time there was a logical step to be taken. At times they attempted to help the people they conquered, until they themselves became so corrupt that the Roman Empire fell.

As long as there is a threat or danger to a country which can be counteracted by accepting America's domination, the people of that country may accept it. However, when that threat exists no longer, Americans will be hated. We forced Japan to open her doors, aided her during a period of disaster, helped build her industries, only to have the Japanese turn against us. Why? We have been the big fish in the Americas for a century, but our Good Neighbor policy is a farce. At one time, we were considered the champion of small nations, but the little nations have become disillusioned. Why? What has happened to our principles? Where does one start? Is settling down in a job enough? Can you and I utilize our experiences of the past few years to an advantage now?

First, we must find ourselves, that is true. Even that takes time, consideration, and plenty of effort. Sometime I may be satisfied to live peacefully and quietly; but at the moment I see such a huge problem before us and feel so darn small and inadequate. Not only do I not have the mechanics (language, historical background, knowledge of social trends, etc.) but also, I am not spiritually qualified for the task. In many ways, I have aged in the past year. In many ways I am not as happy as I was when we left New York. The answers are no longer simple.

Madeleine, even my writing reflects the way in which I am going in circles. Still, there is always a focal point which has been strengthened every time I begin to wander and that is my pacifism, my firm belief in something of God in every man.

April 17, 1947 ~ Red in Warsaw to Madeleine in Solingen

What a lovely spring. Last evening was the first spring evening we have had, and I did so want to write to you. I felt guilty for having written you that last letter and wanted to tell you that something has happened. What? I do not know, but inwardly it was like a beautiful day after many rainy ones and I was happy. For the first time in the last two or three weeks, I was really satisfied that you are in Germany and I am in Poland; lately I have been so selfish and small.

The mail dam has broken, and today two letters arrived. Another time your reaction to Maja might have caused a disturbance, but not today. I am sorry that the letter caused you anxiety; it is my fault for not explaining myself more clearly. Possibly I should have waited until I could have told you personally and given you the reassurance that is needed at a time like that; however, I was impatient and wanted you to know. Maja means no more to me than any other person that I might be fortunate enough to meet and like very much. I took more time and pains to tell you about her because she is a woman and I am a man, which brings in the possibility of a relationship.

Maja is a person I like looking at just as I like looking at the picture of Mr. Batoris' wife. In their parlor there is a huge picture of her, and invariably I sit so that I can see it during the course of an evening. It does not mean that I have designs on his wife; neither would I were he away. The fact that I had a wonderful time in Prague was caused by my having met Maja, so naturally I was grateful; however, it did not mean that I did not wish you had been there with me. I would like to have shared that day with you, just as I would like to share a day in the mountains with you. The only way I could do it was telling you about Maja.

Madeleine, I value our relationship far too much to let anyone or anything come between us, unless it is something greater than ourselves. That greatness I hope we can find together rather than separately. We have made great strides, and we are growing and we shall continue growing together.

As far as the supper and spider, that was handled with a great deal of tact; enough so that we have been in each other's company on several occasions without embarrassment to either. I told her quite frankly that we cannot have the relationship she desires without killing the friendship we have already established. Also, she understands why I shun any attempt for us to be alone. I still insist that relationships can be a great temptation for me; however, as long as I love you as I do now, the temptation is only a physical one, which alone is not enough. Yet I make no guarantees that this situation will remain any more than I am confident that I shall always remain a pacifist, even though my pacifism has been strengthened in the past year.

That letter of yours is one that I shall treasure; letters are that way, the same as experiences. You retain a warmer spot for some places and some experiences than others. This letter has more of you in it than many of the others; I felt as though we were digging for that understanding that is necessary, that unity of spirit. My only regret was that I fumbled and hurt you. My sweet, I know not how to make up for that at such a distance; were you here, I would kiss away your tears. You struck at much that Gibran has said: "Joys and sorrows come from that same filled well."

April 18, 1947 ~ Red in Warsaw to Madeleine in Solingen

Your letter written on the tenth arrived today. Just think, only seven days! Shall I be efficient and answer you points one by one? Here goes.

My sweet, as was said time and again in London, I am not concerned about when we get married. I would prefer to be married before we return; however, trying to make all arrangements, getting married, making some adjustments, and then parting within two weeks seems fast work. If we should be somewhere alone, then many of the reasons for being married in Switzerland have been eliminated, although I like the idea of being married amongst friends.

My favorite color is blue, a pretty bright blue, and I would love to help you pick out a dress.

Leave. Peter wishes to go on leave the last two weeks in July and the first week of August, so I should be back by the end of the first week in July. In addition, Philip hopes to come in June, but we do not know when. Therefore I suggest you decide when it is best for you and hope that does not conflict with Philip's visit here. The sooner the better suits me. And the Alps do sound wonderful; I am getting excited!

About the job. More and more I think of doing something to help to resolve the racial problem in America, but I'd also like to concentrate on working toward a world government with authority over nations.

Yes, I know how much a few quiet months would mean to us. Yet how is that done without an income? Maybe we could get a few good books, a small mountain cabin, and camp with $100 or so. Honestly, I am open to most any kind of a suggestion at the moment.

Steve Cary has already been informed of our marital intentions. I told him that we were not making announcements of the fact.

Yes, I have received a very sweet letter from your mother; I would like to write to your brother, Walt, too. I am glad to know that they are not disappointed at the prospects of their darling daughter being married in Europe. I have mentioned this possibility to my family; however, I do not think I shall have difficulties on this point, as they would expect me to be married at your home anyway. Sis has sent the family a picture of you which you had sent to her.

April 19, 1947 ~ Madeleine in Solingen to Red in Warsaw

I came back here three days ago from Soltau to find spring bursting out everywhere—forsythia and cherry and tulips and hyacinths—and even a spring lamb gamboling in our garden! Then unaccountably I was sick one day, but that was a wonder, too, for our room is full of flowers, and through the big open window I could see the sky, pale as anemones in the dawn, sunlit blue all day and starry all night. The next day I took a 158-mile truck trip and felt better at the end than at the beginning, so you see I am quite cured.

On our trip, we saw spring all over the hills and smelled the ploughed fields—it reminded me strongly of spring on the way to Marseille. I saw Cologne for the first time. And after half an hour winding through the horribly ruined streets (and I have seen a good deal of ruin already) where spring trees are blooming among the debris, I saw the twin-towered cathedral standing lonely against the sky and the arches of a once-mighty bridge plunging into the Rhine, and I was almost physically ill. It took a greening wood and a quiet talk with Kjell to make me feel alive and hopeful once more.

And then your letters arrived. Oh Red, each one makes you seem closer and dearer, and in each one I feel you know more about me, too. There's a poet hidden somewhere inside of that man Stephenson, and when he talks about stars and rain, it gives me pause to wonder. The stars have been brilliant these nights, and just now, after an afternoon lying about in the garden—all of us with two babies from the neighborhood and the cat and the lamb and the sweet grass—there's been a swift, warm rain, the kind that's pregnant with life.

The more I know Grete Ravn, the more I wish to. I'm happy that you like Ted so much; he needs to be a splendid man to match her—she's devilish and devoted, hard-working and full of fun, courageous and changeful, and altogether lovable. We've talked a good bit in the few days I've been back, and so much of her experience matches mine. She and Ted didn't have long together either, and both of them were anxious, I think, before their meeting in Denmark. They don't know either where they'll go or what they'll do, and they don't worry about it. They're hoping to be married in August, when they are both through with FRS. Oh Red, do you suppose there's the smallest chance of our going to Sweden and Denmark from Warsaw? We could see them (unless they plan to go right away to England) and Kjell and his fiancée. Golly, marriages are busting out all over! I'm beginning to feel quite in the swim.

I told you in another letter that I'd write you more about Kjell Nahnfeldt, one of our team members from Sweden. Someday you must know him, Red; I count him with the very few remarkable men I know—a rollicking person (It's he who sings us awake with his lute and Swedish folksongs on Sunday morning and does handstands with the mechanics.) with an extraordinary spiritual sensitiveness. His expression of things spiritual takes an almost evangelical form, but his face, his bearing, his life, so illuminate and illustrate that expression that he is entirely convincing. And it is to Kjell that I owe some of the springtime I now experience. His conviction that life will live itself through us if we only let it, that all that is needed is for us to will to be willed through, has come to me at a ripe time, and I am feeling at once a stillness and a joy that I cannot remember knowing before. What he has spoken of in our few talks together is nothing new; I've read it hundreds of times before and yearned after it and not found it, at least not for long. But the expression of it by someone who lives it in the present is infinitely more compelling and vital.

And in another way Kjell has added to our thinking, Red—about relationships with other people. He conceives of it in terms of responsibility; one does love more than one person, and should, if that love is all-embracing, but the responsibility implied in sexual love is reserved for one person. Toward other people, love is expressed just as creatively but in a different manner. It's an approach in some respects new to me, but it's a rich and possibly a promising one.

It seems a long time since I wrote you about the discordance in the team; during the time I was away (they didn't need me for a peacemaker after all), the situation became much more easy and under-standing, and since I'm back, the atmosphere within the house matches the beauty outside. It's quite wonderful.

Two of the people I'm most fond of, Muriel and Kjell, leave in a week; I hope the new arrivals from England will fit in well, so we can go on in this way. As for the work, I'm having to start again from scratch. Although I feel as though I've learned something about Germany in this month, I don't know any more about the work here than when I arrived. But I'm easier in my mind about finding what I should do; if I can be open and not impatient, it will come.

May 1, 1947 ~ Madeleine in Solingen to Red in Warsaw

It's a long while since you've had a letter, but you have been in my thoughts and speaking more than usual. Even now, I am not sure I can tell you what is on my heart. I want only to see you, and for us to talk and be silent together.

It's been a pregnant time, these two weeks past, Red, and I do not yet know what will come of them. Much has to do with Kjell. I wish instead of my telling you about him, you could meet him. Someday I think you will. Red, Kjell has found something for which we are look-ing—that harmony with the universe of which you write, that deep inner security which is the source of fruitful action. To me, he was like a spring of living water, a tangible assurance that there is such a thing as the grace of God, a divine guidance. The way he feels and says this is not the way you and I have. Perhaps someday, in pridelessness, we shall come to the same way.

I was glad for your letter, the one you called a "terrible" letter. I think it must be significant that the letters each of us thinks poor and inadequate are most precious and revealing to the other. Perhaps we have not learned yet to show ourselves quite simply and unashamedly to the other. But seldom have I felt closer to you than when reading that letter. It was, as you say, no love letter. Red, I don't want that just now. That's part of a change that almost frightens me. This concern about the direction the world (and especially our country) is taking, and our relation to it, and most of all, our relation to God, is so absorbing my thoughts and feelings that there is room for little else. Red, this something bigger than ourselves—we have got to find it. I hope we may find it together, for it is the strongest bond that could exist between us. But find it we must, whatever the cost.

There is another way in which Kjell has helped—this problem of relationships between men and women. There was between us, almost from the first, a strong attraction. We are very much cut from the same cloth. I think it is right to say that it is a spiritual attraction, but it had a physical basis as well. I think probably that was more true of Kjell, but as soon as he was aware of it, he set himself to transform that into an expression of love that would enrich us both, and through me, you, and through him, his fiancée. And it is true to say that he did, Red. I think I have never had such guidance and understanding from anyone in such a short space of time. We even (and do you know me well enough to know how extremely rare this is?) prayed once together. And it is something like this that I think we must achieve together, Red. Not because we must follow the pattern set by another. It will have to be in our own way. But the selflessness, the seeking, the willingness to be led, must be the same, I believe.

You will think this all very gloomy, my dear; you will think there is no spring here. It has been a very hard winter, and now there is a spring such as one rarely sees—everything at once. We are bowered in beauty: lilacs under our bedroom window, apple blossoms reaching into the kitchen, a circle of white birches on the lawn with narcissus in the grass—heart's truth, 'tis Paradise! And woods and streams and country houses only five minutes walk from us in every direction! Oh Red, I wish you could share it! I ache to think that another spring may not be so lovely, but each one is newly astonishing.

And the team seems, at least to my happy eyes, to be reborn too. Three members have left, and their farewells drew us all closer together. Two new trainees have come out, the old animosities seem to have disappeared, and sometimes we are so richly gay together that it almost hurts. I regret often and often, Red, that you haven't the benefit of a team life. Sometimes I think living with only one person must of necessity be dull after this hectic hilarity.

I've taken over the supervision of clothing and food stores, which will be quite a job until I get them reorganized. Besides prying open crates and saying "No" ten times a day to unfillable requests, I am to do some refugee work, some youth work, as well as keep up with the "contacts" that one makes everywhere, even on the street. In some ways I feel more rooted, more needed here than ever in France. People are so spiritually hungry that, at the slightest occasion, they pour out their hearts and look to us for hope and understanding. Almost I regret already the prospect of leaving in August. But I think we will feel when we get back home that it is right; then our job will be correlating the two worlds we have come to know. I shall have lots of stories and experiences to match with you come June.

May 4, 1947 ~ Red in Warsaw to Madeleine in Solingen

The past week has been one of the most difficult times I have experienced in many a month. It all started two weeks ago today when four of us took a day train to Czerwonka. Then we had four very good days. I missed you terribly, because I was able to putter in a garden a bit. We sorted clothes and had a clothing distribution. I was really beginning to enjoy it when it was time to return. Thursday night meant fifteen hours in a train; Friday night Henry and I obtained a normal night's sleep, but since then it's been six hours each night; in addition, someone slept in my room four of them. I was exhausted, and yet the tension of having visitors here meant that I could not relax.

I hope never to be that tired again. It was difficult for me to keep an even keel; I found myself cutting words with Peter. Fortunately, he understood and said nothing but rather was his patient self.

Some of the difficulty has come about because I have found myself swallowed up in the machinery of administration and cannot shake it loose. There have been times when we thought we had everything running smoothly; then something happens to throw us backward. I have to take care of most of the details of purchases, transport, finance, visas, etc. With twenty vehicles and twenty-nine people, it is a full-time job, with little time for making and developing those contacts one would like so much to make. I become frustrated, because I find it impossible to meet engagements that could so easily be made. It clearly shows my inadequacy in holding this job and developing it into a place of real significance. I had dreamed of Peter and I making contacts here that might lead to something more permanent in Warsaw, but that has not been the case. Now I find myself with more work even than previously.

One thing is certain—I am not one to live away from nature. The city was not made by men like me. I like the city, yet I do not care to live in it. There is something about it that is too artificial; give me the wide open places with plenty of trees, a brook, a few hills, and some flowers.

Maybe I would like the city better if my work was more creative than going from one office to another like an errand boy. Maybe Peter and I lack imagination; however, I am afraid that we are reacting to the drastic cuts in our budget and what they have done to the imagination that we once had. For instance, Bill told us that he thought we could figure on $200,000 for next year; only yesterday we receive a cable saying it possibly would be $100,000. And that after having a budget of $600,000 this year!

They ask us to use our imagination in utilizing what personnel we have. This is a country which is in drastic need of first stage relief. We are making inroads on the more permanent types of work, but this government is still thinking in terms of supplies, and why should they not? Just recently the Polish government used nine million dollars of its very limited foreign credits in order to buy wheat, yet the Americans will tell

CHILDREN HELPING WITH GARDENING IN LUCIMA, POLAND. 1946.
-PHOTOGRAPH BY JOHN ROBBINS

you that there is enough food here if only there were an adequate rationing system.

In the Mazurska area, black bread costs 60 zlotys per kilo. When he can get work, a man makes 200 to 250 zlotys per day, yet there is little work. There are no potatoes left. The central and southern areas are faring better, but we do not know for how long. The orphans are really suffering, and the ration cards have been revised because the government did not have enough food to furnish all of those who held cards. Yet they ask us to use our imagination in establishing service projects! Somehow I do not have the heart unless we can get more supplies, but from where?

I do not feel righteously indignant as I have at times, but rather I am tremendously hurt. I love Poland. It hurts me deeply to see America and Poland at each other's throats when one needs the help of the other so much, and each needs to understand the other. How is that done?

May 6-7, 1947 ~ Red in Warsaw to Madeleine in Solingen

Madeleine, my dear, this is no letter to be writing to a girl whom you expect to marry in a few weeks, yet you might as well know that this redhead does not always ride high. You would not have been proud of me yesterday when Van Cleve and I became quite emotional while discussing the coming conference. Both of us felt like kids afterwards. It all arose over the fact that Peter and I were inviting only one representative from each team instead of the usual two, because we shall have ten people in Warsaw and the additional team members would make thirteen. The housing situation is extremely bad here, and we have no promises of rooms for even the ten yet.

I am reluctant to accept any proposals that cast more work on us, and since Peter is to be away until the day before the conference, I knew it was up to me to provide those rooms and make arrangements for food and everything else for three additional people. I finally gave in, but it does mean that we have one more good reason for asking a third person to come help us in Warsaw. This is something both Peter and I have been fighting a losing battle on, as our budget is being cut, and we cannot see increasing our overhead in view of that. Do you know how many people work on administration in other missions? We have twenty-nine people here with two in Warsaw plus one Polish secretary. How does that compare with others. Much of my work is dealing with spare parts, repairing truck parts, renewing visas, obtaining visas for traveling, and so on, in addition to the normal amount of administrative duties.

Has Mother written to you since we told them we were planning to get married? Do not be disturbed if she has not. She is old-fashioned enough to want to meet you before giving us her blessing, yet she is wise enough to know that she and Daddy have interfered with their children's affairs too much already. There is no fear of your not being accepted by everyone, particularly Mother and Daddy.

There is some wonderful Polish music floating through the window from the courtyard. Earlier today, two men playing violins, two playing accordions, two playing guitars, one playing a hand saw, and one playing mandolin held a regular concert on the street, taking a collection from the passersby.

May 12, 1947 ~ Madeleine in Solingen to Red in Warsaw

It's a lovely afternoon; a blooming chestnut (remember Paris in the spring) just outside my window, with a bird singing in it.

It's warm, and I'm grubby, having shifted clothes and cases and swept out our clothing room for four old dears who came to sort this afternoon. Four of us lost "face" with the Germans today by trudging up and down the street with arms full of ground sheets and dirty canvas sacks, no truck being around. It's funny; they resent our being here, and yet they feel we should act the part of people in authority. Such waiting on I've never had in my life. Going back to America will be tough; I can't live there in the manner to which I have become accustomed!

A very good friend of mine, Dr. Lydia Hauck, who kept me supplied with parcels in France, has asked for the names of women doctors who are in need of help. There is a large committee, the Medical Women's Alliance, which is ready and anxious to help such women who are in need. I am practically stymied at this end because, like so many Americans, they won't consider helping a German unless it is proved that she was in a concentration camp or deported or something. The offer is much too good to pass up, and I'm wondering if you could somehow make contact with women in Poland who would be eligible for such help as the Alliance is ready to give. Chiefly it would be food parcels, but I am sure they could manage medical supplies, instruments, clothing, and other things. The important thing is to establish a sound contact; I think it would be well if you would write a short introduction for each person whose name you suggest. The human interest angle is all-important, as you know. Once that's established, supplies just flow out.

Grete and I often talk of what it will be like to return to a "normal" life again, and we wonder if it will be harder than we imagine. When you stop to think about it, we do have power and prestige here, however much we may romp through the streets and sing in our lorries and meet people as naturally as we would anywhere. Still, at home we are not accustomed to walking into a mayor's office and being deferred to by government officials and waved on by policemen and bowed and clicked to by all comers. It all seems part of the fun now, but if one were in it too long, it might become a real danger. "Power corrupts," and yet someone must have power. Maybe the test of our having it is being able to put it aside easily.

May 13, 1947 ~ Red in Warsaw to Madeleine in Solingen

Your letter written in longhand arrived today; it had a most sobering effect on me. Recently, I have had periods of extreme depression to high elation. Although I am no closer to the Truth than before, here is that knowledge that you are not only willing to be patient with me but are anxious for us to find ourselves before moving too quickly.

I have come to feel I cannot leave Warsaw soon enough. Each day I want to escape. Never before have I felt so much as though I were in a trap. I have been playing tennis, and the physical exercise has helped. Yet it was your letter which made me admit that I am refusing to search for the truth. Oh darling, I do feel so inadequate. If ever I have envied you a friendship, it is now. Kjell is the type of person I have been looking for several months without success.

On several occasions some of us in CPS attempted to form groups for the purpose of meditation and silent searching. Each time I would gain something and then become stale and dull. There have been times when I would set aside a period in each day for my own meditation only to find that soon it became mechanical and hence of no profit. Yet whenever periods of trouble arise, there is always a sense of satisfaction in retiring by myself wherever there might be beauty. Somehow most of my attempts to rise to heights greater than myself have been when something was disturbing me enough to force me to seek outside strength. Is not that so often true with so many? We are prone to using crutches instead of searching for the causes so that we can dispose of the crutches.

It seems strange for both of us to be disturbed and confused at the same time; however, you have something with which you can start working. You may have to go back through some of it with me. How long will you be able to be with Kjell?

Since starting this letter, I have been for a walk and came back down Makatowska Street. It was in semidarkness with an occasional street light hanging from an arm extended from a high iron post. It reminded me very much of an etching by Andre Smith. His drawing shows a street stretching into infinity bordered on each side with only the fronts of the buildings held up by props in the back. Along the street are telephone and electric wires running from one post to another until they run together. The only living thing in the picture is Christ sitting beside one of the posts like a forlorn man. Tonight I wondered if Christ and what he stood for have not been forsaken in the ruins of these streets.

Darling, I am not happy. Maybe it is a good thing, because it is preparing me well for the meeting this weekend which should decide the direction of our program for the next year. If everyone comes as disturbed and open as I feel now, it should be a meaningful meeting.

May 15, 1947 ~ Red in Warsaw to Madeleine in Solingen

We have just completed our conference. AFSC and FRS are going to be surprised. Next year we have a budget of only $100,000 from AFSC and, of course, reduced supplies from FRS. In spite of this we are planning to carry on the Czerwonka child feeding, with added social and medical attention; the Kozienice medical clinics, plus social work involving case work and youth clubs; the transport team plus a nurse; the work at Krakow with an additional truck; continued work with students in Gdynia; a possible third person in Warsaw; and plans for at least two work camps next summer!

It has been most difficult to come to these decisions because the immediate needs are so great and this allows only half of our budget for food supplies. When everyone is talking about the possible threat of starvation in this country this summer, when fear can be seen more clearly in the faces and expressions of people, one has less heart to double his efforts in social work when our supplies are being cut so drastically.

Madeleine, I have talked with Bill Huntington, and he says that the Peace Section surely would be willing and anxious to have us spend some time working for them. Bill himself seems to have done something of the same thing that I have done—left a technical job in order to work with those things which seem urgent. He is anxious to see a world government and has accepted the job with AFSC as a means by which to become more familiar with some of the problems of Europe. His approach is not political but rather an attempt to recognize the rights of individuals and work for the fulfillment of those rights.

I am so anxious for June and a few really free days with you.

May 27, 1947 ~ Madeleine's journal

Berlin is the last desolation. I walked through the Reich's chancellery yesterday, and if it had been bombed and plundered a thousand years ago, it could not have had more of the chill and smell of death about it. I suppose the ruins of Athens are more alive than these, for there at least the spirit of a noble age must linger. The wide, imposing capital of a nation slid into heaps of dust and broken stone; straggling little vegetable patches where once there were great avenues of trees and buildings; twisted girders and twisted trees against the sunset. One doesn't feel pity, only a numb horror and the inevitability of a moral nemesis.

May 28, 1947 ~ Madeleine in Berlin to Red in Warsaw

In Berlin, of all places, I'm finding the time and the quiet to write to you. I got here Saturday evening to find that Bill Huntington had just arrived, having just left you in Warsaw. He was sure you would have hopped on, too, if you had known I was here, but I'm not disturbed over that. With the pressure of work and the short time I have here, it wouldn't have done at all for the kind of meeting and talking we want to do. But I do feel like having a fling, and it would be fun if you were here. In a few months, we'll have a fling all over Europe!

Your last letters have touched me very deeply, and though I am sorry for your unhappiness, I know from my own that it is often a fruitful thing if it drives us to look for the foundations of our living. I am very, very far from those foundations, but I am thankfully happy that we shall so soon be together to try to find ourselves and each other. Bless thee for a warm and understanding and tender heart.

As the time comes nearer for our meeting, I am less and less inclined to try to put things on paper. We must at all costs save a good chunk of time alone; I, too, have three weeks, so we should be able to be by ourselves and still have enough time with the family in Switzerland. Oh Red, I do look forward to walking up the street to Oncle Paul's with you, and looking over the lake from the balcony in my aunts' house. It won't be long now.

June 3, 1947 ~ Red in Warsaw to his parents in North Carolina

Peter left last week for Jelina Gora for ten days of vacation; that means that I am left alone in Warsaw; however, everything is going smoothly at the moment. When he returns, I shall leave for Germany and Switzerland. My plans are to fly to Berlin and then take a train to Dusseldorf, where I shall meet Madeleine. Then we shall travel together to Corcelles and visit a few days with her relatives before going to the mountains.

Tonight I sent a cable asking for my birth certificate to be sent to Paul Gerber. I do hope that this is done in time for us to get married there. We are not sure that we shall; however, we wish to have all necessary papers in case we decide that it is best. Both of us have been working under a great deal of strain, so we wish to be together a bit again before definitely taking the step of matrimony. We are sure that we shall be married sometime in the future but are not sure yet when the best time will be, as both of us want to do some thinking.

Our plans now are for us to be together this June and then return to our respective jobs until the middle of September, when Madeleine will come to Poland. We hope to have about two weeks here before going to Sweden and then on to Denmark. We are booking a sailing date for October for the States, so we should see you in November at the very latest. Naturally, we shall not have a cent of money left by the time we return, but we feel that we are young enough to spend what little we have now in order to see more of Europe and visit some of the many friends we have made since coming here. Madeleine is like myself in being able to acquire friends wherever she is. Everyone loves her.

We have no plans about what we shall do when we return; however, we have written to AFSC asking about traveling for them for a few months before settling down in order to tell people about France, Germany, and Poland, and the Quaker work in those three countries. If you ever thought I had stories to tell when I came home before, you just wait until we get there this time. We shall keep you up until the wee hours of the night telling about how people live, what people eat, many exciting times, people we have met, and so on. Although Madeleine is small physically, she can match me in enthusiasm and energy.

The new understanding and affection we found while you were here have made me realize what a far way there is yet to go. Oh Red, may the day come soon when we can be together so that we can get on with our traveling that way!

-Madeleine

Crisis Draws Us Closer

shall go to the other convent w
your meals are served in your ro
by a deaf-and-dumb sister!
hope I make too much of the
being alone, but it's easy fo
small delegation to get in-gro
and keeping giving each other
tastes of that stale cheese w
call ourselves. There's so much
straighten out.

Red, are you surprised some
at the amount of work it t
to get a very little done? Do
the same in other work too?
just relief work? I begin to
better the need for administra
but it's an awfully fallible
need — it arises from people
inadequacies largely. So mu

1993 ~ Red from Monan's Rill

I was just days from visiting Madeleine in Solingen when on Sunday, June 8, a telegram came from the Paris office: "Madeleine in serious accident; will keep you informed." I sent cables to London and Paris (it wasn't possible to cable to West Germany), asking for more information. Where was Madeleine and how badly was she hurt?

The next day, Monday, the diplomatic plane from Berlin brought a telegram from the AFSC team in Berlin: "Madeleine has a concussion. Come as soon as possible."

I panicked!

The team in Berlin knew I was coming on Thursday. By telling me to come sooner, they were telling me the worst. Madeleine was lying somewhere with a concussion and in very serious condition. If I didn't see her soon, I might never see her again.

I rushed to the American Embassy, but the diplomatic plane from Berlin that brought the second telegram had already returned. The next—a British plane—was due in and out Thursday, and already I had reservations on it. So I went to the United Nations Relief and Rehabilitation Association offices, as they sometimes had unscheduled flights in and out, but to no avail.

In those days, only two years after the war ended, Warsaw's telephone system rarely worked. Oftentimes, we couldn't make a connection, and when we did, we might be cut off at any moment. I drove AFSC's jeep from one embassy to another.

How could I get to Madeleine? I could take a commercial flight going to Sweden, then to London, and finally to Dusseldorf. If all connections were made—which rarely happened—I would arrive there one day ahead of my present arrangements. A Polish friend said, "I know where the Russian freight trains going to Berlin stop in Warsaw. You could ride the rails through East Germany."

His idea was tempting but risky. I'd get to Berlin quickly, but if I got caught, I might never see Madeleine.

We had twenty vehicles in Poland in the Anglo-American Quaker Relief Mission. A team member said, "One of us could drive you to the Polish-Czechoslovakian border and then you could drive through Czechoslovakia and West Germany by yourself."

Several team members were willing to drive me, but we had bought our trucks from the U.S. Army, and many of them had

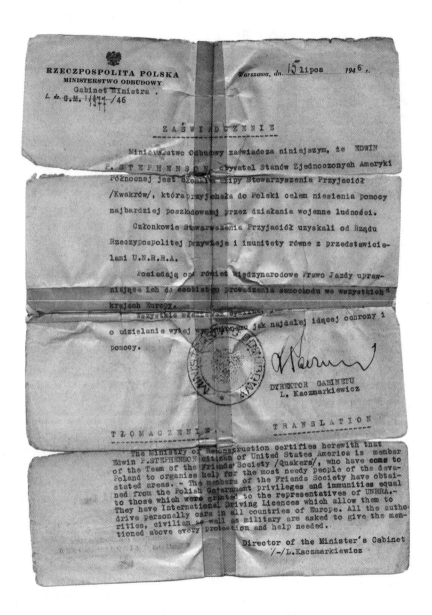

POLISH TRAVEL AUTHORIZATION CARRIED BY RED AT ALL TIMES IN POLAND. 1946-47

seen service in North Africa. Not one vehicle in our mission could withstand my anxious, heavy foot. What would I do if the truck broke down?

On the chance that the British might have another unscheduled plane coming in that week, I drove to the British Embassy. As I explained my predicament to an acquaintance there, he stepped out on the balcony and pointed to a truck idling in the courtyard. He said, "That truck leaves for Berlin in five minutes."

I flew down the stairs and stopped the British lorry driver as he pulled through the gates. He seemed like my last hope. Hastily I explained, "My fiancée has been in a accident and I am trying to get to Solingen, Germany. Will you take me to Berlin?"

"Do you have papers permitting you to cross East Germany?"

"No."

"Then I can't take you." But taking pity on me, he promised, "Tonight I am staying at a hotel in Poznan, Poland. If you can get your papers and meet me there before eight o'clock tomorrow morning, I'll be happy to drive you. If you get to Poznan during the night, come to my room and sleep on the floor."

I dashed to the Russian Consulate. The large two-story building seemed cold and hostile, but fortunately the huge foreboding waiting room was empty. To the young man at the counter, I told my story. He said, "Before we can start the process, we must have a letter from your embassy requesting the papers."

I dashed to the American Embassy and, by chance, met a man I knew. I blurted out, "My fiancée has been in a accident in Germany, and I am desperately trying to get to her. I need a letter from my embassy for the Russians, requesting an emergency visa."

He turned his back to me as he said, "We have had emergency requests in for six weeks with no success. You don't have one chance in a thousand of getting the Russians to act."

Frustrated and furious, I shouted out at him, "I'll take that one chance, and the only damn thing I am asking of you is to write me one measly letter."

Taken aback at my outburst, he didn't even wait for a secretary but sat down at a typewriter and wrote out the letter himself. While typing he said, "My chauffeur writes and speaks Russian. He might be able to help."

When the chauffeur and I arrived at the Russian Consulate the room was full. My heart sank, the lines were so long! But the young man at the desk saw me towering above the crowd and motioned me to the window. After reading the letter and asking me to wait, he went across the street to the Russian Embassy and was back in twenty minutes.

As he approached the counter, he said, "Here are the papers. We just need four pictures."

I thought all was lost. In those days, nearly all traveling papers had to have a photo attached to each copy. "I have a stack of pictures at my hotel room, but I have none with me."

"That's fine. I'll just hold the papers here until you return."

Looking at my watch, I nearly collapsed. "There isn't time to go to the hotel, come back here, and still catch my train to Poznan."

"Here take the papers and have your chauffeur bring the pictures back to me after you have left. May you and your fiancée have a long and happy life."

Suddenly, I was on my way to see Madeleine! I caught the train to Poznan and stumbled into the truck driver's room early the next morning. As I rode in the back of his covered lorry through East Germany, my anxiety dragged out the miles.

Finally, late that afternoon, he dropped me at an intersection in West Berlin, where the AFSC team picked me up. There were two trains a day from Berlin to Dusseldorf, near Iserlohn where Madeleine lay in a British Army hospital. They had been making reservations for me on every train, canceling when I did not arrive and making reservations on the next train. Therefore, I had a reservation for the overnight train.

They took me to their quarters and tried to get me to eat something. But to all my questions—"How is Madeleine? When did you last hear from her?"—they said nothing. Later I realized that they didn't wish to lie to me but wanted to avoid telling me just how close to death she was.

As we were leaving to catch the train for Dusseldorf, the telephone rang. Someone called out and said, "Wait! This may be from Iserlohn." We waited, but the telephone connection wasn't made. Minutes ticked by. I was so afraid of what the call might tell me, but I had to know. The driver kept saying, "We have to go, we'll miss the train."

Finally, we left for the train station, still with no word about Madeleine's condition.

The next morning, Wednesday, I arrived in Dusseldorf and was met by members from Madeleine's team. They, too, kept a conspirator's silence about Madeleine's condition as they drove me to the hospital.

Mid-afternoon Wednesday, I walked into Madeleine's room. She opened her eyes and gave me a weak smile. Later I learned this was her first conscious moment since the accident four days before!

June 15, 1947 ~ William Huntington to Madeleine in Iserlohn

(William Huntington was an AFSC Commissioner in Europe)

For the past week we have all been thinking of you every hour—a pleasant practice to continue to be sure as you get better and better and go on into years of good health, but an anxious one the first few days until we heard that you could at last be said to be out of danger. I hope that you are now well enough to read this or at least to have Red read it to you.

It was certainly bad luck for this accident to happen to you. So many of our people when they heard of it said with a sigh, "But we've been so lucky this hasn't happened before." But such resignation to the law of averages is poor consolation to the unfortunate victim! Still, it does give us all an intimate share in your suffering and a humility of conscience in that we are each in our part to blame. When I heard it was a skid, I thought immediately of a ride in a similar truck I had recently when we swerved crazily from side to side and only escaped by the skill of the driver and the grace of God.

It isn't the sort of vacation that you and Red were planning, but it will be an experience for both of you that you will always remember—one that will bring you closer together, more deeply perhaps than all the happy hours in Switzerland could have done. And those will come later, too. Who knows but God why things happen as they do?

Carry on the noble struggle your good physique has been putting up to pull you through. Relax and resign yourself to a good long rest. (With the same happy ending, I hope, that was planned before!) Consider yourself awarded the Purple Heart with oak leaves and cherry blossoms and orchids and all the ribbons of the spectrum.

And believe me, were this New York, I should have the florists send you daily bouquets to brighten your bedside. Blessings upon you and a swift recovery.

June 23, 1947 ~ William Huntington to Julia Branson in Philadelphia

(Julia Branson was the Director of Foreign Service for The American Friends Service Committee)
Saturday, June 21, I borrowed the Frankfurt jeep and made an all-day round trip to Iserlohn to see Madeleine. I had two hours in Iserlohn and talked with her, with Red Stephenson, and with her doctor. I was happy and relieved to find her well out of danger and making extraordinary progress toward what the doctor believes will be complete recovery.

She was resting comfortably in bed in a small pleasant ward in the British Eighth Army Hospital, weak but cheerful. The problem at present, in fact, is to get her to stay quiet. A couple of days before, too much activity had brought on a hemorrhage, and great care was being taken to prevent this recurring. Her head and face were still slightly swollen and her eyes were black, one very bloodshot, but they told me that she was looking ever so much better than before. The scar just above her right temple seemed to be healing well and will not be noticeable, I should say, in ordinary appearance. Her right hand was black and blue and had a mild fracture in the little finger; no displacement of bones. This hand had been x-rayed before, but the plates had not yet been developed.

I did not get a detailed story of the accident. Madeleine remembers nothing, not even the beginning of the skid. Deborah Alexander of FRS (a member of the Solingen team), who has been in the same room in the hospital with bruises and cuts on her knees and who was leaving the day I was there, was driving the truck at the time, but I did not ask her about it. Madeleine said Deborah was a very good driver and is sure it was not her fault. The truck skidded on a wet cobbled road between rows of big trees. There were apparently pedestrians and bicycles on the road, preventing free manipulation of the wheel, which might have otherwise recovered from the skid. The truck spun into the trees and the ditch and was totally wrecked. A German doctor first took care of Madeleine and Deborah and is, I gathered, to be largely credited for their survival. The ambulance from the hospital reached them about an hour after the accident. Madeleine was in very serious condition, bleeding heavily from her head and face, and very near death.

Red told me Major Woods, Madeleine's doctor, has had long experience, especially with head injuries. He impressed me as being very competent. He assured me that Madeleine had no other injuries other than the skull fracture and the hand fracture, and that the way she was recovering indicated that she should have the minimum of complications resulting from the severe wound to the brain. He said that in ten days she should be up in a wheelchair and in three or four months she should be back to her pre-accident self. He said that it has to be expected that she will be subject to headaches and dizziness for some time. It cannot be predicted how long. Eventually she should get over them altogether.

After talking to the doctor, I discussed with Red what plans he and Madeleine had best make. I said I thought that Madeleine should abandon all idea of going back to Solingen for more work, and that I would write FRS confirming this. Also we agreed that she should give up all idea of visiting Poland, as had been their plan. Furthermore, we agreed that Red's return to Poland should be, if possible, adjusted to the best interests of Madeleine's recovery. If he is useful in aiding in the rehabilitation period and the doctor welcomes his staying there, it would be best, I think, for him to stay until she is ready to be taken to Switzerland. He then could go back to Warsaw for August (assuming she left Iserlohn at the end of July) and as much of September as necessary to wind up his responsibilities there and to turn them over efficiently to Louis Taylor.

In a week or two it may be clearer just when the best time for these movements to take place will be. These suggestions now are only estimates based on the doctor's best judgment at this early stage. I told Red, however, that I feel his plans for the time being should be subordinated to what is best for Madeleine, and this means subordinating his work as a member of our Polish mission likewise. I am confident that you will agree that this is the right hypothesis and that the Polish mission will be able to adjust itself to this emergency for her sake.

June 23, 1947 ~ Red in Iserlohn to his parents in North Carolina

Dearest Mother and Daddy, Sorry not to have written lately, but our plans have been changed drastically because of an accident in which Madeleine was involved. Sunday before I was to leave Poland I received a telegram saying that Madeleine had been in an accident and had received a fractured skull. The next day I received a second telegram asking me to come to Germany as soon as possible. I left the same afternoon, getting to the hospital on Wednesday afternoon.

Madeleine had finally regained consciousness, but she was still considered dangerously ill. It is a remarkable thing that she is even alive, but Dr. Wood says that she will have a complete recovery if she will take a long rest. Our plans now are for her to remain here until the end of July and then go to Switzerland and wait until I can finish my job in Poland. Then we shall sail from France in October.

It has been a real ordeal for both of us. Only in the past few days has she realized how badly hurt she has been. Never have I suffered as I did the seventy-five hours when I was trying to get to her. Now it is she who must endure the hardship of lying quietly when she feels like getting up and going out into the sunshine.

Everyone has been kind to both of us. German friends have sent her flowers and fruit; they are not allowed to visit in the military hospital. Bill Huntington drove over from Frankfurt yesterday. People from her team come over about two days out of every three. The nurses are very pleasant and allow me in to see her most any time during the afternoon and evening. I am living in the officers' mess, so I am getting to know most of the doctors.

We have kept her family pretty well informed. Three cables were sent to them before I arrived, and I have sent two and just now finished a second letter.

This is going to make returning to Poland very difficult for me, but Bill has told me to stay with her as long as she needs me. He is writing to Peter to find out if I may stay until Madeleine leaves for Switzerland, but even though Peter may consent to this, we are not sure that I should. Madeleine knows that I should be back to work and does not care to detain me if it means terrible hardships on those in the mission. She is a real Trojan, and this tragedy has caused us to realize how much we mean to each other.

1993 ~ Madeleine from Monan's Rill

I was only briefly in this "small, pleasant ward" described by Bill Huntington. Grete Ravn, a member of the Solingen team and a nurse, came to see me early on and decreed that I was too ill to be in a ward.

Problem: "But private rooms are only for officers." Solution: I was declared a Civilian Officer and thus eligible for a private room.

My room faced a sunny hillside, golden with ripening grain, where small figures toiled in the fields. For me, the view was like a medieval tapestry, endlessly fascinating. There was one drawback in this idyllic scene—a wood cutter who chopped endlessly, day and night. Often I begged that he be stopped. The noise was, in fact, the characteristic bruit of an aneurysm, caused by the abnormal connection between a vein and an artery resulting from the brain injury. The wood cutter would go on chopping until January 1948 when a miraculous operation in Philadelphia repaired the trauma.

The army hospital had minimal equipment. Not even ice was available. Once, when I had a hemorrhage, a driver was sent out to scour the countryside in hopes of finding some ice, but he returned empty handed. The nursing staff, most of them young women about my age, were competent and caring; several became friends. Red was in constant attendance, helping to feed me, amuse me, cheer me up. The Marshall Plan was being formulated at this time, and I was intensely interested in the details, but after five minutes of serious talk, my attention would flag. Then Red resorted to tricks; he wiggled his ears, gobbled like a turkey, and entertained me as if I were a five-year-old.

July 1, 1947 ~ Red in Iserlohn to his parents in North Carolina

It has been a little more than three weeks since I left Poland, yet now it seems like ages although the time has gone by very rapidly. Madeleine has improved beyond all expectations except her own. She thought she would be up and out within a couple of weeks and is now realizing that she could not take three steps without aid. However, they have let her sit up in a chair for thirty minutes a day for the past two days. They think she will be able to take a few steps within a couple of more days. It is going to be a long, hard battle for her.

With the exception of two days, she has suffered very little considering the fact that she was so badly hurt. One night she had a nose bleed that lasted several hours, and it was most frightening, as they did not seem to be able to stop it. Saturday they had to remove the cast from her arm and hand and put on another. This was a most terrifying experience, as her broken finger had not mended, and they pulled on it in an attempt to remove the old cast.

This past weekend I went back to Solingen, which is the city where Madeleine was working. It was very nice to be with some of her teammates for a few hours. Also, I visited a German friend of hers and attended a Friends Meeting; later in the day two of us took a walk through the woods and across a brook that is one of the most beautiful I have seen. It is where Madeleine used to take her nightly walks after supper.

Before leaving I visited a Polish displaced persons camp in Solingen and was able to spend several hours with the welfare officer looking over the camp and the living conditions of the Polish people there. Their case is one of the saddest of any people during the war. The solution to their problem seems too far away for us to grasp.

Naturally, a trip like this meant that I went for forty-eight hours without seeing Madeleine, and I must admit that I was more than ready to return to her. Just how we shall stay apart for two months while I return to Poland, I am not sure. However, there is work to be done, so we must face it. I shall not feel satisfied until she has arrived safely in Switzerland. She will remain here until the end of July, which means that she will be all alone with very few visitors for about three weeks.

Say, have you sent my birth certificate to Switzerland? We wish to be married in Corcelles and a birth certificate is something that one must have in order to obtain papers in Europe.

Madeleine said to tell you that she has received your letters and that she will answer them as soon as she is able to write again. At present her right hand is in a cast.

Both of us are getting excited about returning home; so you can expect to see us before Christmas. We don't have definite plans about where we shall go when we return, as we shall have to report to Philadelphia, and then we wish to visit you and her people. Keep your fingers crossed, and we shall get there as soon as we can.

July 5, 1947 ~ Red in Iserlohn to his parents in North Carolina

Madeleine is getting along beautifully; in fact, I am planning to leave next Thursday, spend a day in Berlin, and then fly to Warsaw on Saturday. She has really had a tough time of it, yet she does not complain. She wants to get out of this hospital so badly that she would not complain of anything if that would free her any earlier. However, she promises to tell the nurses if she is suffering, so that they will treat her.

I shall certainly hate to leave her, but the doctor thinks that it is just as well for me to go, as she has depended on me so much in the past three weeks that she needs an opportunity to find her independence again.

1997 ~ Red from Monan's Rill

Though her words were cheery, Madeleine's first few letters from the hospital in Iserlohn were very short and written with a shaky crayon scrawl. Gradually, she began to type again, and the letters grew longer as she gained strength.

July 10, 1947 ~ Madeleine in Iserlohn to Red en route to Poland

You are a wonder—getting a note and a kiss to me today! I wish this could reach you as quickly.

Ruth bathed me in the tub and let me splash like a kid. The radio had charming harpsichord music—all good for my morale. I feel quite peaceful, love; sure, there's a lump in my throat, too, but the world's good for all that.

July 13, 1947 ~ Red in Gora Pulawska to Madeleine in Iserlohn

It is nearing eleven o'clock on a Sunday night. Peter is sitting beside me eating some wonderful raspberry ice cream (jealous?), fifteen people are talking as hard as they can, someone is lighting a gas burner, and two people are trying to read under the same gas lantern that I am using.

Peter, Lou, and I are planning another conference on the weekend of September 13 and 14. I shall be free to leave as soon as I like after that. In the meantime, I hope to be able to go to Krakow. Ex was disappointed that I came back so soon, as she has been called to Warsaw to help. Since she's here, I shall take the opportunity to do some visiting and resting, because I feel as though I need a rest. I have been very frank with Peter. Really, I do not feel up to par. Part of this is physical and part of it is from the strain of the past few weeks. It's nothing serious, but if Ex is interested in helping us and arrangements have been made for her to do so, I see no reason why I shouldn't take advantage of the setup.

July 13, 1947 ~ Madeleine in Iserlohn to Red in Warsaw

It's Sunday morning, sunny and blue, new flowers bright in the room, the radio playing, and I do wish you were here. Kiss me, love, and lay your cheek beside mine and let us look out at the bright field together.

I have been very bad, as you see by the date. The day after you left was gray, and I felt gray, too. Yesterday was much better; I wangled permission from Mitchell to get up morning and afternoon. The physiotherapist started me on climbing a stool (practice for stairs), deep knee bends, wagging my head from side to side and up and down. Elementary but encouraging. I felt fine, though pleasantly tired. Afternoon: five visitors, thrice welcome now that you're gone, but they stayed long. Today I feel much better, only not so inclined to Susie-Q down the corridor.

FLASH: FEMALE PATIENT NAME OF YAUDE SEEN WALKING ABOUT HOSPITAL GROUNDS THIS PM FULLY DRESSED. STOP. ACCOMPANYING NURSE MOLLY PREPARED TO MAKE SIGNED AFFIDAVIT THAT THIS DID OCCUR. FOR THE TIME OF FIFTEEN MINUTES. STOP. WHY WEREN'T YOU HERE FOR THE BIG EVENT. STOP. DARLING I LOVE YOU. NO STOP.

> There was a young man from Varsovie
> Whose judgment was quite topsy-turvy;
> His love, so 'tis said
> Had a crack in her head,
> She wasn't even particularly curvy!
> —Shakeisbeer

July 14, 1947 ~ Madeleine in Iserlohn to Red in Warsaw

I've spent long moments lying here thinking how to tell you how I miss you. Still I haven't found the words. Tonight I wish for you with an ache that goes clear through me. Sometimes there seems so much of you here that your actual absence seems trivial. Red, whatever you give away, keep that green coat; I remember it vividly from Paris and now here, so that it seems almost a part of my picture of you, like your hair.

Darling, did you know you left Lettice's little book *Of Life and Death* here? Or was it a-purpose? I've had much comfort and some thinks from it.

You asked for details—now take 'em! This afternoon I was up for two hours, helped get the tea ready, climbed a flight of stairs alone, and at the end wasn't nearly as nerve-tired as usual. Wood still hasn't shown up, though he's been back since Friday, so I've asked to see him. Gosh, it's harder to get than an audience with the Pope!

A beautiful letter from Paulet; they hadn't yet received your last one but insisted that I come there to convalesce. Trudel was trying to get permits to come and get me! Oh Red, what with lying about and the food I shall be stuffed with in Suisse, I shall be as plump as a hen; and if you get any gaunter, people will think it's you, not I, who had an accident! (Guess you had an accident at that—you ran into me.)

Your two notes from Berlin came today. It was good to have them, and if as you say you couldn't write what you felt, I understand that better now. Here I am, wanting to tell you so much and only the unimportant things get said. Wanting to tell you how dear to me you are, and all I can say is, I love you. Perhaps some day I can tell you better. For now, I'll just kiss you; maybe the longing and the need and the tenderness and the faith will come through that way.

July 15, 1947 ~ Madeleine in Iserlohn to Red in Warsaw

It's a warm, sweet evening and I've just had a bath—by myself. And as I came back to my room I felt so strongly, "Oh, if Red were waiting there and would take me in his arms."

I have turned some kind of corner today. Gotta say this for Wood—when he does appear, he gives you the green light. I may now stay up all day long, get dressed in the morning and wander about as much as I feel like. I get violet-ray, more exercises. Also dark glasses, for sunlight. Me and Garbo—I TANK I GO HOME.

Gee, Red, I miss you more, in a way, every day that I get better. 'Cause now we could begin to do things. Besides, I'd like to show off for you! And I look more like before; my hair's been washed and curled. With a dress and some lipstick, I'd hardly stop the clock! I feel so much different from the weepy, droopy creature you said good-bye to last week that it seems an age ago!

Dear, this morning with the sun shining and the music playing, I planned a little about our wedding. The thought of it was an extraordinary peace and joy. Oh Red, I never thought I should ever be so ready to marry anyone. I think I feel as much a part of you, as much your wife, as any ceremony could make me feel; but I shall be glad of the ceremony for all that, to give thanks that we came together and were preserved to each other, to say to one another, "I take thee. . . ."

My Red, can you read between the lines the much love and gratitude and faith that are there? I cannot seem yet to say them as I would; perhaps if thee can feel them with me, thee will know, too.

July 17, 1947 ~ Madeleine in Iserlohn to Red in Warsaw

Drop everything and rush out and have two vodkas—one for me and one for thee. The cast is off! And it was painless. My finger is like a small curled-up sausage and is pretty immobile, but it's out!

Two more vodkas (you will be under the table before I'm through); this morning I walked down to Seiler See by myself. And I was given one of the babies to nurse for an hour. He responded nicely to French songs—that is, he went to sleep! Oh Red, it does make me long for one of our own! They are not as fragile as you think, and they're incredibly wonderful. Already, as I feel stronger, I can think about having one with much more equanimity. How would you like us to bring a ready-made one home? The night nurse will sell me a beautiful little girl for ten cigarettes because she cries every night at 4 a.m.

Your cable came yesterday; it was so brief and so right—that you were there and safe, that you love me and are Red—that I sent you one this morning in case the mails are slow.

The weather is glorious; if you were here, I think I could make it up the hill we have looked at so often.

I am not unaware of the fact that my letters are awfully self-centered, my dear. I do think about other things than myself and Red, but I find it hard to get them down. But I've gleaned a couple ideas from my experiences here that I'll share with you sometime. The international situation would gray my hair if I were the graying kind. I've noticed particularly since you have left, a marked tendency to worry unduly over all sorts of things. Worrying over the world is a profitless job at best, but more and more I feel that we must establish ourselves firmly on those foundations which are eternal.

I was rereading your last letters. Red, I seem to know you so much more, to feel you so much more closely, that it is like reading the letters of a new person. I hurt with the perception of you and with love for you. It will be long, I suppose, before I love you all I am able or know you as I wish to. Can you bear with me that time? The new understanding and affection we found while you were here have made me realize what a far way there is yet to go. Oh Red, may the day come soon when we can be together so that we can get on with our traveling on that way!

Much love, dear heart. Now I have two arms to embrace you and two hands to caress you; had I two hearts to love you, you should have them both.

July 18, 1947 ~ Red in Warsaw to Madeleine in Iserlohn

There has been so little time for writing to you in the past week that I left the office before five o'clock today in order to get a letter started. In Berlin I arrived before breakfast and was able to attend Meeting for the first time in many a month besides the short periods we have at the mission conferences. Then after writing you a short note, I took one of the team members to the French sector. It was a beautiful ride and gave me a look at part of Berlin I had not seen before. That afternoon I slept awhile in order to be fit for the dinner with the American Friends. After three weeks in the officers' mess, that was one of the most refreshing evenings I have spent with friends in some time.

The plane left at eight o'clock on Saturday morning. The weather was fair enough for good visibility, but it was rather rough at times, and I was none too happy. However, I was able to enjoy watching the contrast between the area around Berlin and around Warsaw. The crops in Germany were much greener than those in Poland. In fact, they seemed to get worse the farther east we came. I think this might have been caused by the drought, as Poland has been heavily hit this year. Also, I noticed that the land in Poland showed many signs of the war that the farming area of Germany did not show from the air.

Henry Dasenbrock met me at the station and brought me into town, where I met Peter; we soon set off for Gora with a Ford that I doubted seriously would get us there without breaking down. Fortunately, we were able to get to the bottom of the hill where the team lives before we had to stop for car trouble. Exactly forty-eight hours after leaving you, I was sitting down for a conference at Gora Pulawska. You can imagine how much good I was at that meeting.

The meeting went off very smoothly; it was our first attempt to hold a conference at the site of one of the teams. I was able to get in a couple of long walks with Peter; that is the only way one can have any privacy. There are several very nasty problems presenting themselves to us at the moment, but Peter is doing a masterful job in handling them. Our meetings oftentimes drag along; this is laborious, yet neither Peter nor I have cared to give it the direction that Philip gave. You know I talk a lot but the conferences have seen times when I have been silent most of the time.

Leslie took me to Lucima on Monday, as I planned to spend one night with the work camp. Lucima is a very heartening place to see these days, as thirteen houses are going up and more than twenty foundations are being laid. They hope to complete forty houses this summer.

The work camp is going along nicely, in spite of the fact that David was disillusioned when he learned that most of the campers had come in order to improve their English over the summer months. Something I had warned him about in May. To me that does not matter, as they can use that as a basis for coming together and living together as easily as having a project, and because that is what they wish to do, they will have more incentive to practice conversational English in open discussions than otherwise.

Madeleine, why do I go on like this? It is not what I wish to tell you, yet this is easier than telling you all the things I have been thinking this past week. How can I tell you that oftentimes I have felt very much removed from the events at hand, and my mind wanders back to Iserlohn? How can I tell you of a beautiful sunset and the feeling of peace that overcame me? It was like one of your kisses. The same sky, the same sun, the same world, yet different from other sunsets and momentarily I was a part of something else. How can I tell you how elated I am when someone asks about you? A feeling of pride and yet a sadness, rich in happiness tempered with grief.

Once again I find myself not thinking of those kisses and embraces as much as I do those times I would walk into the room and be received with a smile, or those hours I spent at the side of your bed watching you return to life. Aside from those days when you were suffering, I thoroughly enjoyed every minute with you. You taught me much during those days: patience, tenderness, and a capacity to love that I would not have thought possible.

Did I tell you that Ex and Henry are planning to get married before leaving Poland, and then go to Rome? They will be sailing about the same time as we do, so we should at least see each other in Paris and again in Philly, if not on the same boat.

July 20, 1947 ~ Madeleine in Iserlohn to Red in Warsaw

Hi darling, may I have this dance? They're playing "Love Walked In," and I feel for the first time the urge to circle round the room; now if you were here we could settle two things: one, can I dance, and two, can I dance with you?! It's Sunday noon and a dullish day. I feel dullish, too; I'm beginning to wonder how much of the listlessness and depression I feel sometimes is due to my condition and how much to the monotony of the place. I appreciate better your feeling stale here. It's beginning to get me, too. What I'd give occasionally for a keen, stimulating person to talk with.

The sisters are unfailingly pleasant and sometimes chat just for fun, even the medical officers do; in fact, I think I'm becoming more of a person and less of a patient, which is an achievement all around. I felt quite pleased when, the other morning going out the gate, I made small talk with a bunch of soldiers. You know, one has to relearn one's social touch as well as the use of one's legs and arms.

Friday, Grete walked in with a big, pleasant guy in FRS gray; I was sure I'd seen him before—and it was Ted! Red, I am happy for them. In just a few minutes, I was sure he was right for Grete. And that means a lot, for I'm very fond of her and think much of her. I enjoyed Ted's conversation more, I think, than anyone's who has been here. He seems to have a keen, observant, fair mind, and his comments on the German and Polish situation were illuminating to me. I realized while he was talking how little I'd asked you of all the things that had been in my mind about Poland. There were several times when my mind was full of questions and ideas but listening and discussing a complex, abstract problem seemed a huge effort. Curious, how one retreats from what is difficult or demanding. Now I feel much more ready to take on something like that. It seems to me that there's been so much change and progress in the week since you left.

I had a lovely letter from your mother, and I wrote one back to reassure her. She said the latchstring is out for us, which gave me a warm glow. My family is so happy about you, Red, that I wish your family might feel as easy, too. I hate to think of their feeling apprehensive or worried about their new daughter. Not that they're getting a perfect one, by any means, but I wish they knew that with all her failings, she does love and appreciate their Edwin.

July 22, 1947 ~ Red in Warsaw to Madeleine in Iserlohn

Today is a holiday in Poland, the anniversary of the formation of the Lublin Government. Peter is invited to a reception this evening, but since he is away, Ex and I are planning to go. I'm not sure who will be there, but the invitations were issued by the president of the Minister's Cabinet. Parades began yesterday, and I expect are going on today. You should see the streets lined with red and white flags. Large billboards show graphically the increase in production over the past two years. Last night there were fireworks with colored rockets.

Yesterday, darling, I was feeling pretty low for some reason. About supper time, Henry came over and asked if I wanted to go with him and Ex to Hotel Polonia for dinner and dancing, but I turned it down and said that I preferred to go for a walk. However, I walked back to Hotel Central with him in order to speak to Ex and to my great surprise found a letter from you. You have no idea how much it meant! How did you do it, type with your left hand? I was hoping that you would get Grete or someone to write to me before the cast came off, but I was not expecting a letter from you for another week.

After reading your letter, I went for a walk along Jerozalimske to the bridge. It was late evening and turning to dusk; lights were coming on in the apartments. The amazing thing to me was some of the places from which a light came. In one building, there was only one window left and that was a half-cellar room, yet there was a light. In another there were two rooms on the second floor, and nothing underneath except burned walls. The encouraging thing was to see new wooden frames going into buildings that were only burned and not blasted.

The river was as low as I have ever seen it, but there was a steamer going up, which means going south. That is my favorite view, because it is away from the city, and I feel as though I can release myself in that direction, whereas in the opposite I am caught up in the outline of the hollow buildings. Yet when the sky turned red in the northwest, I turned and watched it.

I thought of all the blood that was spilt over this city, and for what? If one could be certain that that was the last time, then one might justify the slaughter, yet here in the midst of the ruins one hears talk of war.

Madeleine, that was a scene I would like to have shared with you. I have seen one painting made from the bridge as the artist looked back at the city of ruins, but last night it was more colorful than any artist would be able to capture: the lights slowly coming on, first in one black building and then another; the sky fiery red; smoke coming from factories to the north; cars and trucks passing with their lights; fireworks bursting from among the ruins. The city of dead has risen, but the Earth is not at peace.

A man with a mandolin has walked into the courtyard singing "The Red Poppy of Monte Casino." He has a terrible voice and is a worse player, but he is so typical of many of the beggars who go around playing and singing. Only last night, Henry and I were observing one little fellow who used to play an accordion with bellows he pumped with his feet. It was a horrible thing, and one could never tell what tune he was trying to play. Last night he had a regular accordion, much better looking but rather cheap. He had on clean clothes that looked well made though not new, and he was much healthier looking. I was amazed, and we decided these beggars must make a reasonable living.

It is a common thing to see several men standing together to form a band and playing an assortment of instruments. One member of the group stands across the street from the band, so they can beg from everyone passing. One day, a group of five came into the courtyard. They were really good, and I enjoyed them so much that I threw money out to them—something I rarely do.

Two days ago I stopped to buy some cherries from a man with a pushcart. Just as I had made the purchase and his mother had taken my money, someone further along the street hollered. He started off with his pushcart in a run; not only him, but all the others there who were selling produce, too. I was amazed, as it was obvious that they were doing something illegal, because within the time I stopped to see what was happening the pushcarts started slowly coming back. Within five minutes, they were shouting their wares again. They are supposed to have a license to sell on the streets away from the marketplace; however, they are so well organized that the police cannot catch them.

I received a letter from Paulet and Trudel. Paulet suggested that Trudel go to Germany and come back to Corcelles with you. He wrote this before he received the letter asking about your visiting them for six weeks. I shall not answer him for a couple of days yet, as I figure that you might still get someone to go with you from the team.

July 24, 1947 ~ Madeleine in Iserlohn to Red in Warsaw

Last night late there was a brilliant new moon and a sprinkle of stars and sweet warm air. Ever since the Marseille trip, I think, crescent moons have reminded me sharply of you—and so for a bit last night, I missed you more poignantly than usual. Red, the next new moon but one we should see together, coming up over the mountains.

My social life is becoming a whirl. Shortly I won't even have time to write you! Twenty patients were invited by the Colonel to go to a play in the Iserlohn Garrison Theatre called *Hasty Heart*. Transport was laid on here and beer in the theater lounge, and the beer was cold. The play is excellent—had two years' London run—and was well produced. But for the boys and Chris and me, it would have been OK in any case, for it was a takeoff on life in a British military hospital. The setting was Burma, but the beds were made and tucked up endlessly just like in Iserlohn. Everybody went into a flap at the Colonel's inspection, and the crack that brought down the house was, "This is a British military hospital—you're not supposed to be comfortable!"

When I'm around the ward, I'm considered available Yaude, which bucks me no end. I can wait on the other patients, mind babies, accompany patients for X-rays, and help Miss Cram (the chatty lady who used to arrive with a huge basket of magazines—remember?). Miss C has turned out to be not a bad egg when she stops chin-wagging; we had a long and remarkably sensible conversation this morning about Quakerism, conscientious objectors, and the future of America—all topics not very current around this joint, as you well know. Meanwhile, I cut out purple deer from felt, for other patients to sew together. (This was also parodied in the play, to the great delight of the boys, who howled at the fat man laboriously embroidering blue buttercups!)

Golly, Red, I do wish you could see me; the change since you left seems so tremendous. I can walk forty-five minutes round the countryside. I finally got up on the hill opposite my room and picked some of the pink flowers I looked at for so long. Noises bother me very little; the wood chopper sticks around, but he's fainter and easy to ignore. As I feel stronger I feel more cheerful, and so the happy circle goes on.

My exercises include playing catch with a tennis ball (you can toss for me) and jumping up and down. This all sounds elementary, but you were around long enough to know how revolutionary it is for a woozy floozy like me! The ultraviolet treatment is giving me a nice tan in ten easy minutes a day. The only thing which is not clearing up fast is my right eye, which has become bloodshot again. I am sure that the sight, or at least the movement, of that eye is impaired; the eye specialist will check it soon. I've had to do some considering of the possibility that I may have to get along with something less than the perfect eye I once had or with wearing glasses again. Neither of these is anything to moan over, but eyes are pretty important and sort of personal possessions. One would rather have them pull their own weight, so to speak. Still, there's plenty of time for improvement, I should think, and if it doesn't improve, we shall fix it up as well as possible and go on from there.

The little finger is still somewhat sore and fat (It will be overgrown for a couple of years, apparently.), but it's coming straighter and stronger each day. I have invaded the Chapel to use the hideously out-of-tune piano there and can manage not-too-rapid passages for about five minutes. I reckon it will be quite a while before I get back to prewar agility, but I just can't worry about it; walking and riding are too absorbing and too wonderful for the moment.

Red, I've been especially glad and thankful for the improvement because of you. I know you will hoot at this, but it was in my mind often in the days after you left. I didn't want you to have an ailing wife who couldn't take her share of the family's responsibilities and work. I still don't want you to have a wife like that, but I'm daily cheered by the prospect that I shall be an almost-good-as-new woman. In some ways, I shall probably be dependent on you for some months yet for good advice and encouragement in regard to my health, but I hope the time won't be long. Dependent on each other we shall always be, and should be to some extent, but I'd like it to be dependent in ways that are essential and growing.

Perhaps after two months of health and strength, I shall find the understanding and the words to tell you what it was to have you here. Perhaps I can never explain, yet you know. The greatest gifts one can't thank for; one can be thankful, that is all. It's like the sunshine that gives us life and touches us with joy, that we accept and need and are happy for, almost without knowing it. So was your coming and your staying—a light of love and courage round about me that I needed, accepted, and blessed almost unknowing, because it was so natural and so necessary.

July 24, 1947 ~ Red in Warsaw to Madeleine in Iserlohn

Tonight I feel lousy, although I do not know why I should. When I read your one letter that has come or when I talk with someone about you, life comes back into this wretched soul. Saturday I leave for Gora's anniversary, then to Kozienice for one night, then to the work camp for a couple of days, and maybe on to Krakow. This place is dead to me, and I have to force myself to work.

Even shaking hands with the Prime Minister did not thrill me. Ex Williams and I went to the reception given by the President of the minister's cabinet. We passed by three armed guards at various points and then into the mansion. At one time, it must have been one of the most luxurious places in Warsaw. They have cleaned away the smoke and done a cheap job of repainting and refurnishing; however, one could still tell something of its graciousness by the marble floors, beautiful stairway, the high ceilings, and the large doors and windows.

There was a new scarlet carpet, which we followed through several halls until we arrived at a huge hall, where we were introduced to the Prime Minister and his new wife as "the Quakers."

It looked as though all the important people of Warsaw were there, except the ambassadors from the English and American embassies. Some of the lesser dignitaries represented those nations. You should see an English officer in formal uniform! Gee, kid, there is nothing like it in all eastern Europe with all of its color and glory.

July 28, 1947 ~ Madeleine in Iserlohn to Red in Warsaw

I don't feel like writing you this evening. I'd far rather walk with you up the road that goes past my window, toward the east where there are fields of new-cut wheat and cool woods and half-timbered cottages built into the curve of the hill. And when we'd walked a few miles, we'd sit against a tree and feel the softness of the summer night rise around us.

But writing is the only sharing we have at the moment, and there is great news. This is probably my last letter to you from Iserlohn. Wednesday morning, July 30, I may leave the hospital! I wish you were here to celebrate the moment. This morning, coming back from seeing Wood, I threw all my newspapers up to the ceiling in a burst of excitement, and then, unaccountably, I began to cry, just a little.

I'm better than I'd ever hoped to be at this stage, and I think better than he expected to see me. This convalescence in Switzerland is going to be a long holiday as far as I can see, and at the end of it, I'll be better than ever before. I may do as much as I please without getting too tired; I may swim, dance, climb. In fact, the only things he has forbidden me are diving, riding, and wild, late parties. Since my very few attempts at diving have resembled a frog flopping, and the only time I was ever on a horse was when my father held me on one at the age of four, and late, wild parties are few and far between in my young life, I can't say that I feel seriously restricted.

Since you go for the details, dear: Wood says the little finger will probably give more trouble than anything else. That may be, as it's still rather bent and sore, but I'm damned if I can find time to worry over a little finger! It will need lots of exercise, that's all. The eye Wood is not concerned about; says the redness will go of its own accord in a month or so. Apparently it's still too early to test the vision. Everything else seems OK. I have to listen hard for the wood chopper during the day (he's still noticeable when I'm trying to get to sleep). I asked Wood about having a baby, and he said medically there was no reason why I shouldn't begin a few months after September. But after having two new babies in my room the last nights, I think we'd be smart to wait until we have a huge house, so that the baby can howl in one corner of the top floor, and we can sit in the opposite corner of the basement! But I'm getting lots of lessons in baby care.

I've been concerned over you; you mentioned not feeling up to par at Gora and hoping to have a little time off since Ex is anxious to help in Warsaw. It's not at all surprising after the strain of the weeks here. After all, you have planned for a vacation in June, instead of which you got anxiety, uncertainty, and a constant drain on your nervous energy. By the time you get to Switzerland, it's I who will be taking care of you! I hope you will be able to take care of yourself a bit, and regain your good health and good spirits, even while you're doing a job. You know, it's been a curious pleasure to think of you back in Warsaw; I think you love that city a good deal, and it must have been good to see it again and all the people there who mean much to you. I truly wish you happiness in your last weeks there.

July 31, 1947 ~ Red in Warsaw to Madeleine in Iserlohn

Madeleine, my dearest, if only you could be with us now. I have been taking what possibly will be my last visit to Lucima, and I kept wondering how I ever would be able to share with you all the pleasures and headaches of the experiences here. Last night, I wanted to write to you while sitting beside the Vistula; however, all of us were very much concerned about Van Cleve. He is seriously ill with measles, and of all things, he must lie under a canvas on a cot beside the river! Luckily we have two very young Polish girls who have just finished their medical studies, and we have most of the medicines that they wish. Last night, he had a very high temperature and was much too sick to be moved; now he is better, but still too weak to move over these roads. In fact, we have the choice of taking him to Kozienice, a ride of four hours over very bad roads, taking him to Warsaw, a ride of five hours, or leaving him where he is. Oh, what to do!

The work camp is going along nicely. In fact, there are some who are already talking of having camps again next year. One boy had already planned to attend a Polish work camp for ten days in September, so we are pleased to know that he has the benefit of this one and will be able to use some of his experience in the purely Polish one. Also, one Polish boy and one Swiss girl wish to work with the Mission. I think the boy will join the transport team, and I would like to see the girl join the new team forming at Nawiady.

She has studied Polish for two years and speaks bits of Swedish and Danish, also Italian, plus her French, English, and German. And only twenty-one years of age! If there ever was an ideal international work camper, she is it. She is capable of doing many things, having worked in a hospital for four years, and she is heavy enough to be handy with manual labor. She has a keen insight into human relationships and seems to draw the best out of the people around her.

For what's mis-said or left out or bungled, use
your love for understanding

-Madeleine

The Moment of Arrival

our work is making up for our
shortcomings, misunderstandings,
mistakes .... not to mention that
the people with whom we try to
work. I'm not discouraged so much
as surprised. Times! Is that
how the world gets on — a slow
sort of progress but one where
I can have a hand in too. You
see, my dear, however childish
this may sound, I've always been
in awe of people of affairs.
I'm beginning to see that people
do things and take decisions
not so much because they
know more than others as because
they have the courage or the energy
to try, or lack the imagination
for fear! sort of fools rush in

August 3, 1947 ~ Madeleine in Solingen to Red in Warsaw

You will know by now that I left Iserlohn on July 30 and am now back in Solingen. Curiously, although I had gotten used to your absence from the hospital, I missed you acutely again when I came here— walking in our garden, visiting the neighbors, sitting at meals—all the things I had planned to do with you seemed suddenly empty and a little lonely. Still, nothing could dim the pleasure of being back, and it was a lovely homecoming. I found my room full of flowers from the staff and friends—beautiful roses of a tender pink just opening out, and many others. I'm being shamefully spoiled with breakfast in bed (Old Warhorse Wood wouldn't approve.), and I spend my days like a "lidy," glancing at magazines, packing, visiting friends, lying in the garden. Oh gosh, what I wouldn't give to do a good day's work! This life is getting me down. I keep feeling that I ought to be able to do more, but I can't seem to find the push. I don't get the almost painful weariness that I used to have in the hospital when there had been too many visitors; I just feel, after a couple of hours, totally disinclined to do anything at all. I reckon this is one of the things to be "expected," and it's certainly not a very bad aftereffect, only it gets my goat sometimes.

You know, love, the longer I'm away from Iserlohn, the more I marvel at our time there together. In many ways it seems to me I was more keen and interested and eager then than now. Perhaps it is the alchemy of love that it could transform so shut-in a time, mentally and physically, into so happy an interlude. I feel a lack of affection and understanding in the team now that I'm here. It is not really a lack, only my hypersensitivity, and the fact that you've probably spoiled me. I am now quite reconciled to the fact of leaving Solingen; a team is no place for a convalescent. If it is a healthy group, it fills in the vacant place, takes up the slack, and goes on, and anyone who is not actively in the work inevitably feels out of it. The world wags on, and so it should.

August 5, 1947 ~ Red in Warsaw to Madeleine in Corcelles

This is one of those nights that I would like to talk on and on; I am bubbling over with all sorts of things. This a.m. Leslie and I returned from Krakow—a marvelous trip—and now I feel the best since returning to Poland. Best of all was to return and find so many letters...from July 14 to July 28...waiting for me! It was like having part of you here to greet me on my return.

I wanted to shout with joy when I read some of the passages telling about the wonderful, marvelous things you are doing. Then I wanted to cry because I was so happy. It is as though I were regaining life along with you, my dear. It was as though I walked along with you and plucked a flower and placed it in your hair, or helped you toss the papers around the room in celebration of your leaving the hospital. I imagined our leaving there together with beaming faces as we said good-bye to our friends. A letter from Ted says that possibly you will be leaving for Switzerland tomorrow with Frieda.

August 10, 1947 ～ Madeleine in Corcelles to Red in Warsaw

It's Sunday afternoon in Corcelles—the rest you can perhaps imagine better than I can tell you—the peacefulness of it, the bright gardens beneath my windows, the blue mass of the humped hill at the end of the lake, the feeling of being at last at home. Only one thing lacks and that is your being here. Oh Red, Oncle Paul's house is full of you, where you slept and what you said and did and how much fun they had with you. All of them think you quite perfect, which is as much sweet music to my ears. They approve of you, and I approve of their approving, and so the happy circle goes on.

Two of your letters were waiting for me. Oh my dear, I wish I had the wisdom to help you over the next month. But for me, too, the days, however pleasant in themselves, are a time of waiting. I think that to a degree it is inevitable and perhaps right that this should be so. The event we are waiting for is a momentous as well as a joyous one; I remember reading once that one's choice of a mate is as important as his choice of parents! Still, I hate the sensation of marching through a set of days like an automaton, simply because I must. I've been rereading, with greatly deepened appreciation, the pamphlet on marriage and parenthood that you got in London. Speaking of the difficulties of the period of the engagement, it says, "It is possible to 'come over' the difficulties, to 'walk cheerfully over the world, answering that of God in every man.'" Those are oft-repeated words, Red, and they may not speak to your condition just now, but I pray that they, or others, may; they did speak to mine when I read them again a few days ago.

As for the books, if all other persuasion fails, you can think of them as a preparation for auditing the Stephenson-Yaude accounts! I'll try to keep careful notes, but between what AFSC pays and what comes out of our travel and personal allowances, and three or four kinds of currency I feel "confoosed." Also, prices here are exorbitant—far worse than I had imagined. I shall try to be circumspect, but a wedding dress and a little wedding lingerie I do need. I fear your bride is not going to be very bedecked! Shall you mind?

You'll want to know about the trip. It went off famously and was twenty times more fun than ever I dreamed it could be in Iserlohn. Frieda went with me and we climbed on the train at 4:30 p.m. We had a magnificent meal (or so I thought until I had a Swiss meal). Then we retired to the cleverest, coziest sleeper I have ever seen. If we have the shadow of an excuse to get a sleeper on the Continent, let's do it, Red. They're sharp. I slept reasonably well,

MADELEINE AND COUSIN CLAUDINE ON A TRAIN TO BASLE. 1947
-PHOTOGRAPHER UNKNOWN

and at 6 a.m. we were in Basle where Claudine met us.

We slept most of the morning, Frieda fixed me a lunch, and then we set off to see the sights. There, just two months after the crash, I sat on a balcony over the street, watching the world go by, eating with lingering appreciation a strawberry ice, and missing you like hell!

I'm home now. Already I feel better today than I did yesterday, and I'm far happier than in Solingen. There are lots of little things to do in the garden: blackberries to pick and beans to string and dishes to wipe and the floor to sweep. Little things, but they occupy one's time and one's fingers and bring back the habit of doing useful things. I guess that sounds awfully simple, Red, but this convalescing seems half physical and half mental. It may be physical weakness, but I realize I fuss over small things that aren't worth the worry, but as one part of me gets stronger the other does, too. And so it progresses. The idea is to improve me so much that you won't recognize me when I come to meet you!

August 10, 1947 ~ Red in Warsaw to Madeleine in Corcelles

As I begin this, soldiers are marching past the hotel singing—a common sight on a Sunday in Warsaw. The more I see of them, the more I dislike the idea of a country wasting its manpower on something that seems as useless as an army. Just what could these poorly clad and equipped soldiers do in case of an invasion? Would it not be better to give them all short courses in first aid, means of evacuating a city, situation precautions for camp life, and so on, and let them work for the rebuilding of Poland? The best men in the country are serving in the army.

Your attitude about your recovery is most pleasing to me, particularly the balance that you seem to have about possible future handicaps. Although I trust they will not be permanent, it made me realize what a great person you are. Yes, I know what you mean about having our dependence on one another be the kind that is growing. You may now realize some of the torment that I went through during those three days trying to reach your bedside, wondering if you would be permanently injured, if you would be an invalid. Yet I knew that I would always be happy with you if only you were capable of knowing that I love you and would be able to return that love. You may know now how joyful and thankful I was when it became evident that not only could you still smile and have a twinkle in your eye that had meaning, but that also you would be able to share worldly pleasures. Madeleine, there is much within you and much that you would have to give even if you were confined within four walls. Life after all is within us and the external things only stimulate that life and give it food for growing.

I have just reread Gibran's words on marriage and somehow I have better understanding of what he means. "Love one another, but make not a bond of love." Yes, there shall be a bond, but it will be through something more lasting than our existence on this earth.

Madeleine, this is not a conventional love letter; however, it is Red, happy and more at peace with himself than he has been in a long time. The next six weeks will not be hard for me. I hope that they are pleasant and happy ones for you.

August 15, 1947 ~ Madeleine in Corcelles to Red in Warsaw

I've just heard Kreisler's "Liebesfreud" on the radio, and it sounded like us, merry and slightly crackers; I almost saw you coming in the door and grinning at me!

I am overflowing towards thee, and yet the more I feel the less I am able to say. Words have always been facile for me, and this is a new experience. So is what I feel for you, Red; perhaps that is why the words come hard. I think we have had, and are still having, a tremendous experience, one that will probably change us both, and it seems as if the magnitude of it is too much to take in all at once. At least that is so for me; much of what I have thought and felt and become aware of these past two months will return, I think, in years to come.

At the moment, I cannot seem to fit all the pain and joy and new expanses of understanding into what I know now. For thee, it seems to me that a maturity and a great wisdom of love and life have come already. Red, your last letter made me pause in awe. Truly, for a love like that I do not know any words; I can only be still and thank God and love you more. I used to be able to write poetry—not too bad either—but it's years now since I have. I wish I might once again, for you. When you come, I hope I may be able to tell you in the poetry of bodies and souls what it is to know a love like yours.

I couldn't help feeling a little sorry for myself last night, for I had to have your letter read to me, and the somewhat inharmonious voice of M. Charles blended strangely with the sentences written out of your heart.

Darling, I'm not a great person, not yet, by a long shot. I'm sometimes a scared kid. You see, my right eye is making trouble, and I can scarcely read at all now. For distances it's still all right, but anything small or close just doesn't work. All week before I left Iserlohn, the eye was swollen and red; Wood saw it and said it would clear up in time. But in Solingen and then here, it seemed to get worse instead of better, and finally I went to a specialist in Neuchâtel two days ago. He didn't seem very pleased with what he saw; said probably the optic nerve was being pressed and that caused the inflammation. He has taken an X-ray and sent to Germany for their X-rays and a case history. It is possible that an operation will be necessary to relieve the pressure on the nerve, but it is too soon to tell as yet.

Red, I planned at first not to tell you about it. You have had so much cause for worry and grief already, and God knows I don't wish to add to it. But after thinking about it, it seemed not right to keep it from you; it's as if it were your eye, too, if you see what I mean. I'd rather not go ahead without telling you. And I must admit that I have longed for your support these past days. It was rather a blow at first; I was so sure that I was well on the way now. And so I am, in every other respect.

It's just a week since I've come, and you would be pleased and amazed. I'm nice and round, if not fat; I have a good color and a good appetite, and I gad about a good bit, with no ill effects. I go easily a long morning without a rest, and once I managed all day. I putter around in the kitchen—just you wait, Tante Anna is making a good Swiss Hausfrau out of me. I'm accumulating a book full of recipes and firsthand experience. I help pick fruit and vegetables; I clean my room and wash dishes and go to the post office and visit the relations and take jaunts into Neuchâtel—it's lively life! And I've learned to greet everyone, old and young, that I meet, whether or not I know them. Tiens, darling, you're going to have a little provincial waiting for you!

About the eye: there's no cause for despair. It still has lots of kick in it, and if something must be done, I feel confident that this man is capable. Only I do lose courage occasionally, largely because of weakness, and I picture myself going about always unable to read. It's fantastic how much of our civilization is based on letters! Luckily I can touch-type, so I can continue to write. Uncle Paul and Tante Anna and Paulet couldn't be kinder. The serene, down-to-earth atmosphere of this home is a wonderful one to be in. I don't expect my uncle and aunt ever studied any psychology, but they know instinctively how to put people at ease and make them feel normal and useful, and to give them little things to do that help bring one back into the routine of living.

There was one sentence in your letter that made me catch my breath, dear. You said the next six weeks. Is it really as long as that? I had counted on the middle of September, which is just a month away today. I feel torn, Red; you know I'd want you to finish up the job in the way you think right, and indeed, I often feel as if it is I who am working there and contributing something, because you are there. And at the same time, I long for your coming, almost desperately sometimes when this eye business looks black to me. I'll send you further news as soon as I have it, and then you arrange things as it seems best to you.

Don't be upset, my dearest; I know when I'm being foolish. It's just that I can't seem to help it sometimes. I realize full well that I am a walking miracle; two months ago today I doubt if anyone would have been rash enough to say that I'd be as nearly recovered as I am now. But I am stiff-necked, like most humans. One is ready enough to say it is the grace and goodness of God, when one has recovered from an illness or an accident, but rare is the person who says that at the time when the illness comes.

August 19, 1947 ~ Madeleine in Corcelles to Red in Warsaw

The letters are really flying now, figuratively as well as actually. Your letter came yesterday, and my friend from Rochester, who is studying at Lausanne this summer, read it to me. I still greatly prefer to read thy letters myself, but Henry was a good deal more sympathetic than M. Charles. It was a wonderful letter, and it gave me courage and hope from the deep springs of living. For often it seems to me, the ills that beset us both come from our not being at home in the universe, from not understanding or accepting the conditions and disciplines of the abundant life.

First of all I'd like to reassure you and to beg your pardon if I caused you any alarm by my last letter. You have so very much more on your shoulders these days than I have, as I realized afresh from your letter, that I feel thoroughly ashamed of myself for having troubled you with my difficulties. Not that I don't believe in husbands and wives sharing their troubles as well as their joys, but this is one time when I can do little to help you except perhaps to buoy up your spirits, and I don't think I helped you much by worrying you over my eye.

I went again today to see the doctor, and he was more pleased with the look of the eye. He thinks now, after the first X-rays, that the nerve is not being pressed, but that there is perhaps scar tissue from the profuse bleeding which is causing the trouble. These may disappear of themselves or it may be necessary to disengage them from the nerves so that they do not hinder the functioning of the eye. In any case, he will not decide in a hurry. There is much to be discussed in such cases, he says, and he will ask for a consultation with a professor of medicine in Geneva who is supposed to be one of the best men in Europe.

Meanwhile, I can go about life quite as usual, with the exception that I can read scarcely anything. But with the house and the vineyard and the fascination of the countryside, that is not a great privation, although I do feel it rather keenly when I can't read letters—especially thine. But in the end it may well turn out that I've had a free trip to Geneva out of this and nothing worse! In any case, you know that I am having the best of care and the best of moral support from the folks here.

Bill Huntington stopped by on Saturday—and thereby hangs a tale. I told him about the eye difficulty, and he says the insurance in the States will cover any expenses. If necessary, he said, call in four or five or six specialists to make sure the utmost is being done.

Bill, his wife (and isn't she charming), and three kids, plus their camping equipment, tent, and pots and pans, arrived in Corcelles in the middle of the afternoon, to the great amazement and interest of all the neighbors. They were in old clothes, and covered with dust and sweat. Oncle Paul and Tante Anna took them in, as they take everyone in, let them have a wash, gave them a magnificent tea, and we had a wonderful time.

But afterwards one of the little girls next door came over to inquire who the American savages were! The big girl, announced our little neighbor, was not very neat! Oh, Tante Anna explained, they came all the way from America in a car, and you understand, on the sea the winds blew hard and mussed their hair and their clothes! Our small friend departed open-mouthed.

I suggest that when you arrive, we gather all the American savages together, put feathers in our hair, do a war dance, and give them a run for their money!

Our money is going to have to stretch a long way. Tante Anna was talking over possible plans for a wedding supper or tea or something; she's willing to have a small affair here, but I'd want to pay for the food and wine, and that mounts up surprisingly fast. I am writing to my folks to send me $100 if it can be transferred; I have more than that in the States and can pay them back. Jeepers, it's so long since I had to spend any money that it strikes me all of a heap!

I've been wondering about Saturday, September 27 for a wedding date. It falls on my birthday, but that is incidental. That would give you time to rest and relax and give us a little while to plan some things together. On the other hand, the grape harvest comes early this year, and Oncle Paul doesn't think they'll be through until the beginning of October. If our sailing date isn't too close, and if you are willing to wait, we could fix the date for the following Saturday, the fourth. What do you think?

August 20, 1947 ~ Red in Warsaw to Madeleine in Corcelles

It is most difficult to even start this letter. Your letter telling about trouble with your eye came this morning, just after I had sent off the worst letter I think I have ever written to you. Since then I have sent you a cable saying that I possibly could be in Basle on September 9. Ex asked me if I should raise your hopes like that, and I answered that I would meet that date or have some excellent reasons for not doing so.

Oh Madeleine, I sit and wring my hands for lack of something to do. There is much that could be done, visiting, writing, reading, refiling reports, but honestly, how can one do those things that are not really pressing when one only exists here, and his real self is miles away with a lovely girl. My heart skipped a beat when I read "for I had to have your letter read to me." And then the way you went on to tell about your eye in such a matter-of-fact manner. You are great. Yes, I know you feel like a scared kid at times.

Madeleine, did you realize that for once you wrote a letter with a great deal of life and happiness and never once mentioned the beauty of some flowers, or a mountain, or something blue. Instead it was full of things you were doing and what you were thinking, about cooking and hopes for the future, until it was so full of richness that I did not miss the sight of the lake nor the green of the vineyard. Yes, I know you are able to see, and somehow I think your right eye will be OK. It may take an operation, but that will be done with me nearby, I hope. Not that I can help any medically, but it would help me a great deal to be close to you at a time like that. The main thing is, Madeleine, that you have found something in the past two months. You will have to wait for me to catch up again, because your redhead has been going stale since coming back to Poland; it's not permanent, only you must have some patience.

Today I received a wonderful letter from your family. I feel as though it were really my family, too. Madeleine, how can I ever live up to what they think of me? Or should I go ahead just being Red and let them really see what kind of guy they have for a son, and then all of us can enjoy the fun of knowing each other.

Of all your letters, I think this one speaks to my condition at the moment more than any. You, too, are grasping for words when words are inadequate. Sometimes I just sit at the table and write nothing, thinking, dreaming, wondering. Sometimes I think that, if I left a large blank space, it would have more meaning than the jumble of words I put down.

I would say to you, "Pause in silence and join me in that spirit that is wordless." And that is the way I often feel, my sweet, after having sat here alone silently. Just as though you might have reached over and kissed me on the forehead and a smile would cross my face.

August 24, 1947 ~ Madeleine in Corcelles to Red in Warsaw

You went on a Sunday walk with me this morning, did you know? It's a perfect day, sunny and with a fresh breeze. The sky is as blue as in the Midi, the lake glistens, and the vineyards are green and heavy with harvest. I started off through Cormondreche, just across the railroad, and wound through lanes between gray walls. I sat awhile in the sun thinking of many things—and thee. Finally I happened on the pretty, ancient village of Auvernier beside the lake, with its Roman road and flowered fountains and old yellow tower. We'll go there, Red—soon. Oh my love, I feel intensely your need for rest and renewing, and I know you can find it here. The countryside breathes peace and beauty; more than that, it breathes order and industry and human striving. I long for you to be here and for the chance to do something for thee, for once.

I came home at noon to a magnificent dinner: soup, rabbit, new potatoes with parsley, cucumbers and tomatoes fresh out of the garden, melon, nut cake (which I hear you are partial to), and coffee. You'll get back your three kilos and more in Switzerland.

Your telegram came late Thursday, and Saturday I sent you a reply after having seen the doctor. Your message cheered me greatly, but I was saddened, too, to feel that I had caused you so much anxiety. We both know how much I'd like to see you in Basle September 9, but I cannot see now that circumstances make it necessary for you to change your plans to that extent. I am sure Ex is a great help and support to you; perhaps that is why you feel you can leave earlier. But your letter, which arrived yesterday, says that you hope to reach Basle by the sixteenth. If that is the date that will allow you to finish up things in a thorough, unhurried way, I should stick to it.

The last four or five days, the eye seems to be less red, particularly in the mornings, and by evening the swelling is almost entirely absent. What particularly bucks me is that I can now read—not for long, but the sight is definitely better. I read your letter and Ex's yesterday, and a long, hilarious letter from Connie Madgen telling me of the closing of the refugee program. The doctor has not seen the latest X-rays, but he feels now that the matter is not as pressing as he thought at first, and he says there is a very good chance the eye may take care of itself. He is watching it closely to make sure that nothing develops that might injure the optic nerve. I go to him again on Tuesday, and he will then call Geneva to make an appointment for me to see a specialist there.

It may very well be that this is just one of the things that Wood said was to be "expected." In every other respect, I feel an improvement day by day—even my hair is getting better! But honestly, Red, if one had sat down and mapped out a place for me to convalesce, he couldn't have drawn up a more perfect set of conditions than those here. As my body gets stronger, it should have a salutary effect on the eye as well, and as I feel better, my morale rises. That's really been the trouble, I think; I've been scared by this eye more than anything else. But I have myself much more in hand now, and much as I should love to have you here sooner, immediately, if it were possible, I don't think you should come running whenever I get the jitters! Of course I shall let you know at once if the doctors decide that an operation is advisable, but aside from that, I'm inclined to let the whole thing drop and get on with plans for the wedding. OK?

Tell Ex her letter raised my spirits like a ton of TNT! She sure hasn't lost the old touch. I've been sort of mentally writing her a letter ever since she's been in Poland, and it's not there yet. But do tell her I still love her, wish her very well, and am as pleased for her and Henry as I am for me and Red. Of course, have them come to the wedding. Drag 'em in, if necessary. I gather they're going to need some refreshment, liquid or otherwise, after that do-or-die tour of Europe they're planning. There's just one thing, Red; if the wedding is the twenty-seventh, that is to say during the harvest, I am not sure we can offer them a bed with one of our relatives. Tante Anna's house, for example, will be full of people working in the vineyards. Mimi is coming to work and will share my room; you, poor dear, will sleep at the aunt's, I'm afraid. Never mind, I'll come up the street every morning early and throw out the lifeline!

I lie awake nights thinking of running to meet you at the station in Basle. Claudine would love to have us spend some time there, and we can have a good time in Basle, just waltzing up and down the streets. I should love to show you that pink town hall! And will you buy me all the ice cream I can eat? It costs a lot, and I am developing an enormous appetite.

Oh darling, what else can I say? The nearer your coming, the less I can put on paper. It all seems to stay in my heart, waiting for you to touch it and release it. Like you, Red, I have great confidence for the future. I can hardly imagine a problem that will seem really grave once we can live and work and play and love together.

August 26, 1947 ~ Red in Warsaw to Madeleine in Corcelles

Your telegram arrived saying your eye was improving; yet it does not satisfy me. My plans are to leave here September 7 subject to the approval of Peter. I shall cable you a week today when I expect to leave.

August 29, 1947 ~ Red in Warsaw to Madeleine in Corcelles

A three-page letter arrived from you yesterday. Oh, how wonderful it was to learn that your eye is improving, and more than that, my sweet, you are full of life and love. It makes me ever the more anxious to join you. The days go slowly, but gradually the day of departing from Poland is approaching. Then, my heart, we shall dance and sing and cry for joy!

Tomorrow I go to Gora and attend Henry's and Ex's wedding on Sunday. They think they can make Switzerland for our wedding.

Do you think that I might help some during the harvest? I know nothing about gathering grapes, and I can't do a full day's work; however, there should be some physical labor that needs to be done. I shall not be happy doing nothing, particularly if everyone else is working.

September at last ~ Red in Warsaw to Madeleine in Corcelles

By the time you receive this, you should have received a telegram saying that I am arriving on the ninth at Basle. This will be a busy week, but even so I was tempted to try and make the Friday night train. This will give me time to collect a few loose ends over Saturday and Sunday and then have two days and nights on a train before seeing you. What sweet thoughts—the sight of you as the train pulls into Basle. I do hope that you can make the trip. If not, I shall contact Claudine and then come to you as quickly as possible.

Saturday I received a letter saying that we have bookings on the Queen Mary for October 18! Darling, we are lucky. Now we must go to England again. If we get married on the twenty-seventh, we shall have only three weeks before the boat sails. Shall it be a week in Switzerland, a week in Paris, and a week in London?

Yesterday Ex Williams became ex-Williams. They are duly and officially married. The weather was very nasty, and there were more than sixty people in that little barrack, but everything went off very smoothly. Even the angel-food cake was excellent. You have no idea what a feat that was for Ralph when he did not have proper cake pans, oven, cream of tartar, or anything.

September 7, 1947 ~ Red in Warsaw to his parents in North Carolina

This is a hasty note just before the train leaves; the past two weeks have been hectic. I am leaving here tonight, arriving in Basle, Switzerland, forty-six hours later. We plan to be married at Corcelles on September 27, arrive in Paris about October 4, London about October 11, and sail on the *Queen Mary* October 18, arriving in New York about October 23 or 24.

Mother, I have not forgotten your birthday; however, if you will wait until November, I shall present you with a new daughter, OK?

-With much love, Red

September 13, 1947 ~ Red in Geneva to his parents in North Carolina

If only you could take a vacation like this! Wonderful air, excellent food, beautiful scenery, clean and orderly streets and buildings, modern conveniences!

Madeleine is sleeping, and I am on the balcony where it is light and cool.

Last evening we had tea with Algie and Eva Newlin, professor of history from Guilford College. While we were there, five Americans we knew in Germany arrived. They are spending their leaves in Switzerland and hope to come to our wedding. Last night I had dinner with Philip

Zealey; he leaves next week for Warsaw as the representative for World Student Relief.

Today Madeleine and I talked with someone about working for the Program Committee, the UN's Food and Agriculture Organization for the International Refugee Organization, but they are looking for people to begin work in October, so we are not interested. Maybe we shall apply later. Monday we talk to the personnel director of UNO. The chances are small, but we have to start looking for a job pretty soon. We don't think we shall ask for an assignment until after the first of the year, as Madeleine still needs much rest and I need a break.

We are in Geneva because Madeleine had to come back and see a neurosurgeon. He says she must be careful—no excessive activity, no running, no alcohol, and no flying because of the altitude. The bad news is that she could go blind in any five-day period, so he's given us referrals to neurosurgeons in Paris, London, New York, and Philadelphia. He says we must be patient as it will take time for her to heal. We return to see him again on the twenty-second but are still hoping to get married on the twenty-seventh.

Though this is a heavy burden, we are grateful that Madeleine is alive, and we will not let this news dampen our spirits. The past four days have been the happiest of our lives. In fact, it is as though we have lived a lifetime in four days. Each day we become more anxious to come home and meet each other's families. You will love Madeleine.

1995 ～ Red from Monan's Rill

In those days, official documents were needed to travel and many more were needed to get married: birth certificates from North Carolina and New York, notarized documents from Poland and Germany assuring residence in those countries. We went to Berne to deliver these papers to the American Consulate and obtain the proper American documents to satisfy the Swiss authorities. And then to Corcelles-sur-Neuchâtel where we had to post the banns for four weeks.

Madeleine had been living with her Uncle Paul and Tante Anna Gerber. We assumed they would not let me stay there until after we were married, but would insist on my staying with Madeleine's other aunt in Corcelles. We knew it would be hard to stay in separate houses, but we were not going to upset the family by demanding that we stay together. In late afternoon we arrived by an electric trolley at Uncle Paul's house and lo and behold I was shown a small room on the second floor with an adjoining door to Madeleine's room and a shared bath.

The banns did not permit us to be married until September 27, so we enjoyed walking in the vineyards and through the village with its clean and orderly streets. Of course, there were visits to the neurosurgeon in Geneva where, fortunately, we had friends.

Madeleine was determined not to be married in the gray uniform she had worn for over a year and a half; so when she had the energy, we would go shopping for rings and a wedding dress. Finding two simple gold bands went quickly, but finding a suitable dress that would fit was another problem. After several trips of dashed hopes she was tired and ready to give up when I spotted a bright blue dress. When Madeleine turned up her nose at the gaudy attachments, I pleaded with her to ask the clerk if they could be removed without damaging the dress. She then had a lovely blue dress with the very simple costume jewelry and belt that we added. She was in heaven.

THE WEDDING PARTY: THE BRIDE AND GROOM WITH UNCLE PAUL AND HIS SON PAULET   -PHOTOGRAPH BY A VILLAGER

Many friends in Europe wished to come to our wedding, but Madeleine's first cousin Paulet Gerber took us aside and reminded us that Madeleine and I had neither the money nor the energy for a church wedding. He suggested we take what little money we had to honeymoon on Lake Geneva for a week. Suddenly the village council announced that posting banns for us was useless and allowed us to marry earlier on Saturday, September 20, 1947.

Paulet had assured Madeleine that she could get a bridal bouquet at a nursery in the neighboring village and that the morning of the wedding would be time enough to order flowers. On Saturday, September 20 we were awakened by the bells on the cows as a herd passed underneath our windows going from the village to fields near the lake. Madeleine called the music of the bells the Symphonie de Corcelles. We were up for an early breakfast of hot milk and coffee, homemade bread, butter, cheese and jam. Although the sky was clear blue, we could not see the Alps as we walked through the village into the vineyards, which were still green and

MADELEINE IN HER WEDDING DRESS HOLDING
HER BRIDAL BOUQUET   -PHOTOGRAPH BY RED

had not yet started turning their fall colors. On we went across the railroad tracks and through more vineyards to the nursery: to a nursery without a hot house in late September. We found only field flowers, limited to pink carnations, not one of Madeleine's favorite flowers. Since we were too happy to let pink carnations spoil the day, Madeleine told the man that she wanted a bridal bouquet. She was assured that she would get just that. He went into the field and cut a large bundle of pink carnations and put them together like a sheath of wheat with evenly cut off ends, and handed them to Madeleine. She was distressed at the disappointing bouquet, and tears started to roll down both sides of her face. Feeling devastated I said, "Ask the man to give us some small wire and green ribbon and I'll go home and make you a bridal bouquet."

At the time I was not aware that florists cut off the stems and put a wire through the base of the flower, wrapping green ribbon around the wire to make a flexible nonbreakable stem. Instead I pushed a wire up the center of each of those little stems. Before I was half through, Uncle Paul was yelling up for us to hurry as the magistrate would be waiting. Finally, I did succeed in creating a crescent shaped bridal bouquet, which I laid on Madeleine's left arm. She was most pleased and very happy, even though there was no time for me to shave.

In those days, brides were the only women who attended a civil marriage ceremony; so the wedding party consisted of only Madeleine and myself, Uncle Paul and his son, Paulet. We walked along the same narrow street where only a few hours before the cows had passed, then by a schoolyard where the children stopped playing to watch our small procession, the tall groom and the bride-to-be with a spray of pink carnations on her arm.

The wedding took place in the meeting room of the village council around a large oak table with a picture window looking out to the now visible Alps. Of course, the ceremony was in French, but at one point the magistrate said to me in English, "Do you engage this woman?" To which I readily said, "Yes."

Thus the two wild geese landed and flew off together to

"venture forth, commit yourselves to air,
To trust in that which can never be known
Until the moment of arrival."

For forty-five years I told Madeleine that I had only engaged her, to which she would reply that since I did not understand the French I did not know what I had promised.

Waking At Night

One star, window framed.
Loved body, warm beside me -
Long years of marriage.

-Madeleine

Epilogue

Beech Tree

Sheltering, giant, ancient tree,
~~Reaching~~ going back to the time of our founder.

Reaching —— feet into the sky,
Spreading dense state over —— acre.

~~How many~~ Children play beneath,
among your branches,
Lovers carve initials in your
grey bark,

Vows are exchanged in your presence,
Trysts held in your darkness,
And ~~sending souls~~ meditation
in your shade.

Are you indeed a tree,
Or a monster rooted in earth,
Sending down elephantine ~~trunks~~ legs,
Stretching ~~out~~ out ~~incredible,~~ pliable
trunks
To ~~reach~~ incredible lengths —
seventy feet and more,
Trunks that burgeon in spring
From the tightly ~~neatly~~ rolled, ~~tight~~ pointed brown
packets

Madeleine ~ Here the letters end. We were together, and we didn't need letters any longer. We sailed for home in the luxury of cabin class on the *Queen Mary*, since air travel was out of the question because of my head injury. In January 1948, I underwent a very hazardous brain operation at Jefferson Hospital in Philadelphia to repair the injury sustained in the truck accident. Miraculously, it was a success.

Red ~ The sound of Madeleine's wood chopper, which had receded in Corcelles, increased on our return to the US. I could stand next to Madeleine and hear the chopping myself, though I was several inches away; it was the sound of her heartbeat pounding in the aneurysm. The neurosurgeon told us that without an operation, Madeleine would live no more than six months. Until Madeleine's operation, the procedure had never been performed successfully.

Madeleine ~ In September 1948, we loaded our belongings and some secondhand furniture into an old car and headed west. Red had been invited to work for the American Friends Service Committee regional office in San Francisco to develop a self-help housing project in a Black ghetto in North Richmond across San Francisco Bay. Six weeks after we arrived, we reported that the project would not be feasible.

Still working for AFSC, Red created a community project, North Richmond Neighborhood House, which became known nationally for its innovative programs in community work—working with street gangs, job training and placement, study halls, and other projects for community empowerment.

Both of us were involved in Quaker activities: The American Friends Service Committee, Berkeley Friends Meeting, Friends Committee on Legislation, John Woolman School. It was a sorrow when we found we could not have children, and a joy when we adopted a daughter and a son, Anne Josephine and Robert Paul, named after my aunt and uncle in Switzerland, who had been so involved with us and given us in full measure. We have experienced the joys and pains of being parents, as well as the gift of our grandchildren.

In Berkeley, we were pleased to be able to establish a little community of Quakers where our biracial children found companionship and acceptance. So rich was this twenty-five years of shared living that when our children grew up and moved away, we, with another family in the community, gathered interested Quakers and friends into thinking about another community. After several years of planning and saving for land, fifteen adults found 400 acres in Sonoma County, California, and began an industrious experiment in an intentional community which we named Monan's Rill. Here we have lived for fifteen years—surrounded by beauty, peace, and open spaces—with good friends, old and young, with whom we share values and commitment to one another.

Red ~ Our being a part of the building of Monan's Rill was a continuation of our efforts to create a more peaceful and just world which was the motivation that had earlier carried us to war-torn Europe.

A COMMUNITY GET-TOGETHER AT MONAN'S RILL
-PHOTOGRAPH BY ALAN BARTL

In addition to the things we did together, Madeleine accomplished much in her own right. She developed an interest in Oriental philosophy and attended the American Academy for Asian Studies, where she wrote a Master's Thesis on Oriental Philosophies and Contemporary Quakerism.

In 1954, she renewed her interest in music, studying with concert pianist Julian White and attending the Music School at Hayward State University.

To celebrate the fiftieth anniversary of the American Friends Service Committee, in 1967, Madeleine wrote a Quaker Cantata for full orchestra and chorus. The words she took from the journal of George Fox, the founder of the Quakers. Because of the magnitude of the production, the cantata was not performed until the fiftieth anniversary of the San Francisco Regional Office of AFSC in 1992. Madeleine had worked in this office, served as the Clerk of its Executive Committee, and acted as the executive for a short period.

In 1996, Germany marked the fiftieth anniversary of Quaker assistance after World War II. As part of that celebration, Madeleine's Quaker Cantata was played over German radio.

Madeleine worked on two compositions. She had gathered notes and folk songs of Switzerland, the homeland of her mother and site of our wedding. She also made tapes in hopes of composing a piece on Quaker Meetings.

Though she taught music to children in the neighborhood, Madeleine never promoted herself as a teacher, as she had not felt at ease with any of the teaching methods she had studied until she took a summer course on the teaching methods of Hungarian composer Kodály. She earned a Master's Degree in Music from Holy Names College in Oakland specializing in Kodály's methods, and began teaching music in earnest.

Madeleine fell in love with Pendle Hill, a Quaker retreat and learning institution in Pennsylvania, the first time she visited there in

MADELEINE AND RED, 1990   -PHOTOGRAPH BY NANCY RICHARD

1943. Later in our lives, she was able to attend a summer session at Pendle Hill, and then in 1990 we returned for a time as Friends in Residence. That is when and where this book began.

Madeleine ~ In 1989, when I developed a rare blood disease, the physician in Santa Rosa to whom I fortunately found my way was Dr. Marek Bozdech, who was born in Wild Flecken, a refugee camp near Bavaria. That was not a camp in which I worked, but close enough to our relief effort in Germany to satisfy my feelings that life had gone full circle.

Red ~ Late in summer 1993, Madeleine was facing death once again. More than two months before, she had been told she had only two months to live.

Madeleine's Journal ~ August 5, 1993

After the developments of today— preparing to go to the clinic and another visit with Dr. Bozdech, a pleasant drive with our Bob, Amy, and Elijah—I reflected, half asleep, on the wonders of my life. Surrounded by so much love, by such skillful care, I feel I am the focus of much affection, care, and concern. It is overwhelming. In my relaxed state, I picture them all coming together over me. I raised my arms in heavenly bliss over my head, seeking to express in movement the converging of this love and attention.

Such concern and support and love are indeed what the whole world needs, but why should so much be concentrated on me? I enjoy it, I take courage from it, I am grateful for it. But so many are so needful of what I have in such abundance, why does so much flow into me? Will I do something with it? Can I share it? Can I understand it? I feel I am on the edge of an understanding such as I have longed for, with no idea at all of what it is. I am about to enter a strange, frightening, and mysterious promised place.

Red ~ On September 5, 1993, Madeleine Yaude Stephenson died of acute leukemia, leaving behind family and friends who love her, a world made richer by her having been a part of it, and this book.